Doing Media Research

An Introduction

2nd Edition

Susanna Hornig Priest

University of Nevada, Las Vegas

 **SAGE**

Los Angeles • London • New Delhi • Singapore • Washington DC

For information:

SAGE Publications, Inc.
2455 Teller Road
Thousand Oaks, California 91320
E-mail: order@sagepub.com

SAGE Publications Ltd.
1 Oliver's Yard
55 City Road
London EC1Y 1SP
United Kingdom

SAGE Publications India Pvt. Ltd.
B 1/I 1 Mohan Cooperative
  Industrial Area
Mathura Road, New Delhi 110 044
India

SAGE Publications Asia-Pacific Pte. Ltd.
33 Pekin Street #02-01
Far East Square
Singapore 048763

Printed in the United States of America

Priest, Susanna Hornig.
Doing media research: An introduction/Susanna Hornig Priest.—2nd ed.
    p. cm.
Includes bibliographical references and index.
ISBN 978-1-4129-6097-7 (pbk.)
  1. Mass media—Research—Methodology. 2. Social sciences—Methodology.
I. Title.

P91.3.P75 2009
302.23072—dc22   2008036294

Printed on acid-free paper

09 10 11 12 13 10 9 8 7 6 5 4 3 2 1

Acquiring Editor:	Todd R. Armstrong
Editorial Assistant:	Aja Baker
Production Editor:	Sarah K. Quesenberry
Copy Editor:	Melinda Masson
Proofreader:	Wendy Jo Dymond
Typesetter:	C&M Digitals (P) Ltd.
Cover Designer:	Edgar Abarca
Marketing Manager:	Carmel Schrire

'TE'

Doing Media Research

2nd Edition

To my sons, Andy and Wes, who probably no longer remember the many evenings of their childhood when I was busy with the first edition of this book.

Brief Contents

Part IV ~ Research in Broader Context: Contemporary Trends and the Dissemination of Research Results

Detailed Contents

**Part II ~ Asking Questions and Collecting Data:
Creating a Research Plan**

Part III ~ Approaches to Data Analysis: Basic Tools

About the Author

Susanna Hornig Priest is a professor of journalism and media studies at the University of Nevada, Las Vegas. She has taught mass communication theory and research methods at the undergraduate and graduate levels since 1989. She holds a doctoral degree in communications from the University of Washington, a master's degree in sociology from the University of Nevada, Las Vegas, and a bachelor's degree in anthropology from the University of California, Berkeley. Her own research is centered on the role of science in American society and culture, its expression in the mass media, public engagement in science and science policy, and public opinion formation. She is also interested in the social roles of new media technologies.

Priest has served as a member of the Research and Publications committees of the Association for Education in Journalism and Mass Communication and as chair and research chair of the association's Science Communication Interest Group. She is a fellow of the American Association for the Advancement of Science, past associate editor of the journal *Public Understanding of Science*, and current editor of the journal *Science Communication*. She regularly serves as an advisor to a wide range of academic projects, government agencies, and private organizations on communication, public engagement, and public opinion issues and reviews research submissions for a variety of academic organizations and scholarly journals. Her current research is supported by grants from the National Science Foundation and other sources.

Her publications include more than 30 refereed research articles and nearly 20 book chapters, plus two books. She is currently editing the *Encyclopedia of Science and Technology Communication*.

About This Book

Information for Instructors and Students

This is a book about social science research methods written primarily for mass communication and media studies students. Its goal is to help beginning research students understand methodological options and start doing meaningful small-scale studies. While studying research methods can be a lifetime occupation, everyone needs to begin with a grounding in what research is about, why it is important, and how it is done. This book will help mass communication students do just that—get started—whether as undergraduates or as beginning graduate students. It is also designed to encourage them to learn by doing rather than by studying methods only in the abstract. The philosophy of this book is simple: Research is a lot of fun, so let's go do some!

Just as journalism and media studies are most often classified as social sciences, our methods are most often drawn from social sciences, such as anthropology, sociology, and psychology. Methods for empirical research, both qualitative and quantitative, that originated in these three disciplines are therefore the core of this book, just as they are the original core of our field. In recent years, methods from other disciplines, including literary and rhetorical criticism, history, and economics, as well as the blend of theory and method sometimes referred to as the "critical cultural" approach, have increasingly enriched our studies. So, although the traditional empirical methods of social science are emphasized in this book and its scope does not include an exhaustive survey of the many alternatives to these methods, I've also tried to make regular mention of the existence of a broader range of choices. In discussing those that are drawn from these core social sciences, I have been careful not to privilege quantitative techniques over qualitative ones.

In relying on the historical separation between the social sciences and the humanities as one guideline to determine what should go into this book, I recognize that the line between the two is getting less and less distinct, especially in communication studies. Further, new media technologies, such alternative perspectives as those from feminist scholarship, and other new insights and issues continually challenge the methods of traditional social science as applied to mass media issues. The "objectivity" of both science and journalism is increasingly subject to critique. At the same time, however, I don't think we have exhausted the usefulness of empirical social science (qualitative as well as quantitative) for exploring the media's role and influence. I have tried to balance a strong statement that studying contemporary media issues presents compelling new challenges with an equally strong invitation to draw from the best that our traditional methods have to offer in rising to meet these challenges.

The emphasis on the scholarly origins of our traditional methods results from many years of teaching students who may have no statistics or methods background and in many cases have only the most minimal grounding in the social sciences. Part I of this book is devoted to discussing these outside origins—most methods texts available to media research students pay relatively little attention to them. The communication research community has been trying hard to establish its own independence; perhaps this has made us reluctant to emphasize how we've borrowed our methods from fields with different histories and objectives. But contemporary sociology of knowledge tells us that scientific method and social purpose are inseparable. To understand research methods *and their limits* and to fully understand the contemporary critiques of our traditional methods, we need to understand their historical origins, not just how they work.

This book attempts to introduce complex issues as simply as possible, using simple language and straightforward examples, and to encourage student researchers to go right to work on problems they find interesting. Although oversimplification is necessarily a risk of this approach, students in those social sciences from which we've borrowed all begin to learn research methods at the undergraduate level, and each of these fields has found ways to let students participate in the research process from the start. It's time we did the same in mass communication and media studies.

This new revision of the book has been undertaken with a number of goals in mind. The first edition did not have enough information on media content analysis, a set of approaches central to the field, so more detail on this has been added. Of course, new communication technologies have been evolving and changing at an incredible rate over the past decade, so this new edition includes much more discussion of those trends. The material in Part I of the original book has been shortened and streamlined, as well as tied more closely to contemporary media issues. Finally, the hands-on exercises that follow most of the chapters have been updated and revised.

The following reviewers provided important input that helped shape the development of this revision; their insights are gratefully acknowledged: Kendra L. Gale, University of Colorado at Boulder; Laurel Hellerstein, Endicott College; Lee Joliffe, Drake University; Antonio C. La Pastina, Texas A&M University; Rashmi Luthra, University of Michigan-Dearborn; Amy Kiste Nyberg, Seton Hall University; Gregg A. Payne, Chapman University; Michael Ryan, University of Houston; David W. Worley, Indiana State University. If this book contains errors and omissions (as I am sure it must, despite my best efforts), I hope they will inspire my colleagues to join in the attempt to communicate what we're about ever more clearly and simply. As *communication* researchers, we have a special obligation to do this even better than our colleagues in the other social sciences!

—Susanna Hornig Priest
Las Vegas, Nevada

PART I

Roots

Social Science Foundations

CHAPTER 1

A Philosophy of Social "Science"

Doing research about anything is an exciting journey of discovery. Media messages themselves help us see this, not just through programs about research like *NOVA* or science magazines like *Discover* but also in films like the Indiana Jones movies, which turn archaeology into an exotic adventure, or television series like *CSI: Crime Scene Investigation*, in which laboratory science plays the key role in solving crime mysteries. This book will help you start doing research about the media and its influences on society. But just what is "scientific" about social science, and where does media research fit into this picture?

Some controversy exists about whether social science is actually "science" at all. One of the earliest sociologists was the 19th-century scholar Auguste Comte, who first thought of society as being like a biological organism—divided into parts that function together. (We can think of our media institutions as one of these parts.) This was an analogy derived directly from biological science. Strict reliance on an **empirical**[1] (or data-based) **research method** in social science continues to be associated with Comte's **positivist** philosophy, which held that it was both possible and desirable to develop a "science" of society.

As the social sciences developed, the argument that society could best be understood by applying the methods of science, based on systematic direct observation, continued to be made. Science had come to be thought of as objective (free from opinion, prejudice, and outside influence)—at least ideally. Social science has often aspired to copy this by concentrating on collecting objective data about observable phenomena. Historically, the emphasis in science on using evidence from direct observations to settle issues of truth had arisen in part as a reaction against reliance on traditional beliefs, intuition, or personal opinion. Surely, social science could develop most fruitfully by relying on the same approach, or so many social scientists believed.

Over time, though, others began to question the usefulness of the scientific model for social science. Some began to see the positivist position as a weak point or limiting factor rather than a strength of social scientific inquiry. How is it possible, these scholars asked, to study important social phenomena "objectively" when "subjective" individual thought and interpretation are so characteristically human? Can social science researchers ever really claim to be doing anything other than personal interpretation? How can they be sure they are actually measuring abstractions like attitudes and beliefs in the same sense that a physicist might measure the strength of an electric field or a chemist might assess the acidity of a compound? The study of human activity by human beings has a special dimension called **reflexivity**, the particular challenge of turning the lens of scientific inquiry inward to make one's own species the object of study.

The assertion that it is possible and desirable to measure or assess, in a scientifically accurate way, *everything* that is of interest to a social scientist is still controversial but probably cannot be supported. Some **quantitative** research in mass communication—that is, research that uses numerical measures to investigate social phenomena—has been criticized for making just this positivistic assertion. A quantitative approach limits investigation to factors that can be measured; this can mean ignoring important aspects of human social behavior, such as meaning itself, that may be difficult or impossible to quantify.

For these reasons, mass communication researchers sometimes question the field's past overreliance on quantitative methods. In practice, these methods are excellent choices for some types of problems but less useful for others. Today, researchers are more likely to recognize that **interpretive** methods—that is, methods that make use of (rather than seek to eliminate) the human feelings, reactions, and insights of the researcher—also have value. Interpretive methods, sometimes called naturalistic methods, are generally **qualitative**; the results are expressed in language rather than in numbers. Both qualitative social science work and quantitative social science work are empirical in the sense that they rely on systematic observations. Further, *both* kinds of data actually require interpretation. What most clearly distinguishes any social science from the humanities is the systematic reliance on data, whether qualitative or quantitative.

Scientific thinking actually changes in revolutionary leaps and bounds, not just evolutionary increments, as Thomas Kuhn (1970) was the first to point out. Today's truth may be rejected tomorrow. The instruments and techniques available to scientists affect the kinds of experiments they can do and therefore have powerful effects on what kind of new knowledge is created. So do politics, history, and culture. Media research is no different.

For example, just as nuclear weapons were created by a society desperate to win a war, while the new science of ecology has emerged in an era of concern over environmental problems, concern with propaganda during World War II set the research agenda for much of the pioneering early work in the field of mass communication. Then, in the 1950s and 1960s, concern over the effects of television, especially televised violence, became more important as society's interests and priorities shifted from winning a war and toward understanding internal conflict and other domestic problems. Earlier work on persuasion and propaganda was put to new uses in political communication, public relations, and advertising.

Regardless of the extent to which social and political factors influence the choice of research problems or what methodological approaches are used to study these problems, the underlying strategies that have made science so useful in modern societies have not changed. *Good science uses theory well, gathers evidence systematically, and contributes to the accumulation of knowledge.* This continues to be the basis of good science—and of good social science. Good social scientists, whether positivists or interpretive researchers, using qualitative or quantitative methods, follow these same principles.

The best social science often sounds like common sense when it's finished. If it doesn't "ring true," there's likely a false assumption somewhere. However, this doesn't mean that we can jump to good social scientific conclusions based solely on our intuition. Good researchers gather empirical evidence carefully, evaluate it systematically, and present it cautiously.

QUALITATIVE VERSUS QUANTITATIVE METHODS

A research **method** is a general approach to a research problem; a **technique** is a more specific procedure that is part of a particular method. The distinction between qualitative and quantitative methods is important, although it is often overemphasized. Nevertheless, a majority of social science researchers, including those that study the mass media, tend to be specialists who use one of these types of methods more regularly than the other.

The Argument for Qualitative Methods

Qualitative methods are designed to explore and assess things that cannot easily be summarized numerically. Descriptive observations of conditions and practices in another culture, interviews that use open-ended questions, and analysis of the structure or the arguments in a set of newspaper editorials are all examples of qualitative research. Many of the most important methods discussed in this book are qualitative—that is, they rely on the interpretation and analysis of what people do and say without making heavy use of measurement or numerical analysis as quantitative methods do.

Qualitative researchers may actively reject the positivist assumption that everything of interest can be measured. Their training and experience have taught them the value of looking at subtle aspects of human social life that are best described in words; furthermore, there is not necessarily a single, accurate description that we'd all agree on. The use of language and symbols is a key characteristic of human beings. How can people and their communication be studied in a meaningful way if we limit ourselves to looking at only those aspects that can be captured by numerical representations? Qualitative social science researchers may see quantitative research as flawed by a tendency toward **reductionism,** or artificially simplifying complex social phenomena.

Instead of seeing investigators' personal insights and responses to what goes on around them as interfering with accurate observation, qualitative researchers doing interpretive research try to make use of those insights and responses in a systematic way. They may also argue that quantitative researchers tend toward **reification** of the objects of their study—that is, they trick themselves into thinking that abstractions like attitudes, values, and content themes are objectively real when they are actually just convenient categories invented by the researcher. Qualitative researchers generally look for truth in the development of insightful descriptions of how something in social life works, rather than statistics or equations.

The Argument for Quantitative Methods

Quantitative methods, simply put, use numbers. Most public opinion research, many kinds of psychological experiments, and studies that count the different sources quoted in newspaper stories or the exact proportion of entertainment versus educational programming on television are all examples of quantitative research.

You've already learned that quantitative methods are associated with the positivist assumption that the things scientists (including social scientists) are interested in can always be measured. From this viewpoint, the accuracy and adequacy of scientific measurement instruments (whether survey question-naires or laboratory equipment) is a central focus of concern. An important underlying assumption here is that, if only those instruments could be made powerful enough, we could determine an exact value for anything we might want to measure—*a number we could all agree on*. This is how quantitative methods are sometimes argued to be more objective than qualitative ones, which leads to the criticism that qualitative methods are too subjective, depending too much on the individual researcher's point of view.

Numerical methods are an extremely useful tool for summarizing a large quantity of data and establishing relationships among different factors with a known degree of certainty, whether the topic is the relationship between read-ing a particular magazine and buying certain products or the relationship between the hours spent watching television and obesity. Human society invented numbers over thousands of years because of their usefulness in keep-ing track of large groups of items, whether migrating herds of game animals or money in a bank account. Research often benefits by making use of these valuable tools.

Combining Methods and Achieving Consensus

While the world of social science sometimes seems rather sharply divided between proponents of qualitative methods and proponents of quantitative methods, in fact both are useful in particular cases, and the two types of methods can be combined. Many of the best studies, often done by teams of researchers rather than individuals, combine quantitative and qualitative methods.

Different researchers do come to different conclusions at times, regardless of what methods are used. This happens in science as well as social science. Scientists may have different answers to questions ranging from how quickly the globe is really warming to how likely it is that we will find life on other planets. Social scientists continue to disagree over what really causes crime and just how powerful the media are in shaping children's beliefs and behavior.

Over time, many such differences are resolved by the emergence of a "sci-entific consensus" reflecting the results of many studies and the outcome of ongoing conversations and discussions among researchers about the meaning of these results. For example, thousands of studies suggest that mediated violence may influence people to engage in violence in real life, although researchers continue to disagree about the strength of this relationship. It is very rare for any single study, using whatever methods, to provide the final solution for such a complex problem.

BOX 1.1

Mixing Methods

Let's say you are interested in how the images of gender roles—expectations for how women and men are expected to behave and what kinds of jobs they are likely to have—presented in children's television programming might influence young minds. In a quantitative approach, one researcher might propose that children's attitudes and beliefs about gender be measured and related to the type and amount of television they watch. As you'll see later on, establishing causation for this kind of problem is quite difficult. Nevertheless, this quantitative study could certainly yield important insights. Another researcher might prefer to talk to children individually about what they watch, who their heroes are, and why. This qualitative approach could yield a rich understanding of their world that numerical measures would be unlikely to capture—but possibly at some loss of precision. For this problem, the best solution may be to combine quantitative and qualitative methods. If both studies showed the same sorts of influence taking place, or if neither showed any influence taking place, that would provide especially powerful evidence on which to base a conclusion. The use of multiple methods in a single study is called **triangulation.**

DEDUCTIVE VERSUS INDUCTIVE LOGIC

Another distinction useful in understanding the forms that social science research can take is the distinction between **deductive** and **inductive** logic (that is, reasoning). What many people first think of as "scientific" research uses a deductive model in which the researcher *reasons from the general to the specific.* This means that the researcher begins with a **theory**, an abstract **explanatory** idea that the researcher believes can predict what will happen in a new situation. Working from such a theory, or general proposition, the researcher derives a **hypothesis**, or specific proposition, that can be tested by collecting a certain kind of data. If the new data support the hypothesis, the theory is upheld. If the data suggest the hypothesis is wrong, questions are raised about the adequacy of the theory.

"Cultivation theory" is an important example of a general theory in media studies; this theory, from the work of George Gerbner and his colleagues, states that our perceptions of reality are "cultivated" or encouraged to grow in a certain direction by what we read or see in the media (Gerbner, Gross, Morgan, & Signorielli, 1986). A hypothesis that came from this theory is the assertion that the more violent television we watch, the more we believe that the world is a violent place. This hypothesis has been tested extensively by collecting data on television-viewing habits, media content, and people's beliefs about the world and then looking for a relationship among these.

For the most part, the hypothesis, and therefore cultivation theory in general, has been supported by investigations of this relationship, although some questions certainly remain about the adequacy of the methods used by cultivation researchers (Potter, 1994). The proliferation of new media will be a major challenge to future researchers trying to clarify this question, since almost every viewer can now access different content through cable or satellite television and the Internet. As a practical matter, measuring the types of material people have been exposed to, necessary to testing the cultivation hypothesis, has become enormously more complicated.

Inductive logic, on the other hand, involves reasoning from data on a specific case or situation to a general theoretical conclusion. A researcher who begins with only a general theoretical understanding to guide the development of specific questions is using an inductive approach. Perhaps the researcher believes that media are important to developing a strong sense of community identity but does not really have a specific hypothesis about how this works. He or she might gather data on media use and community identity without a clear preconception of the relationship between them. This type of work, sometimes called **exploratory** research, is common when a new area of research is developing. Sometimes it is difficult to determine whether this type of **case study** might apply in other situations (such as another community). It can remain simply a **descriptive** study that does not make a contribution to general theory.

Often, however, the study of data from a particular case will stimulate thinking that will result in the formation of a new theory, even though the researcher began with only a general question—not with one or more specific, well-defined hypotheses. The researcher in this example might discover that media use in the community being studied seems to vary a great deal depending on ethnic group membership. This could lead to the development of a new theory that would explain media use in terms of cultural identity rather than identification with a particular geographic community. This would be an example of inductive reasoning in research. The new theory could then be tested in additional communities—deductively.

The inductive-deductive distinction is not as clear-cut as the preceding examples may make it sound, though. Most good research, even exploratory research, begins with at least a general notion of the kinds of explanation the researcher thinks are likely (theory) and asks whether the data found fit those expectations or not (hypothesis testing). Conversely, strict adherence to the logic of the deductive model is probably not the norm. Observations gathered to test a hypothesis can send the researcher off in a new direction entirely. If the data do not support the hypothesis, an explanation might be found that is consistent with both the theory and the new data, or an error may be identified in the original logic or the data gathering itself. So out-and-out rejection of a theory on the basis of a single study is rare. Nevertheless, the distinction between deduction and induction is still useful in trying to grasp the underlying logic of any research. Deductive, hypothesis-testing research is almost always quantitative, whereas inductive, theory-generating research can be either qualitative or quantitative.

APPLIED VERSUS BASIC RESEARCH

A final distinction that is very important in mass communication studies is one between **applied** and **basic research**. Basic research is driven primarily by interest in a theory or theoretical idea. It is research undertaken to improve our general understanding of how something works rather than in response to an immediate practical need. The research testing cultivation theory discussed in the previous section is an example of basic research. Applied research is designed to find answers to questions that have arisen when making immediate, practical decisions. Since mass communication is in large part a professional discipline, a good share of our research is applied. Examples include everything from questions about readership that might be asked by a newspaper editor to questions about the effectiveness of children's educational programming that might be asked by members of the U.S. Congress. This is a continuum, not a strict division. Basic research can have important implications for policy or practice, while good applied research almost always uses some theory.

In applied research, using theory well helps the researcher design a useful project. For example, a newspaper editor interested in readership for his or her publication might want primarily to increase the paper's circulation but could still make good use of a theory that suggested that readership has something to do with cultural or community identity, and a congressional committee interested in the educational value of children's television might make good use of cultivation theory in understanding how TV can modify our perceptions of the world. Applied research that uses theory can also help refine the theory and add to our accumulated stock of scientific knowledge.

The best media research almost always has both applied and basic elements; it may be inspired by a practical problem but draws from theory and contributes to our accumulated knowledge. Unfortunately, applied researchers sometimes think that basic researchers don't understand the importance of solving real-world problems, whereas basic researchers may believe that applied researchers ignore the importance of theory. The truth is that both are necessary and important, and the best of one is not so different from the best of the other.

THE LIMITS OF SOCIAL SCIENCE RESEARCH

Throughout this book, you'll learn to take these abstract distinctions—qualitative versus quantitative methods, "objective" versus interpretive research, inductive versus deductive logic—and apply them to both theoretical and applied research about real-world questions and problems. But there is always a certain level of frustration built into attempts to tease apart the relationship between mass media and society, no matter how simple the question and how well developed the research technique. This is because the mass media are, of course, *a part* of that society, and it is very hard to separate one part of a complex system for study. The extent of Comte's commitment to positivism may be outdated, but his recognition that societies are complex wholes has withstood the test of time.

Each particular piece of research that a social scientist completes can provide only a partial answer, and each has limits. Further, some of the questions we would most like research to answer may never be settled by the evidence. They remain matters of social conscience and collective judgment. It is a characteristic of our culture that we would like scientific answers to important social questions, but that doesn't mean they are always available. Many issues are more a matter of what we as a society value than things social science can fully illuminate for us. Others depend heavily on the context. For instance, whether television or the Internet helps children learn or warps their perspectives probably depends on other elements of their lives, such as the influences of friends, family, and teachers. Social science cannot provide definitive answers to all social questions.

As the issues that we as a society consider most important shift over time, and as social scientists gain new insights and develop new tools for understanding them, new research questions are constantly being invented. We can see this very dramatically right now as the media landscape shifts from the "mass" media of a few years ago to the myriad of new technological choices now before us. Even though social science cannot usually provide complete answers, it can almost always provide useful insights. The process of creatively asking and answering new questions is ongoing; no one can expect the underlying issues to be settled "once and for all," but for those of us who have learned that social scientific research can be a lot of fun, perhaps this is not such a bad thing.

Important Terms and Concepts

Applied research	Deductive
Basic research	Descriptive
Case study	Empirical

Explanatory	Quantitative
Exploratory	Reductionism
Hypothesis	Reflexivity
Inductive	Reification
Interpretive	Research method
Method	Technique
Positivist	Theory
Qualitative	Triangulation

Exercise

In some ways, journalism is like social science; in other ways, the two fields are quite different. To better understand the points of this introductory chapter, think through the answers to these questions. Your instructor may want to use some of these as the basis for a class discussion.

1. Does the idea of "journalistic objectivity" sound like the same sort of "objectivity" we are concerned with in science? How are they alike, and how are they different?

2. In gathering information, when do journalists rely on quantitative information, and when do they rely on qualitative information? What are the advantages and disadvantages of each? Give specific examples.

3. Editorials are obviously interpretations of a situation, not objective accounts, but they are not the only form of interpretive journalism. Can you think of some other situations to which this term (*interpretive*) applies?

4. How do journalists make use of theories or hypotheses? What about triangulation (or the use of multiple methods) in journalism? How do these uses seem to parallel and not parallel what social scientists do?

Note

1. Terms appearing in **boldface**, which are also listed in the "Important Terms and Concepts" section at the end of each chapter, are defined in the Glossary at the end of the book.

CHAPTER 2

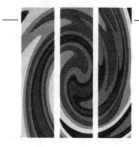

Foundational Disciplines

While media research draws its methods from many sources and has invented some of its own, three of the earlier social science disciplines provide especially crucial methodological foundations for our field. These three—cultural anthropology, experimental psychology, and sociology—are briefly introduced in this chapter. As you'll see, in each case, the methods used arose from the type of theory and overarching research questions characteristic of each field.

ANTHROPOLOGY AND THE RANGE OF HUMAN EXPERIENCE

As late as the early 20th century, before the advent of today's "global village" in which nearly all human beings have at least some access to information about the rest of the world, a large portion of the people around the globe knew only their own way of life. Many people practiced forms of marriage other than monogamy; some groups seemed peaceful and some perpetually at war; some, such as the Inuit of North America and the Bushmen of South Africa, had made extraordinary adaptations to extremes of climate, whereas others seemed to have an easier life.

Studying the variation in how people make their livings, how they are organized as societies, what their beliefs are, how tasks and leadership roles are distributed, and how the differences between men and women, adults and children, and leaders and followers are conceptualized is the subject matter of *cultural anthropology*. Cultural anthropologists begin with the knowledge that all human beings are part of the same species; their genetic makeup is very much the same despite superficial variation in such things as skin color and body type. So how can the extensive variation in human groups be explained? The answer is in a group's **culture**, or the way of life its members have learned.

What exactly is a culture? Many definitions have been proposed, but one useful definition is that culture consists of *the knowledge necessary to act as a member of a given social group*. To be an accepted member of a social group, we have to know what's expected of us—what the **norms** or rules for behavior are, including what is expected on ceremonial occasions and in everyday interaction with others. This does not only mean we need to know the laws; we must also understand what behavior everyone in the group takes for granted. For example, we need to know to wear certain kinds of clothes on some occasions but not others. We have to know a particular language, how to make a living in the society, and what is considered polite or rude behavior. Members of the same culture also generally embrace the same underlying values and have the same basic beliefs.

Anthropologists are often "cultural relativists" to at least some degree; that is, they avoid assuming that one culture is "better" than another or evaluating a particular group's value system by comparing it to their own, and instead they try to understand each culture on its own terms. **Cultural relativism** is the idea that the validity of beliefs, including ethical principles, depends on the cultural context. What is considered the ethical norm in one culture may be rejected in another. **Ethnocentrism** is approximately the opposite, the belief that one's own culture is best and that all other cultures should be judged accordingly.

Different cultures not only have different beliefs about the world around them; they also have very different expectations for how people should behave in a particular **social role**, such as mother or brother, soldier or healer, leader or outcast. For example, the definition of mental illness and how the mentally ill person is expected to behave—let alone beliefs about what causes the mentally ill to behave in unusual ways, whether childhood trauma or witchcraft—varies greatly from one culture to another. Appropriate roles for men and women also vary greatly around the globe. Whether or not there is any biological foundation for the existence of these different roles, the forms they take are very much socially determined.

Language and Culture

Languages around the world vary not only in the words and grammar used but also in the understanding of the world that they imply. We cannot translate jokes, poetry, or sometimes even simple statements successfully from one language to another simply by substituting words and making grammatical adjustments. Often, two languages lack equivalent vocabulary. A message can be seen as inappropriate, nonsensical, or unintentionally funny if translated literally—an important principle for advertisers hoping to tap into linguistically distinct markets, such as the growing Spanish-speaking market in the United States. This principle applies to **nonverbal communication,** such as gestures and "body language," as well as to what is spoken in words. The branch of anthropology that studies the relationship between language and culture is called linguistic anthropology and may be of special interest for communication researchers.

From an anthropologist's perspective, minority cultures and languages within a pluralistic society, such as the United States, are not "lesser" just because they differ from the mainstream. African American dialect and culture constitute a rich, independent tradition, for example. Other specialized variations of mainstream language—from the slang of urban teens to the terminology of theoretical physics—are important symbols of group identification, as well as a reflection of the specialized needs of the particular groups or **subcultures.**

Conversely, the same material can be interpreted quite differently by different subcultural groups. The concept of **interpretive community** has come into media studies from literary criticism and captures this idea. An interpretive community, whether based on religion, lifestyle, generation, ethnicity, socioeconomic status, political ideology, or geography, has a distinct shared worldview and values that its members bring to the interpretation of any given media message.

BOX 2.1

Sapir–Whorf Hypothesis

Early American linguistic anthropologists Edward Sapir and Benjamin Whorf were struck by the divisions of shape and time they found in Native American languages. European languages divide all objects into male and female; adjectives and pronouns must reflect agreement with the gender of the relevant noun. But in North America, Sapir and Whorf found

(Continued)

(Continued)

groups who divided objects into quite different classificatory schemes, based on shape, and who used verb tenses that suggested a quite different concept of time from those of European culture.

Sapir and Whorf hypothesized that by learning a particular language, a child learns important things about the structure of the world and that this culturally derived lesson varies from language to language and from group to group. Learning to speak a language that makes particular distinctions structures the cognition of the speaker in ways compatible with a particular cultural tradition. In the same way, a researcher's learning the language of a group of people can yield important clues as to how those people think about the world.

Today it seems less certain that this influence is absolute, since languages can be observed to grow and change. Nevertheless, language (including slang, the "cutting edge" of language where new words and expressions are being formed) remains intimately related to culture.

Participant Observation and Depth Interviews

In today's globalized world, fewer and fewer cultural groups remain isolated from the influence of other cultures, with the media acting as a key source of this intercultural influence. But the research methods originally developed by cultural anthropologists to study cultures distant from their own remain extremely valuable. Two key research methods in this category are **participant observation** and the **depth interview**. Both can contribute to the development of an **ethnography**, or a systematic description of a social group and its way of life. These methods can also be used in other types of studies, however, and are sometimes combined with quantitative approaches.

Participant observation is learning about a social group and its culture (or subculture) through engaging in the group as a member. The researcher's reactions (and occasional mistakes) are useful clues as to what is importantly "different" about the culture. The difficult field conditions experienced by early cultural anthropologists limited what they could do; surveys and experiments were not practical alternatives. Instead, participant observers (now as then) try to become a part of the group they are studying. By making systematic notes about their experiences and observations (what is being said and done) on a regular basis, they try to grasp what everyday life is like in the group they are studying without imposing their own expectations. They try to understand the various social roles that they observe: who the leaders and the followers are; what men, women, and children are expected to do; and how the group is organized. They pay attention to beliefs and to important ceremonies, as well as to the material culture or possessions of the group—from functional tools to expressive art.

A key principle of ethnographic work is **holism**—the assertion that cultures must be understood as whole systems, not isolated parts. All parts of a cultural system depend on each other, and cultural values and beliefs tend to be internally consistent even where individual aspects of them may appear irrational to the outsider. This principle has proved its usefulness over and over again. Isolated practices or beliefs may seem odd to the uninformed, but to the insider (the member of the culture of which these practices or beliefs are a part), they will make sense. The researcher's task, then, is not to explain the apparent oddities but to look for the internal consistency that weaves them together—from an insider point of view.

But observation, even participant observation, does not always tell the whole story. Ethnographers often rely heavily on individuals willing to give up their time to explain what is going on. Such an individual is called an **informant**—not to be confused with a police informer—or sometimes a "key" informant, especially when chosen for a particular kind of expertise. Imagine going to a country other than your own, one with a different language, without a map, guide, or host! Although finding reliable informants is not a trivial problem, the ethnographer is not trying to sample a **population** (the entire category of people being studied) randomly like a survey researcher would but rather is trying to gain access to *shared cultural knowledge* that every member of the group commands.

Depth interviews with one or more informants are the second key method used by ethnographers and other qualitative researchers. The depth interview is an open-ended conversational exploration of an individual's worldview or some aspect of it. Unlike a survey questionnaire, the depth interview does not have a rigidly preset structure, although the interviewer may rely on a list of topics or general questions as a guide. For this reason, these are sometimes called "semistructured" interviews. The interviewer is free to ask follow-up questions or to rephrase a question to get a more complete answer, unlike a survey procedure where each person must be asked exactly the same question. This requires well-developed interview skills.

The results of participant observation and depth interviews, along with other data gathered on the group (for example, its size and composition), are generally combined into a holistic description of the group and its way of life. (The term *ethnography* refers to both the general method and the resulting descriptive report.) Analyzing and writing up the results of an ethnographic project—even a small one—is a difficult task. Although the ethnographer need not strive to be "objective" in the sense that a chemist, a biologist, or an experimental psychologist must, there is still the obligation to be as systematic as possible and to strive to make the written description as true as possible to the ethnographer's observations and experiences. Well-written ethnographies make good reading, but they are not constructed easily.

Early anthropologists studying entire, previously undocumented cultures often wrote book-length ethnographies organized according to various spheres of life, such as religion, work, family and children, social structure, economy, and technology. Today, there are really no entirely new unexamined cultures left to study, although there are plenty of ever-evolving subcultures worthy of study. The modern ethnographer is more likely to be studying an institution, an organization, or a profession—perhaps a mass media organization or profession—and to have a more specific research question in mind. Even though the principle of cultural holism still guides the work, the end product of the research is likely to be less comprehensive and more focused.

A specialized analytical approach called the **constant comparative method** (Glaser & Strauss, 1967) is sometimes used by ethnographers and other qualitative researchers to extract recurring themes from a large body of verbal or textual material (such as a set of interview transcripts) in a systematic way. The task is to reduce a mass of descriptive detail into a coherent description that pulls out the key characteristics or themes of the research setting. This often means classifying observations or statements without the aid of predetermined categories that might too easily impose the researcher's worldview on the data. Instead, the researcher allows the thematic categories to emerge from the actual data being analyzed by adding, eliminating, or refining categories as necessary.

BOX 2.2

The Ethics of Ethnography

When anthropologists' descriptions were most often of isolated groups with no written language and no access to today's mass media, an individual researcher's description would never be read by those described in it. The situation is quite different today. What are the researcher's obligations to produce a description that will "ring true" to members of the culture being described?

Generally, ethnographic researchers feel they have strong obligations to respect the wishes of those who allow them into their lives. Although the group being studied may not need (or want) to know every detail of the study, the research must be done in an open way, and those being studied must be given a choice as to whether to participate.

Occasionally, ethnographic methods are used to study groups that are underground or even illegal. Clearly, this holds very special potential for ethical conflicts. While rare in mass communication studies, we might imagine these conflicts arising in a study of illegal sharing of music files among teens or of the production and distribution of pornography in a major city.

Mass Communication Applications

Qualitative methods in general, and ethnographic description using participant observation and depth interviews in particular, have enjoyed something of a renaissance in mass communication studies. These are ideal
methods for understanding the role of media in everyday life in ways that
experimental or survey research, without the rich contextual detail and
holistic approach of ethnography, cannot duplicate. However, some of the
earliest mass communication studies also used participant observation and
other qualitative techniques.

White's (1950) study of newsroom practices—one of the studies that helped
establish media research as a field and helped develop the very important concept of "gatekeeping" in the newsroom—was also one of the first mass
communication applications of ethnography. This study was conducted by a
researcher sitting at the elbow of newspaper editors, observing their
decision-making work from an insider perspective, and trying to understand
(from the editors' point of view) why certain stories were chosen while others
were left aside. Tuchman (1978) later used elements of ethnography to understand how newsrooms, as distinctive social organizations, produce a particular
version of social events.

Ethnography is also important in audience studies. Janice Radway, in
her well-known 1984 book *Reading the Romance,* used ethnographic techniques to document the reasons why women read romance novels. She
spent time in a bookstore that specialized in romantic fiction, used the
storekeeper as a key informant, and, with input from the readers of this
fiction, tried to understand how the activity of romance reading fit into
their daily lives and what it meant for them. Radway is only one of a growing number of media researchers who understand and use ethnographic
techniques, many of whom base their work on that of anthropologists such
as Clifford Geertz (1973).

Made possible by the expansion of broadcast bandwidth, the proliferation
of specialized media material catering to particular ethnic and language
groups—not to mention special-interest programming for everyone from
sports fans to homeowners—helps illustrate the degree of cultural pluralism in
many modern societies. Why do people watch football games or soap operas?
What roles do newspapers, computers, or video games play in individuals'
everyday lives? Above all, what meanings do these messages and experiences
hold for members of particular cultural worlds?

Ethnography is a good way to approach answering these questions.
Everyday social life is rich with opportunities to increase our understanding
of the relationship between media and society using ethnographic methods.

PSYCHOLOGY AND THE EXPERIMENTAL METHOD

In some ways, experimental psychology is at the opposite end of the social science spectrum from cultural anthropology because it tends to be very quantitative (sometimes elaborately so) rather than qualitative and tends to focus on the individual rather than on broader cultural or social influences. As is true for anthropology, however, there are historical reasons why psychological methods developed in the direction they did.

Some early theory in psychology, such as that of the famous Sigmund Freud, was developed largely on the basis of observations of patients in clinical settings for treating observed problems, rather than on data collected specifically for research. While many psychologists and psychiatrists whose primary work is treating patients rather than doing research continue to find Freud's **psychoanalytic** theories (and the related family of theories that came later) useful, others became increasingly concerned that these theories were difficult to test against research data. Feminist scholars have also pointed out that Freud's ideas about women were heavily colored by the Victorian times in which he lived.

The **behaviorist** movement in mid-20th-century American psychology was a reaction against the psychoanalytic approach, based on the perception that theory building in the Freudian tradition (even if useful for treating patients) was not scientifically rigorous enough. Behaviorists, such as American researcher B. F. Skinner, argued that it was best to limit the social scientific study of human behavior to factors that could be directly observed and measured under laboratory conditions.

Behaviorism was thus explicitly positivist in its orientation. How could psychology advance as a scientific discipline, these researchers asked, unless it could develop testable hypotheses based on direct measurement? If there was no way to determine whether one psychologist's interpretation was better than another's, no accumulated body of accepted knowledge could be developed. This emphasis on collecting experimental data under controlled laboratory conditions has been a powerful influence in the field of psychology that certainly continues today.

Behaviorism's influence can also be seen very clearly in American mass communication studies in the early (World War II and immediate postwar) years. What's now called "magic bullet" thinking in mass media theory—the mistaken idea that there is a simple, direct relationship between media content and what people think—has much in common with behaviorism's emphasis on the direct relationship between an observable **stimulus**, or environmental cause, and a measurable **response** made by an organism to its environment. However, researchers can use experimental methods without making the reductionist assumption that communication can best be understood in terms of stimuli and responses alone.

Some types of media-related questions (although certainly not all) can be approached very effectively with experimental methods borrowed from psychology, especially questions of the media's short-term effects on perception and behavior. And today's experimental psychology, which uses many different theories that are potentially helpful for understanding how media information is received by individuals, is much broader than the earlier behaviorist tradition. For example, the field of cognitive psychology has contributed a great deal to our understanding of how people process the information they receive from the media, and social cognitive theory helps us understand how this might translate into social behavior.

A strict behaviorist might not have seen much meaning in the term **attitude**, usually defined as a stable or persistent positive or negative orientation toward some object, idea, or group. Attitudes can be measured only indirectly, usually through the use of questionnaires, or be inferred through particular behaviors, such as attraction or repulsion, or answers offered to the researcher's questions. Yet, both psychologists and media researchers work with attitudinal data quite regularly, sometimes using the methods of experimental psychology along with data from public opinion surveys.

Interpretive and other qualitative researchers may distrust attitudinal research for entirely different reasons; they feel that getting answers to survey questions is a poor way to understand someone's point of view in any meaningful sense. Whether from a behaviorist or an interpretive perspective, it's worth asking from time to time whether things like attitudes are real or only reified. However, the concept of attitude has been a useful one in understanding the formation of public opinion and its application in fields ranging from political communication to market research.

Methodological Limitations

All human communication depends heavily on the manipulation and interpretation of symbols, whether verbal or visual. Many elements of these defy easy measurement using numerical scales. Regardless of the shortcomings of Freud's ideas, which emphasized unconscious symbolic meaning, behaviorism in its narrowest sense was equally flawed from the point of view of communication research. However, the experimental methods behaviorism helped develop represent a valuable legacy for media research.

Whenever a researcher is dealing with reasonably well-understood and readily observable or otherwise measurable phenomena and is interested in fairly clear-cut cause-and-effect relationships among them, experimental methods are a good choice. They can help determine, for example, whether male or female news anchors are more credible, whether viewing violent films results in short-term physiological or behavioral changes, which of several messages about an issue is the most persuasive, or whether one computer interface takes longer to master than another.

Used creatively and cautiously, experimental methods can provide valuable answers to these and many other questions. The trick is to remember their origins—and limitations. They will not provide answers to questions about long-term effects, nor can they reveal what effects might occur outside of laboratory conditions. These results do not always carry over well into real life. Longer-term influences, such as those suggested by cultivation theory, require other approaches.

The Concept of Experimental Control

The great power of the **controlled experiment** is its ability to focus on a limited number of variables of interest. Children, for example, grow up under the influence of teachers, parents, friends, and siblings—and mass communication messages. These influences continue to accumulate over a lifetime. Sorting out, through research, which elements have what kinds of effect is not an easy task. Using a controlled experiment, researchers can look at the short-term influence of a small number of these possible causative factors, or **independent variables**, at one time.

This is accomplished in part by holding constant, or "controlling," as many other influences as possible. Those outcomes (whether perceptions, attitudes, or behaviors) that are expected to change as a result of variation in the independent variables are called **dependent variables**.

For example, a researcher interested in seeing the extent to which a musical soundtrack changes the effectiveness of a political advertisement would want to test several identical ads, each with different kinds of music, on audiences that are as alike as possible. One ad might have no music at all. In this example, the ads with different music would be referred to as different "conditions" or "treatments." The ad with no music, used for comparison, would be called the "control" or "control condition."

Three options are available to achieve control in an experiment: laboratory conditions, choice of participants, and statistical manipulation. The most important of these is probably the use of controlled laboratory conditions.

Participants in psychological experiments are usually tested in a special research setting, not in their homes. Each **subject** (the term used in psychology to refer to a research participant) is treated exactly the same, which minimizes the chance that a difference in room color, temperature, the order in which events occur, the way a question is asked or a task explained, or something else about the subject's interaction with the researcher, the research setting, or the research staff has an influence on the dependent variable that might be different from one subject to another.

In the example above of music in political advertising, it would be important to be certain that each subject had a nearly identical viewing experience, with the single exception of the music used in the ad "treatment."

The second means of control is through the choice of subjects (participants), the people who will be tested in the experiment. One way to do this is to limit the subject pool. For example, if you want to rule out the influence of gender, you could study only men or only women. Unfortunately, in this case, the results would apply to only half of the population, because results obtained for one gender might not apply to the other. Control achieved by limiting participation is possible but should be used with caution.

University researchers often use students as subjects. This helps eliminate the possibility of age or level of education affecting the results but opens the researcher to the very common criticism that his or her results do not apply to people who are *not* college students. Nevertheless, sometimes this convenient form of control is appropriate.

Another element of subject selection involves assignment to different treatments or conditions. In the political communication example, one option would be to randomly assign each subject to view one of the ads. Subsequent checks can easily confirm whether the random assignments have created groups that are equivalent in terms of key demographics.

The third type of control is statistical. Almost always done with computer software, modern techniques for statistical analysis can do a good job of estimating the effects of different "candidate" independent variables and therefore compensate for treatment groups that are not perfectly equivalent.

However well controlled, experimental methods are designed to investigate cause-and-effect relationships. In real life, media act as both cause and effect at the same time. If media influence public attitudes, public attitudes are also reflected in the media. One key characteristic of communication media content is that it reflects what some members of a society and culture are thinking, doing, and feeling—at the same time as it influences the thinking, doing, and feeling of others. Experimental methods allow researchers to work around this but run the risk of reifying the idea that media influence is a one-way street.

In today's world of rapidly expanding media alternatives, audience members choose content based on their own preferences. Laboratory experiments rarely reflect this.

Experimental work is subject to two other important criticisms. It usually measures only short-term effects, whereas many important media effects are cumulative and take place over a lifetime of exposure. Also, the way people act and react in laboratory situations, while perhaps satisfying the experimenter's need for controlled conditions, may not be very much like the way they would act and react in actual everyday life. This is especially true for mass media studies. Persons watching TV at home while doing the dishes or surrounded by family or friends could react to the programming quite differently than they would in a research setting.

BOX 2,3

The Challenges of Experimental Control

Say you want to study whether information obtained from television or information obtained from print is better remembered. This seems simple enough. You would probably want to have one group of subjects watch a television program (or, perhaps, a commercial) and a second group read the same information in printed form. To control for information content, you'd have to make sure that exactly the same information was presented in the printed and visual forms. But how can you? Visual media contain images that cannot be duplicated in printed text. Only the soundtrack can be made to match the text. The visual images may be quite powerful, but because they contain additional information, this experiment would not completely "control for" information content. We may be able to tell which presentation is better remembered, but we wouldn't know exactly why without additional research.

More on Choosing Subjects

Literally dozens of factors can affect experimental results: age; education; gender; ethnicity; religion; region or nationality; whether our subjects are urban or rural residents; their personalities, socioeconomic status, attitudes, beliefs, and political affiliations—the list is almost endless. Often, researchers cannot eliminate many of these factors as possible influences on dependent variables. To solve this problem, researchers typically rely on random selection of participants from a larger population. Done properly, this allows the researcher to conclude that the results apply to (or are "generalizable to") that larger population.

Many types of random sampling techniques are used, but the simplest, called **probability sampling,** may be the one most people think of as truly "random." In a probability sample, each member of the population under study (say, all adults of voting age in the United States) would have exactly the same chance of being included. Now, all you would need is a list of all these folks. Then, we could just put all their names into a giant hat and draw out as many as we need!

Well, that's the idea, anyway. In practice, unfortunately, such a list simply doesn't exist. Even if it did, most of those chosen from our "giant hat" would probably not agree to participate. This is an increasing problem in all kinds of research. In experimental research, some degree of compromise is required.

In both surveys and experiments, people are sometimes paid for participating or offered a chance at a prize. However, those who agree to participate—for whatever reason—are not likely to be identical in social demographics, personality profile, and so on to the general population as a whole. They may be more cooperative, more interested in research, or more in need of any rewards offered; have more time on their hands; and so on. In fact, almost any recruitment strategy guarantees that something other than truly random selection is occurring.

Human Subjects Issues

While *all* university-affiliated research involving people requires approval by an Institutional Review Board (IRB) for human subjects (or equivalent), ethical issues are especially sensitive for experiments. The potential for psychological harm to participants is most obvious when the research takes place in a laboratory setting, in which the subjects may not always feel free to get up and walk away. Some experimental research can involve (and has involved) putting people in difficult or embarrassing situations, asking them personal questions, or deceiving them about the actual research purpose, and it is difficult or impossible to guarantee such experiences will not have lasting effects.

Do these issues apply to media experiments? Absolutely. For example, researchers who believe that exposure to violent or pornographic material has negative effects on people will be hard pressed to establish that experiments with such material do not cause harm to those who participate. This is especially important when children are involved. Clever designs may help; for example, Alfred Bandura's classic (1977) study put children with dolls instead of with other children to study how youngsters behave after watching violent entertainment. Still, can it be guaranteed that such experiences do not have a lasting or even permanent effect on the children who participate?

Researchers (including student researchers) should always think about the ethics of their work and its possible, if inadvertent, effects on subjects. This obligation extends beyond the necessity of meeting applicable IRB requirements. Sometimes, IRB paperwork is a significant bureaucratic burden; other times, IRB offices overlook potential harms. In the end, researchers must take personal responsibility for ensuring their procedures are as ethically sound as they can make them.

Mass Communication Applications

Because of the power of controlled experiments to demonstrate or rule out causal relationships, the evidence they produce is persuasive (even though it may not always apply outside of the laboratory or equally to different groups). Experiments are a common and respected way of investigating media influences and effects. Even though experiments can demonstrate only short-term effects, with the potential for overstating these while overlooking "sleeper" effects that might appear later or long-term effects that happen only as a result of repeated message exposure, they often produce the most clear-cut evidence on a number of important questions.

Literally thousands of studies have been done of the relationship between exposure to media violence and subsequent behaviors and beliefs. Many of these studies, perhaps the majority, have used experimental methods. Of course, in real life, many other factors come into play, including the influences of family, peers, and community. Nevertheless, the most powerful evidence of media influence has accumulated through these experimental studies.

Studies conducted on propaganda and persuasion effects, beginning in the World War II period, have relied heavily on experimental methods. These have demonstrated many factors, such as the influence of source credibility, the effects of content placement within a message, and the persuasiveness of particular messages for particular types of audiences. For obvious reasons, the experimental approach to studying message persuasiveness continues to appeal to advertisers, whether they are concerned with encouraging product purchases, influencing voting behavior, promoting more healthy choices, or changing attitudes on issues.

Work on the process of agenda setting—how issues that are prominent in the media become prominent in the minds of readers and audiences—also commonly uses experimental methods. Agenda setting is now well established as a mass media effect, with laboratory experiments providing strong evidence of this. Research is ongoing to understand these effects in more detail.

These are only a few of the more prominent examples of the many topics that media researchers have investigated using experimental methods. New communication technology is now presenting opportunities to extend this work in significant ways. Do source credibility and agenda setting work the same way when the message is delivered over the Internet on a computer screen—and audiences make more active choices of which message to view? How are the effects of violent video games on children the same as, or different from, the effects of violent television on children?

SOCIOLOGY AND THE STUDY OF HUMAN SOCIAL GROUPS

The third major contributor to the methodological repertoire of media research is the field of sociology. While anthropology concentrates on understanding cultural variation and psychology concentrates on understanding individuals, sociology concentrates on understanding the nature of human social groups, from small organizations to large "mass" societies. To a sociologist, understanding society means more than understanding individual-level processes—it means understanding how *groups* of individuals are organized, interact, and mutually influence one another.

Methodologically, sociology is diverse. Sociologists make use of both qualitative methods (some drawn from cultural anthropology) and quantitative methods. Since sociology is concerned in part with group or **collective behavior**, the study of public opinion formation has been an important area of research in the field—and one that clearly has strong links to the study of media influences. This interest in public opinion was the motivation for sociologists to develop and refine survey research methods. Early mass communication research was very heavily influenced by sociologists.

Sociological Theory and Media Studies

Sociological theory has provided many insights into the "mass" in mass communication. Influential theorists in sociology include Émile Durkheim (1858–1917), who saw modern society as a *system* characterized by an increasingly complex division of labor; Max Weber (1864–1920), who saw modern society as driven by distinctive *values;* and Karl Marx (1818–1883), who saw modern society as marked by *conflict* between owners and workers. Note that all three of these influential theorists were attempting to understand the major changes in 19th-century European society as the Industrial Age unfolded.

All three of these streams of thought have found their way into mass communication studies. Following the thinking of Durkheim, media scholars continue to do **functionalist** analysis of the roles media institutions play in keeping complex modern societies going by maintaining social order. Early mass communication scholars, such as Harold Lasswell and Charles Wright, identified many of the media's most important social functions; others have continued to add to this list.

Others (influenced in a general way by Marx) are **conflict theorists** who have been more concerned with the media's role with respect to the unequal distribution of power in these societies. The British **cultural studies** tradition, reflected in the work of such scholars as Stuart Hall, focuses specifically on issues of power and conflict as played out in the media; some American media scholars, including Herbert Schiller and Todd Gitlin, have also been concerned with these issues.

Every society rests on a **value system** that is widely shared by its members. Sociologist Herbert Gans (1979) found a series of "enduring values" in American society, such as individualism (a focus on the leadership of individuals), moderatism (a distaste for extreme views), and pastoralism (a positive view of rural life), reflected in the way media present the news. Media can certainly serve to perpetuate old values and beliefs, including racial and gender stereotypes, but they can also participate in changing them.

Social psychology is the psychology of human social interactions. **Symbolic interactionism**, originating in the work of George Herbert Mead (1863–1931), specifically focuses on human interaction as a source of meaning and identity. This important branch of sociology also has implications for understanding media, which often have influences similar to face-to-face interactions among people. Symbolic interactionists have developed the term **labeling theory** to describe the way we categorize certain activities or individuals as normal or abnormal; this process also takes place through the media.

More generally, our perception of reality itself is largely learned from the society around us, through social interaction with others. This idea of the **social construction** of reality (sometimes called "constructivism") was developed by Berger and Luckmann (1966), who argue that we live in a world literally defined by our own perceptions and expectations, derived from the society and culture in which we live. The media are an enormously important source of these perceptions and expectations, and constructivist thinking has become a big influence in media studies.

A few media researchers have adopted a branch of constructivism called **ethnomethodology**, associated with the work of sociologist Harold Garfinkel and others, that is specifically concerned with how individuals actively make sense of their everyday lives (sometimes called "sense-making"). Despite its difficult name, this area of research is not a methodology at all but tries to characterize the "methodology" that ordinary people use to interpret everyday events and interactions—including media messages.

Public Opinion Studies

Methodologically, one of the most unique and most important contributions of sociology to mass communication research is the development of survey research. Many media messages are actively intended to influence public opinion; in other cases, the influence may not be intentional but is no less powerful. Survey research, sometimes combined with content data, has become very important in mass communication studies, especially for political communication specialists. Media representations may have important implications for how public opinion is formed through suggesting to people what others are thinking (Noelle-Neumann, 1984), as well as through more direct influence.

While survey research may seem easy and is often the first thing beginning researchers think of when they are imagining a study they might conduct, doing a good survey that will yield useful information is quite difficult. Telephone surveys are convenient and had largely replaced in-person and mail surveys until lower response rates and the popularity of cell phones complicated the picture. Fewer people are willing to participate in surveys today than ever before, and because not everyone owns a traditional "land-line" telephone, not everyone can be reached by most phone surveys. Internet-based surveys are emerging to fill this gap, but not everyone uses the Internet or has e-mail—and those who do may be too overwhelmed with junk e-mails to respond to legitimate research surveys.

Other technical problems involve the challenges of writing clear questions that mean the same thing to everyone, putting them in an order that does not lead the **respondent** (the person responding to the survey) to a particular conclusion, and finding ways to distinguish thoughtful opinions from the opinions of those who have no prior knowledge of the survey subject.

Some argue persuasively that public opinion surveys are—at best—only a superficial means of understanding a complex aspect of collective behavior, but they do "take the pulse" of public thinking in a useful way. In practice, an opinion generally represents no more and no less than what people express when they are asked a question in a survey, often the result of an unexpected phone call or e-mail. As with attitudes, it is worthwhile to consider whether such "opinions" are real or only reified.

Nevertheless, survey research methods used in public opinion work constitute an important contribution from sociology, not only to media studies but to political science and other fields as well. As a practical matter, advertisers, politicians, marketers, health promoters, and others who hope to influence society through media messages find survey work an invaluable tool.

Other Methodological Contributions

A number of other alternatives have been adopted by media studies scholars that (while not necessarily derived exclusively from the work of sociologists) were developed in sociology before becoming popular choices in media research. These include **unobtrusive observation, focus groups**, and case studies.

Unlike participant observation, where the researcher is a visible member of a group, unobtrusive observation refers to a research strategy in which the observation is not known to those whose behavior is being observed. This sounds a lot like spying, and in fact, if it is carried out in places where people expect to be in private (such as a restroom or their home) rather than in public (such as a park, shopping mall, or pub), it can be a violation of privacy law in addition to IRB rules. Observing people in public places is generally permitted, however, so long as observed individuals cannot be identified in the published research report, and furthermore, unobtrusive observation is a broad category that also includes indirect indicators of people's actual behaviors.

A simple example would be counting the cars parked in a discount store parking lot the day after a mass advertising mailer was distributed in the local community. While not particularly common in media studies, this approach could be very useful. Watching what magazine or newspaper stories people peruse while waiting in line at the grocery store, for example, could yield useful information. For many examples of unobtrusive observation studies in sociology, see Webb (1966).

Often used in market research, a focus group is a group of people brought together to gather their *collective* reactions to an idea or a product. Questions are asked of the assembled group rather than of individuals one at a time (by using depth interviews, for example) because the actions and reactions of the group members produce different responses. Ignoring the presence of the moderator may also be easier for group members than for individuals in an interview situation. Although focus groups are sometimes loosely termed "group interviews," this is not correct because the whole point is to tap into interpersonal dynamics, not just to gather the opinions of individuals.

Focus groups often deal with emerging issues or potential new products, so group members who have not formed strong opinions often have their thinking stimulated by the comments of the group—without being overly influenced by an interviewer as can happen in a one-on-one situation. Focus group moderators, like depth interviewers, do best if they are highly skilled at managing group interactions without controlling them. This means making sure each individual gets a chance to talk so that a few strong voices do not dominate, without leading the group in a particular direction. These moderators often work with a list of questions or topics similar to the guide for a semistructured interview.

Finally, sociologists and other social scientists have developed the case study approach, which can also be used in media studies. Yin (2008) describes case study research as a "strategy." This might be more accurate than calling it a "method," because case studies can make use of most of the methods that have been discussed in this chapter, especially ethnographic methods, interviews, and in some cases surveys. Case studies also often involve the collection of available data about the social setting under study, such as the demographics of members or workers in an organization. The key thing about the case study is not that it uses unique methods but that it is designed to study a particular example—such as an organization, an agency, or another work setting; media coverage of a specific significant event; or an institution, such as a school or hospital—in considerable depth. The limitation of the case study is that the findings may or may not apply to other similar examples; nevertheless, examining even one specific instance of a social phenomenon in great depth can yield a level of understanding not available from any other approach.

Sociologists also make use of various methods to study media content, both qualitative and quantitative. However, these methods have been developed primarily within media studies rather than borrowed from outside, so they will be discussed in the next chapter (as well as in more detail at several other points in this book).

Important Terms and Concepts

Attitude	Culture
Behaviorist	Dependent variable
Collective behavior	Depth interview
Conflict theorist	Ethnocentrism
Constant comparative method	Ethnography
Controlled experiment	Ethnomethodology
Cultural relativism	Focus group
Cultural studies	Functionalist

Holism	Respondent
Independent variable	Response
Informant	Social construction
Interpretive community	Social psychology
Labeling theory	Social role
Nonverbal communication	Stimulus
Norms	Subculture
Participant observation	Subject
Population	Symbolic interactionism
Probability sampling	Unobtrusive observation
Psychoanalytic	Value system

Exercises

Exercise 1

Successful depth interviews, used in qualitative sociology as well as cultural anthropology, require well-developed interviewing skills. This exercise is designed to give you the opportunity to practice interviewing someone about an aspect of his or her life using this method. Find a volunteer willing to give you at least a half hour to an hour of his or her time for this purpose. Choose someone who is involved in an organization or activity you would like to know more about—playing a sport, pursuing a particular college major, or perhaps participating in a media activity like reporting for the student newspaper.

1. Construct an interview guide that gives you a general list of topic areas to be covered. Your goal is to understand the person's everyday involvement with the activity or organization and what that involvement means to him or her. A good question to start with is "What is it like to . . ." You might also ask the person to explain how he or she originally got involved in the activity.

2. In conducting the interview, choose a relaxing setting. Take notes or record the interaction. Use follow-up questions to keep the person talking, such as "What else can you tell me about that?" and "Why?" Try to create a conversational atmosphere without letting the interview go completely off topic.

3. Afterward, write a summary of what you found out on two to three double-spaced pages (about 600–800 words). It is best to do this as soon as possible after completing the interview so you don't have to rely entirely on your notes. Your instructor may want you to submit this summary for course credit.

4. As the last paragraph of your summary, reflect on how well the interview went. Were there difficulties understanding the activity or organization and its role in your informant's life? Did the conversation go smoothly, and if not, how did you manage the situation? Were there things you wished you had asked but didn't think of at the time? What was the most interesting thing you learned?

Exercise 2

Public opinion research is important to sociologists and mass communication researchers alike; in addition, survey results are often a central topic of media reports, especially around the time of important elections. Yet good survey questions are remarkably difficult to write. To help you think about this dimension, try the following exercise.

1. Choose a current issue about which you believe college students on your campus are likely to have well-developed opinions. (Writing good questions is even more difficult on topics for which people have not yet made up their minds.)

2. Write three clear, succinct survey questions that you believe will assess student opinion on the issue you have chosen in a reasonable, accurate way. Make your questions as unambiguous as possible so that they will mean the same thing to everyone.

3. "Pretest" these questions on at least three of your classmates or friends. Your instructor may want to make this an in-class exercise. Ask your pretest respondents to discuss what they thought each question was getting at, to identify any areas of uncertainty in the wording, and to explain why they answered each question the way that they did.

4. Rewrite the questions in response to this feedback. Are you sure they still measure what you originally intended?

CHAPTER 3

Mass Communication as a Research Field

Among social science fields, mass communication research (or media research) is clearly a latecomer. As shown in Chapter 2, the field borrows most of its methods from other social science fields, including anthropology, sociology, and psychology—as well as history, economics, and another relative latecomer: political science. Ideas from linguistics and from rhetorical and literary studies are also used. But mass communication research has also invented a few approaches of its own, in particular various forms of media **content analysis** (techniques for the systematic study of media content).

Because mass communication research generally takes place within schools and departments that also support professional studies, especially at the undergraduate level, it often has an emphasis on applied research that is related to this professional mission. However, many academic media research specialists are interested primarily in theoretically driven questions, parallel to the questions about media that have been raised by scholars in the foundational disciplines discussed in Chapter 2.

The applied side of media research responds to the practical concerns relevant to mass communication fields, such as public relations and advertising; persuasive political communication; or the design of communication campaigns intended to change human behavior in such areas as health or environment. Other applied work may seek to improve the professional practice of journalism, as well as to identify a market advantage to be gained by doing so. For example, the "civic journalism" movement of recent years was an attempt to make journalism more relevant to society, especially at the local level, but at the same time, it gave news-papers and other media an opportunity to grow and flourish through reaching new markets in ways news consumers found compelling, sometimes as a result of experimenting with novel technology-based approaches.

Research oriented toward these practical purposes exists alongside mass communication research that is driven primarily by theory and that is of interest primarily for its contribution to our understanding of society. Often, this understanding-oriented research includes studies that are critical of existing insti-tutions and taken-for-granted, value-based assumptions, and it may seek to expose the contribution (often indirect and unintended) of professional practice to the maintenance of inequities, the distortion of communication, and other problems in society, as well as to examine the media's potential for improving society by alle-viating some of these problems. This can also be considered a form of application; the distinction between theoretical and applied research is not always clear-cut.

Some scholars explicitly combine the two. As argued in Chapter 1, the best research often combines practical with theoretical goals. Theories about the distribution of power in society and the roots of conflict—sometimes referred to as "critical theory"—may drive analyses that seek to improve, as well as to understand, the social roles of the professional fields of mass communication. Research about human cognition, information-seeking behavior, and persua-sion may be motivated by a desire to understand these processes on a theoret-ical level yet have direct application in applied areas ranging from selling new products to improving Web site navigation. Science communication research may seek to raise public understanding and awareness of science, technology, and associated risks and benefits at the same time as it enhances our theoreti-cal knowledge about how people learn and form opinions on complex subjects; this work has applied, as well as theoretical, purposes.

A degree of dynamic tension between theoretical work, often critical in nature, and instrumental or applied work exists in all social science fields, but it may be more visible in mass communication studies. Theorists and critical scholars can be skeptical of the influence of practical goals on academic research agendas in mass communication, arguing that this leads to shallow instrumental thinking that ignores important "big-picture" issues. But profes-sionals in the mass communication fields also want to find answers to more immediate problems, and universities are increasingly dependent on grant funding (often driven by instrumental goals) to make ends meet. Fortunately, the best research can often—although not always—meet both goals.

Research on how to improve the ways that media organizations serve their audiences can contribute to the business success of newspapers, Web sites, and television stations and at the same time help these organizations raise the degree of involvement ordinary citizens experience with respect to decision making in their local communities. Research on how best to promote a new line of clothing or cars can also help others promote the adoption of healthier eating habits or more environmentally friendly behaviors. While tensions and skepticism remain, good research can combine instrumental and theoretical considerations. Practically by definition, mass communication research almost always has at least some degree of an applied dimension in that its subject matter is almost always relevant to professional practice—even if the research is inspired by purely theoretical considerations or is motivated by a desire to criticize that practice.

ORIGINS OF MASS COMMUNICATION RESEARCH

Scholars often date the origin of mass communication as an independent field of research to the period in the United States between World War I and World War II when the local neighborhood movie theater became increasingly popular. During this period, an important series of studies about film, collectively referred to as the Payne Fund Studies (see Jowett, Jarvie, & Fuller, 1996) attempted to document how exposure to new ideas and lifestyles from Hollywood was changing the values, expectations, and social behavior of American youth. Of course, many other things were changing at the same time—not only did young people attend neighborhood theaters in increasing numbers, but they also increasingly used automobiles to escape from parental supervision for the first time. Network radio broadcasting, also the subject of early mass communication research, arose. In addition, increasing urbanization involving both rural-to-urban migration within the United States and successive waves of immigration into the United States from Europe and elsewhere was changing American culture, creating a much more diverse and mobile society. Today, these processes of urbanization and immigration are global, not simply national, and are creating global markets for media messages alongside those for agricultural and manufactured products.

A second wave of mass communication research, arguably even more influential, was created in response to World War II. The apparent success of Nazi propaganda in influencing the population of Germany focused research attention on the potential persuasive effects of the media. Wartime communication campaigns urged U.S. citizens to purchase war bonds, consume less popular cuts of meat, and otherwise support the war effort, and research into persuasion and the effects of mass communication supported these efforts. Famed Hollywood movie director Frank Capra was personally recruited by the U.S. military to make more effective films promoting America's involvement in the war. An entire generation of women followed "Rosie the Riveter" (a character used in a U.S. government advertising campaign during the World War II era) into factory work to replace the men who had gone off to fight, to support an expanded manufacturing effort that produced the equipment, supplies, and munitions they needed to win. Many women from this era never stopped working outside the home; they had made the transition not merely as a patriotic gesture but because of significant economic needs and a desire for independence that did not end with the war.

And then, just after the war ended, U.S. households were permanently transformed by the diffusion of television programming into the American living room, which created many new and profound questions about media's influence. Both entertainment programming and the advertising supporting it were associated with fundamental, revolutionary changes in how Americans lived, worked, and played—as well as pervasive popular images of how Americans were *supposed* to live, work, and play as presented in dramas and serials. These ranged from the daytime "soaps" with their stereotypical images of the nuclear family (predominantly White and middle-class, two-parent suburban households) to the evening "westerns" that glamorized an equally stereotypical "Wild West" (a vast, untamed, and extremely violent frontier in which the good guys always wore white hats). Concern arose about the apparently limitless influence of television advertising on voting behavior and other political processes, as well as on social values and consumer choices.

The era of media effects research, originally rooted in the assumption of powerful, direct media effects having far-reaching influences on politics as well as consumer behavior and lifestyles, developed as a way to address these issues. These effects were quickly found to be less mighty and more complex than had originally been assumed, and many original theories had to be qualified or abandoned. Interpersonal communication and mass communication were found to interact in complex and interesting ways, whereas independent mass communication effects were found to be weaker than expected under many circumstances. Nevertheless, mass communication research was here to stay. Its original ideas and research methods, borrowed from the social and behavioral sciences, continued to expand and adapt as they were applied to these new problems. And mass communication researchers developed techniques of their own that were specifically designed for summarizing and analyzing the flow of mass communication messages in a systematic and reliable way.

QUALITATIVE VERSUS QUANTITATIVE RESEARCH REVISITED

Media research of the type presented in this book is generally empirical; that is, it relies on systematically gathered data designed to answer (or explore possible answers to) a predetermined question or questions. However, "data" in this context does not always mean numbers. Mass communication research, in borrowing widely from the other social sciences, has incorporated both qualitative and quantitative methods. As presented in Chapter 1, sometimes fierce arguments are waged about which is preferable, with one side claiming that only quantitative or numerical methods are truly "scientific" measurement while the other side claims that only qualitative or nonnumerical methods are adequate for understanding the full range of human experience.

Regardless of this ongoing dialogue, media research and mass communication studies are well accustomed to using both; for example, historical research about journalism and communication technology is primarily qualitative, while experimental research about media effects more often uses carefully controlled experiments and well-calibrated measurements. Scholars following these two paths may happily occupy adjoining offices in the typical journalism or communication department, and over the course of an undergraduate career, the typical student may take courses from each of them without necessarily noticing this particular difference between them.

Nevertheless, some qualitative researchers report they have had to struggle to achieve credibility in the field. In their early years, mass communication programs may have leaned too far in the direction of preferring quantitative over qualitative methods for two reasons. First, quantitative methods bring with them the prestige of being seen as scientific rather than humanistic, an important factor for a new social science discipline trying to establish itself in a university setting. Second, qualitative research is sometimes confused with journalistic work, which (rightly or wrongly) does not earn the same prestige in an academic research setting. In reality, doing qualitative research right is no less technical or time-consuming than doing quantitative research.

This book tries to do justice to both forms of media research and will return to these questions about qualitative versus quantitative methods at a number of points. If a few extra pages are devoted to quantitative methods than to qualitative methods, it is because this book is designed to be used by students who have had no training in statistics.

CONTENT ANALYSIS AS A KEY RESEARCH TOOL

While sociologists and political scientists also use different forms of content analysis to describe the content of media messages, this is a technique that media research can rightfully call its own. No other social science discipline is so directly concerned with examining what is actually being conveyed in mass communication messages—what types of items appear most frequently, how they are presented, who is speaking, and so on. Some social scientists also use the term *content analysis* to describe the analysis of interview material or other records of verbal responses, but this is a subtly different type of project from the analysis of media content.

Media content is generally constructed by a professional communicator according to specific conventions, like the use of named sources and "inverted pyramid style" writing in newspaper stories, whereas speech (as used in a depth interview, for example) is both more fluid and more interactive—not following a prescribed form but generally offering a response to what someone else has asked or stated. This changes the task of summarizing the content for research purposes. Of course, something like talk radio is both conversational in style—though perhaps not entirely like a naturally occurring conversation—and carried over a communication medium.

Just as a survey can utilize specific questions that are numerically scored but also ask for open-ended verbal responses, content analysis can be quantitative or qualitative. Quantitative content analysis seeks a precise estimate of the presence or absence of different features, such as which topics occupy what proportion of the news or how many times certain kinds of sources receive mention. What features are chosen depends on what the researcher wants to find out; quantitative content analysis most often tests specific hypotheses. Qualitative content analysis looks for more general themes and in this way more closely resembles the analysis of interview data. As you will learn later in this book, sometimes researchers use qualitative content analysis to *identify* content themes but also use numbers to count and communicate *how often* particular themes have been found. The line between quantitative and qualitative content analysis is sometimes blurry.

Other times, the analyst does not attempt to assign themes to particular categories so they can be counted but uses a more purely qualitative approach, sometimes described as "textual analysis" or "discourse analysis." Because of the importance of narrative structure that is characteristic of both news stories and entertainment programming—both have beginnings, middles, and ends, and themes may appear only once or dominate an entire story or segment—counts cannot capture everything, so the purely qualitative approach sometimes makes more sense. However, if the researcher wants to compare different types of media content as precisely as possible or to produce a persuasive argument about that content for an audience that might tend to dismiss purely qualitative evidence, numbers can be very useful.

Many of the concepts used in content analysis (especially quantitative content analysis) are borrowed from survey research. If we want to get the best possible idea of what *all* media content from a certain source or period is like without examining every item, we would ideally rely on a probability sample (just as with a survey), in which each media message of the type with which we are concerned has the same chance of appearing in our sample. This is the same principle applied in public opinion survey research in which somewhere between 200 and 2,000 or more randomly chosen people may be used to accurately estimate what everyone in a larger population (such as all adults living in the United Kingdom or all U.S. voters) would answer if asked the same question. Just as with survey research, however, sometimes it is not easy or even possible to meet this criterion of randomness. Later in this book, we consider approaches that do not rely on strict probability sampling, which is not always practical.

One challenge in content analysis that is not as visible in survey work with people is the way that a population and the appropriate **unit of analysis** (see below) are chosen. The term *population* refers to the entire group of things (or people) that the researcher wants to understand, as discussed in Chapter 2. In public opinion surveys related to political campaigns, the researcher is very often concerned with voters, or perhaps only likely voters, as the population. Children too young to vote may not matter if the goal is to predict the election outcome. If the survey is about product preferences, perhaps the population of interest consists only of those likely to have a need for the product—men may not matter if the product in question is something only women are likely to buy.

In media content analysis, the question of population is not quite as clear. Say, for example, we are interested in the content of all the news about climate change the average person in Hometown, California, is likely to read. Would the population consist of all the articles in the local newspaper? What about national newspapers or magazines and television stories, whether local or national? What if there are two competing papers, perhaps one published right in Hometown and one in a nearby city? We might even need to look at some market statistics on circulations and viewer numbers to decide what article population matters most to what we want to study.

The term *unit of analysis* refers to the individual item being described by the data we collect. In the case of a public opinion or consumer survey, the unit of analysis is most commonly the person. Our sample consists of a certain number of persons; we count each person once; and if we want to calculate the percentages that answer a question a certain way, we use that number as the basis of our calculation (3 out of 4 voters, 90% of dentists, and so on). But this is not always the case.

We can imagine a study concerned with a different type of survey population, such as households. We may not care whether a household consists of 1 person, 4 people, or 10 people. We organize our survey and calculate our results in terms of households, not persons. Perhaps we are interested in how many households occupy single-family houses versus apartments versus temporary quarters of some sort in a given city; our results would be talking about the proportions of households, not persons, in each category. The unit of analysis is the household, not the person. If we ask about the number of persons in the household, this is treated as data about the household, not something that changes the unit of analysis. When we state our conclusions, it is in terms of the numbers or proportions of households, not people, living under different circumstances (although we could multiply it out, household by household, to calculate the number of people in each category if this was desired).

However, for media content analysis, the unit of analysis is often murky. Are we talking about counting and analyzing the features of articles, paragraphs, or entire issues of publications? Are we talking about an individual story in an evening newscast or the newscast as a whole? It is one thing to conclude that only 1 in 10 articles is concerned with the local economy and quite another to say that every issue of the local paper for the past 3 years has had some coverage of local economic issues. Both of these statements can be true at the same time; the difference lies entirely in our choice of a unit of analysis.

Other complications occur. What if Hometown is served by two newspapers, and each carries an almost identical article from the Associated Press one day? Does that count as one story or two? New media technologies complicate this further by introducing the element of time. If a news story appears on a newspaper's Web site in three consecutive versions over a 24-hour period, is that one story or is it three? Finally, what if a story about an issue we are studying appears on a general-purpose Web site like www.yahoo.com but has actually been taken from another media source, such as a newspaper or broadcast news program, that also has a Web presence? If we are trying to study the nature of online content about the issue, would this count as two stories or one?

MASS COMMUNICATION AND NEW MEDIA

For somewhere around 50,000 years, or possibly longer, people have made marks on stone and bone that seemed designed to preserve information, but the pace of change for the communication media we utilize has clearly accelerated over time. The 15th-century invention of movable type in Europe was only one step in a prolonged global revolution in communication technology. Wired telegraphy and telephony and then wireless broadcasting (first in code, then in more complex sound, and then in pictures) soon followed. From the initial post–World War II appearance of black-and-white television sets, not only in American homes but spreading quickly around the world, through the invention of color TV and the advent of cable, satellite, and fiber-optic delivery systems; VCR and DVD systems making time shifting of programming a reality; successive generations of music media from LPs to CDs and MP3s; and the transformation of the personal computer into a communication device used to transmit not only data and text but also music and video, the technologies of mass communication have been undergoing continuous reinvention and sometimes revolutionary change.

Today, handheld "personal data assistants," or PDAs; multifunction cell phones that can capture and transmit text, pictures, and video, as well as voice; and portable personal music and video players are everywhere. Bluetooth, BlackBerry, and iPod have become words in our everyday vocabularies—even though their current forms may already have been transformed anew by the time this book is printed.

The traditional printed newspaper is wondering about its future in a world in which increasing numbers of people get their news on a screen, often a computer screen rather than a television screen, sometimes a screen that fits in the palm of someone's hand. Web-based blogs let anyone who can type create and disseminate his or her own news and information, which has created new freedom for many would-be citizen journalists but also new challenges for news consumers since the origins and credibility of much of the information circulating through the "blogosphere" remain hard to determine (see Tremayne, 2006, for discussion). In this "new media" environment, news and entertainment messages are increasingly personalized, offering audiences new degrees of selectivity and choice. Scholars refer to this trend as **demassification** (Rogers, 1986). Where is the "mass" these days in "mass communication"? Some observers have begun to wonder whether the term *mass communication* has actually lost all meaning.

However, just as the theories and research tools of anthropology that were developed to unravel cultures both distant from and foreign to the researchers who studied them are increasingly turned on social phenomena closer to home, the theories and research tools we have developed to analyze the old "mass" media are being tried, tested, and extended to cover today's "new media." Media organizations continue to be in the business of delivering news, information, entertainment, and advertising messages to audiences, even if these audiences are narrower or more specialized than they were a generation or two ago.

Of course, we can no longer think in terms of a single "mass" audience reached by a few dominant "mass" media that ultimately seem destined to create a single global culture. Today's mass media function quite differently than their predecessors did just a few decades ago when the United States had only three major television networks, pan-European television broadcasting had yet to be imagined, much of Asia and Africa lacked television altogether, and the Associated Press held a near-monopoly on world news. But the theories and tools of "mass communication" research still hold many keys to understanding the dynamics of these new trends. Media globalization is certainly continuing—and even accelerating—but in new forms.

Newer media, such as cell phones, e-mail systems, and blogs, are regularly used for activities that occupy a "middle ground" between interpersonal and mass communication in ways that land-line telephones usually do not, significantly blurring the interpersonal communication–mass communication distinction. These also have reached around the globe. We analyze these new trends using many of the tools, techniques, and methods developed by previous generations.

Important Terms and Concepts

Content analysis

Demassification

Unit of analysis

Exercise

You can use your own daily experiences to study how college students make use of today's media and media technologies. You might think of this as an ethnographic study, except that you are studying your own daily life rather than that of other people. Choose a single day that you expect will turn out to be more or less typical for you in order to carry out this exercise. Your instructor may ask you to submit this information in a written report or to bring it to class for purposes of discussion.

1. The day before, create several blank, lined pages on which to take notes, with narrow columns for time of day, period of time, and type of medium, and leave a broader section for notes about media or message content. It will help if you do this in a notebook or on a clipboard, as you'll carry these sheets with you to write on throughout the day.

2. Write down every use you make of communication media during that day, with a few notes about content—what program you watched, what music you listened to, what Web site you visited; who called you on the phone and what he or she wanted to talk about; your text messages and what they were about. For this purpose, define media broadly to include any communication that makes use of technology.

3. You can also use the "message content" column to make any extra notes about how each instance fits into your day. Did a Web site give you great information? Did a message you got have bad news? Did a magazine article keep you from boredom while you waited for the bus or a doctor's appointment?

4. Summarize the amount of time you spent with each kind of communication medium. Now for the hard part: In a few sentences, describe how you would characterize your use of communication media. How does it fit into your day? What does it mean to your lifestyle—what does it allow you to do?

PART II

Asking Questions and Collecting Data

Creating a Research Plan

CHAPTER 4

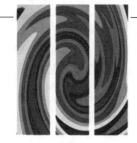

Developing a Research Question, Reviewing the Literature, Exploring Data Sources, and Defining Variables

By now it should be clear that the choice of method depends a lot on the theoretical perspective of the researcher and the type of question being asked. Those who are concerned with the mass media as a causative factor in the acquisition of knowledge or short-term changes in individuals' attitudes, perceptions, behaviors, and opinions are more likely to use experimental methods. Those who are interested in the media's important role in everyday social life and its meaning within a particular cultural context are more likely to choose ethnographic methods. Those who are interested in the interaction of media information with general public opinion will often combine public opinion survey data with data from content analysis. Those who want to understand the mass media's role as a social institution will focus their attention, whatever method they choose, on institutional structure and function—perhaps through a case study of a particular media organization—or on the media content that is itself an outcome of institutional processes. Practical questions about the media are also posed by media managers, educators, advertisers and public relations practitioners, and policy specialists.

None of these perspectives is "wrong" or "right." Mass media research has become an important academic field because of the pervasiveness of the media in modern culture and society. Important studies can be done on many different aspects of the media's various social roles. All of these different questions call for different means to answer them.

A **research question**, whether primarily theoretical or primarily applied, is simply what your research project is designed to explore or answer. Often, the choice of theoretical perspective and preferences about research questions and methods, when not predetermined by particular practical issues, reflect the researcher's training—the ways that he or she has been taught to think about the media—more than anything else. As a student, your understanding of what media research is all about is complicated by the fact that communication researchers have borrowed both theories and methods from fields with widely differing histories and purposes. That is why the first section of this book linked our major social science methods with the fields that developed them.

But these elements of methodological and theoretical diversity are also a great advantage. As a mass communication student, you have the opportunity to develop a better sense of the relationship between theory and method and a deeper understanding of why some methods are chosen over others than students who are taught only how to do experiments, only how to do surveys, or only how to do qualitative studies.

Usually, researchers begin with a general interest in a particular problem. Perhaps it has been unsolved for years, and there's a certain irresistible challenge in it, as with many media effects issues. Perhaps new research on a related issue has suggested a new way to attack an old problem, or the introduction of new technology has changed the media in such a dramatic way that the old conclusions may no longer apply. Perhaps a government agency or private foundation has a special interest in solving a particular problem and makes funds available for research projects in that specific area, such as improving health. Or a manager in a media organization is faced with practical decisions that call for better knowledge of the target population and its response to particular content. In any event, the first step in any research project (after identifying a general direction) is reviewing the academic literature on the issue.

REVIEWING THE ACADEMIC LITERATURE

A review of other researchers' work that has already been published in the academic research literature helps clarify conceptual issues, identify fruitful theories and methods, and rule out "dead ends" that appear to have been thoroughly investigated already, which is why it is first on the list of essential steps in the research process. Sometimes even experienced researchers may be so excited about a project that they want to complete it first and look at the literature later. This might be all right for someone who already knows about most of the scholarship in a particular area, but it can also be a mistake that can lead to a lot of wasted work. Beginning researchers in particular are urged to first understand what others have already discovered about their question. Where you can, plan to build on the work of others rather than trying to reinvent the wheel at every step.

Whether your project turns into a paper submitted for a research course, a thesis or dissertation, or ultimately a published study, the literature review is almost always the first major section after the introductory paragraphs. So it is not just a first research step but an important piece of the final product. This part of the project report summarizes the findings of all the available, closely related research work that has gone before. It is a crucial tool in identifying gaps in our knowledge and in linking a particular research problem to established theory. Not only is the theory helpful in refining your problem and choosing a method, but it also helps link your study to an ongoing stream of studies that ask and answer related questions—making your work a part of an ongoing public dialogue about questions of interest to a community of scholars.

This book is about methods and does not go into theory in depth, but the two are inseparable. More about the role of theory in research is provided in a later section of this chapter.

Sometimes there seems to be no previously published research on a topic, in which case there are several possible explanations. The topic may be difficult or even impossible to investigate using empirical research methods. In other words, it may be a matter of opinion or policy rather than a researchable question (see more discussion of this below). Or the research question may be truly new—an opportunity for exciting discovery! In this case, you must first determine that other research on the question is not "hiding" somewhere in the library. Because media questions interest researchers in a broad range of academic disciplines outside media studies itself (from political science to engineering and psychology to rhetoric), this search can be unusually challenging. A knowledgeable and sympathetic librarian can help enormously here.

Of course, if your study is about something very specific and quite new, such as a particular Web site format that has just been introduced or a piece of technology that has only recently been developed, your literature review is not going to turn up much. By the time this book is in print, quite a number of studies are likely to have appeared about social networking sites, such as

Figure 4.1   Methods without theories are like horsemen without heads. Where does this researcher think she's going?

Facebook or MySpace, but right now (as this is being written), hardly any are available. It usually takes several years for significant studies to be designed, implemented, and published. However, it is also important, even if no published research seems to be available on the specific subject of interest, to identify closely related or analogous studies. What have researchers found out about other Web site formats or earlier but related technologies? Research results that concern earlier related media developments still serve the important purposes of helping clarify theory and suggesting appropriate approaches, by providing some conceptual and practical foundations on which to build.

Modern electronic library indexes have greatly simplified the process of locating appropriate articles and books—but at some risk. Electronic indexes are often incomplete—especially for older material. It may be easy, using these valuable tools, to turn out a bibliography consisting of 100 or even 1,000 references overnight. But what are you going to do with 100 references? You still need to be able to identify which ones are the most important. Those are the ones in which you should invest the time to read, digest, and summarize to inform your own work and to include in your own research report a bit later.

The first edition of this book contained specific suggestions for electronic guides and indexes to the literature most worth consulting. However, this landscape is changing so quickly that it has become difficult to make recommendations likely to remain unchanged for even a few years. Once again, a knowledgeable librarian is vital. All of the literature indexes in modern academic libraries (and most public libraries as well) use a system of keywords, so be sure to start thinking about which keywords are the best for capturing studies relevant to your project (also see the exercise at the end of this chapter).

Another important and perfectly reasonable strategy for locating relevant material is to look at the citations in a few of what appear to be the most important recent articles on your topic, especially those with well-developed literature reviews of their own. Locate the references that appear to be the most crucial in each case, and continue this process using *their* bibliographies until the question seems to be exhausted. Remember that in this strategy you are working backward, however, so you can miss the most recent and therefore most important work. You cannot rely on this strategy by itself, in other words.

What about using search engines to search on the Internet for the literature? There is no harm in trying, but since you are primarily seeking published academic research, this is unlikely to be the most efficient strategy. You will likely turn up too many things that do not fall into this category, you will almost certainly miss some of the relevant publications that would most help you, and you may have to invest a lot of time in sorting the wheat from the chaff—that is, in determining which items are legitimate academic research and which are not. Librarians tell us that this strategy works best for those who are already familiar with the literature in an area and have a pretty good idea of what publications they are looking for. More information about the nature of academic research publications is contained in the next section.

How do you tell when a review of literature is complete? There's no magic trick, and there certainly is no accepted number of citations that is considered appropriate. But there is an important rule of thumb: In doing a thorough review, you'll eventually find that you keep seeing citations to literature that has already been examined. The key academic sources on a specific question are usually reasonably limited in number and often refer to one another.

Writing the review of literature as a section of your final research report is a major task in itself, but it can also be an exhilarating one. Putting the existing literature together in summary form, showing how it relates to a new problem (or a new interpretation of an old one), and identifying gaps and opportunities in the existing research record is both demanding and creative. This skill is at the core of scholarship, and it is every bit as difficult as running a complicated statistical analysis properly or designing the perfect survey. Looking at the literature reviews in a few of the important mass media research journals can give you a good idea of the format (which varies considerably from journal to journal) and style typically used.

Most items cited in your literature review will be journal articles. Of course, books and monographs may also be important, and even popular news articles may provide useful background. But the heart and soul of your literature review will be the academic journal article. For more about this, see below.

THE NATURE OF ACADEMIC PUBLISHING

Why do researchers publish their work anyway? The "publish or perish" imperative in modern universities is sometimes misunderstood and is often the subject of debate. It is true that poor-quality research sometimes comes from professors who seem less interested in the research question they are studying than in getting promoted or getting a new grant. Also, the amount of time that professors devote to writing research articles can interfere with the time they have available for teaching. Yet the most productive researchers are sometimes the very best teachers, partly because they have access to the very latest information. The jobs of university professors generally require them to produce new knowledge, not just pass on the old and worn.

The requirement that university professors publish their work in books and periodicals arose for important reasons and has a long history. It is through publishing—making public—research results that the sciences (including the social sciences) are able to build upon previous results and others' thinking, thus producing an accumulated body of knowledge. Results that have been made public can be scrutinized and tested again, using the same or perhaps a slightly different approach, by other researchers who either confirm or call into question the results. Each generation of researchers is not required to start over but can create new work that rests upon—even though it sometimes reverses—the old.

Published research is usually found in **academic journals**. The term generally refers to periodicals that are devoted primarily (often exclusively) to the publication of research results in a particular area. Before being published, each article typically undergoes a **peer-review** process. The journal editor sends the article out for evaluation by other researchers (the author's "peers") who are specialists in the particular subject matter and methods used. To ensure an objective review, the title page of the manuscript is removed so that reviewers do not know whose work they are looking at. This process is also called a **blind review** because the reviewers are not supposed to know who wrote the article or what institution employs him or her—whether an Ivy League institution or a small state college. (A similar procedure is generally used for conference papers and research grant applications, although grant application reviews may not be blind.)

Reviewers evaluate the strength of the research and recommend to the editor whether to accept or reject the article or, commonly, what revisions would be needed to raise its quality. In this way, they act as the author's silent partners, not just his or her critics. (These days, a lot of this work is done electronically rather than by actually mailing hard copies of manuscripts.) Despite the sincere desire of almost all journal editors to be fair and impartial, the review process also reflects the particular interests and priorities of the journal and its editors. Some publications are more likely to print qualitative work, while others primarily publish quantitative work. Also, each is more interested in studies on some types of research questions than others. The degree of specialization varies but can often be judged by the title (see Box 4.1).

BOX 4.1

Identifying Important Communication Journals

Statistical rankings of journals are an increasingly common tool for judging their quality, although these should be considered only rough indicators. The leading such indicator is probably the Thomson Reuters cross-citation studies (formerly the ISI index). Their communication journal figures for 2007 include a number of publications that are particularly concerned with media or public opinion issues among the top 10: *Public Opinion Quarterly, Journal of Health Communication, Communication Theory, Media Psychology, Science Communication,* and *CyberPsychology & Behavior.* Other top-ranked communication journals, such as *Communication Monographs* and *Communication Research,* regularly include some media studies material along with other types of communication studies articles. These indicators can fluctuate quite a bit from year to year, however.

Another standard is association with a major academic organization in the field. *Journalism & Mass Communication Quarterly* is often considered a leading journal because it is the "flagship" publication of the Association for Education in Journalism and Mass Communication. Similarly, the *Journal of Communication* is associated with the International Communication Association.

Academic journals do not generally make a huge amount of profit, but they must bring in enough revenue to cover their expenses. This means they must consider their readership and strive to present research articles that are likely to be of particular interest to those readers. This tends to encourage and support the existence of communities of scholars with similar interests; in fact, the first academic journals were associated with early scientific societies made up of like-minded researchers. However, it also means that some journals are quite narrow, which can be frustrating to beginning researchers trying to figure out where to send their work—or to understand rejection of what they consider a good paper.

Unlike most commercial print media, academic journals have no formal "query" process in which authors inquire of editors as to their interest in a particular piece. Instead, authors usually make a judgment based on past issues or published guidelines, which are often quite brief, as to where to send their work. However, many journal editors will answer questions about the relevance of a particular manuscript to the journal's interests. Studying the journal itself will also help a great deal.

While no system is perfect, the tried-and-true system of peer review is the best we have. While final publication decisions are up to the journal's editor, he or she generally follows the reviewers' recommendations. The outcome reflects a collective scholarly judgment, not an individual or a commercial one, about the value of the work and its relevance to the area of scholarship the journal serves.

Articles in many of these journals are written in a very dense style that can be quite difficult for the inexperienced researcher to penetrate. Because journal space is at a premium, researchers must write as tersely as possible. Even experienced researchers have trouble writing succinctly yet clearly, which may be one reason why research articles have a reputation for being dull reading. Often providing a minimum of background explanation, they are also written with highly educated and very specialized readers in mind. Try to overlook the style and reach instead for the important information and ideas they offer. And when you find the rare article that is beautifully written as well as offering outstanding scholarship, enjoy!

DEFINING AND REFINING YOUR RESEARCH QUESTION

Before you even begin your literature review, you need some idea of where your project is going—a general topic or at least an area of interest. Reviewing the literature helps identify what other researchers have already resolved and the gaps in our present knowledge, as well as offering ideas for possible approaches and methods. Once you've chosen a general area of interest—say, the role of soap operas in the lives of your fellow college students, the effectiveness of an interactive Web site providing health information, the change in a public figure's popularity following media disclosure of official impropriety, the media representations of war or crisis in another part of the world, the interaction with sources characteristic of modern television journalism, or readership patterns for a local weekly that wants to beef up its circulation—and once the relevant literature has been identified, located, and digested, the next task is to turn this general interest into a researchable problem, represented by one or more specific research questions.

Broad questions about long-term media trends and effects are usually researchable only if reduced to smaller, more specific ones; decades of research, tempered by judgment, are required to actually answer them, and even then the answers will often not be certain. How has the availability of new media for political advertising changed the political system in modern society? What will the eventual influence of the "information superhighway" on public access to information be? How has growing up with video games changed children's attitudes and behavior? Very large, long-term studies are useful in addressing such questions but unlikely to yield definitive answers. These larger studies generally require teams of researchers and substantial funding—unlikely to be available to beginners. Choose something small and specific that you can manage in the time available, whether a single academic term for a course project or a year or so for a master's degree paper.

Usually, defining a researchable question means narrowing a bigger problem and choosing only one aspect of it for immediate study. Are you interested in how the roles of women, as portrayed in popular mass media, have changed over time? Will you study this in print or on television, in entertainment or news? It is better to focus on a thorough study of one particular medium and program genre (say, sitcom dramas or the local evening news) or publication (say, women's magazines) during a specific time. A good project in this area for a course might even focus on several episodes of a single program or several issues of a single magazine. Keep things simple and manageable. You can always add additional data for comparison later.

Comparing two periods, or two programs or publications, can add depth to a small-scale study if it doesn't complicate things too much. In the example above, the research question is about change. If comparing two eras isn't practical, perhaps your literature review has turned up evidence of what things were like 20 years ago that you could use as a basis for comparison with your contemporary data.

If you plan to do research involving people (such as experiments, observations, interviews, or surveys) rather than media content, consult with your instructor at the outset of the project to find out how much time it will take to get human subjects (IRB) permissions. The difficulty of this varies greatly from institution to institution; some institutions make it extremely easy to get permission to do these projects for course credit, and others do not. Deciding to study media content eliminates this hurdle. You might also be able to find survey data from a study someone else has done that you can reanalyze for your project, rather than starting from scratch. This may still require IRB permission in some cases, but it should be a much simpler process.

Bear in mind that some extremely interesting media problems are simply not researchable by the methods of social science. This includes legal, ethical, and policy issues on which social science can shed valuable light but that it cannot ultimately resolve. *Should* televisions be allowed in courtrooms, for example, or *should* children's programming be more aggressively regulated? *Should* parents limit their children's access to the Internet, or *should* news organizations reveal the identities of sexual assault victims? Ultimately, these issues of policy are matters of conscience and societal preference; no study can completely answer them. All "should" questions fall into this category. Social science can provide guidance about the likely effects of a particular decision in some cases, but in order to apply the methods of social science, we must change the "should" in these questions to "what would happen if."

Asking—and answering—a researchable question requires both caution and creativity, both focus and clear thinking, and often a willingness to track down obscure resources, persuade others to participate in and support your study, and sometimes even raise money. Still, asking a simple, if small, question that can be researched on a student budget with readily available tools and resources *can be done*—and also can be a lot of fun! A good trick is to write out your research question on a scrap of paper or a 3 x 5 card and put it where it's constantly in view. One characteristic of a good researcher is a broad interest in all kinds of possible research questions and all sorts of available theories and methods. But actually *finishing* a research project also requires focus.

MORE ABOUT THE ROLE OF THEORY

Up to now, theory has been discussed mostly in general terms. Media theory is often taught as a separate course from methods, but it is generally impossible to produce the very best research without some kind of theoretical idea to guide you. Fortunately, many courses on media and society, even introductory ones, include at least some material about theory. If you have not taken a media theory course, it is especially important that you pay attention to the theories that have been used in the academic literature that you have located on your topic. Refer also to Chapter 2 for an introduction to some basic theoretical ideas contributed by our "foundational" disciplines for methods.

Actually, you probably already know a few theories or at least **theoretical concepts** from other courses or from your reading about media issues. While a theory provides a well-developed explanation that can yield testable hypotheses, a theoretical concept is an abstract idea that can be used to guide research but is not fully developed as a theory. Theoretical concepts can be considered a part of theory and can be almost as useful as complete theories in guiding exploratory or inductive research, even though they do not provide specific hypotheses; however, understanding the distinction between a theory and a theoretical concept can be very helpful to a researcher. Here are some examples.

"Agenda setting" is an example of a theory in media studies. This theory says that when the news media cover an issue, people who read or watch that news will consider the issue more important. Here the cause (media coverage of an issue) is very clearly linked to an effect (people thinking the issue is more important). Many studies have very clearly demonstrated this effect. Agenda setting may be a rather narrow theory, but it is one of our most robust, easily demonstrated explanations for one way that media accounts definitely appear to influence news consumers.

"Framing," on the other hand, is an example of a theoretical concept. This concept captures the idea that in creating a news story or another media product, some elements are inevitably left out, and what is put in is organized in a way that produces a certain impression. Framing undoubtedly contributes to the social construction of reality, discussed in Chapter 2, and some scholars have argued it should be considered a theory. However, framing is really a theoretical concept rather than a fully developed theory because (for example) it does not actually specify which types of frame will produce what impression. Even though framing is best considered a concept and not yet a theory, it is a concept that is providing guidance to quite a number of contemporary studies of media content and its influence. The frames offered by a given body of media content can be studied productively, even though the links between frame and production or frame and impression are not completely understood.

The "uses and gratifications" approach studies what people get out of using the media—what purposes it has and what needs it fills. Sometimes these are not obvious. For example, people may watch television or keep up with the news in order to have something to talk about the next day or to give the appearance of being knowledgeable and informed. News often fulfills entertainment functions as well as informing us, while entertainment actually imparts a lot of information—for example, information about social norms and expectations. Uses and gratifications research is especially useful for studying new media, which often take over the niche of old media. E-mail has replaced personal letter writing in many cases. For many people, Internet surfing has replaced newspaper reading and sometimes entertainment TV. But is "uses and gratifications" a theoretical concept or a theory? Most scholars would probably argue it is a theoretical concept. It is an excellent tool for descriptive studies of media consumption patterns but proposes little in the way of explanation about *why* people choose to use different media for different purposes.

Often, a fully developed theory will make use of several theoretical concepts. The developers of communication campaigns sometimes use the "theory of planned behavior" (see Azjen, 1991, for details). This complex theory uses several theoretical concepts to explain the complicated links between attitudes and behavior. One of these is the concept of "self-efficacy" (Bandura, 1977), which refers to the extent to which people feel they have control over an outcome. Self-efficacy is one element of the theory of planned behavior. For example, I am more likely to eat less if I think that I can do it and that it will really help me lose weight; if I don't believe this, I am unlikely to bother. However, by itself, self-efficacy is not as good an explanation for decisions as when it is combined with other factors, including what other people seem to want us to do, in the larger theory. Once again, some people might see self-efficacy as a theory—it does suggest one narrow element of cause and effect—but it is not as complete an explanation as the broader theory of planned behavior can provide.

An example of a theoretical concept from the critical tradition is "hegemony," which states that the media tend to promote a single monolithic way of looking at things (we might say they promote a single worldview or belief system; critical theorists would use the term *ideology* here). Hegemony occupies a middle ground between a full-blown theory of media's role in promoting a particular set of beliefs and a theoretical concept. In itself, hegemony does not specify why media act this way or what effects they have. However, set in the context of the critical literature on the media, this concept does seem to provide a broad understanding of the role of media in maintaining power structures within society. Hegemony can also be observed, if not actually tested in a formal way, by examining the range of sources and points of view incorporated into media accounts, so while it does not lead to specific hypotheses (hegemony does not tell us what causes it to be complete or incomplete in a given situation, for example), it does provide an explanation of one important type of media influence, and it can provide useful guidance for research.

These examples all help make the point that the distinction between a theory and a theoretical concept is not "black and white" but "shades of gray." Scholars might disagree on particular cases. Nevertheless, the distinction is conceptually useful to researchers: It is helpful to understand whether the theory you are using provides an almost complete, or only a partial or tentative, explanation of what is going on or whether it offers a way to only create an organized description but not test a hypothesis. Literally hundreds of theories and theoretical concepts are available in the scholarly literature on media; this section considers only a few common examples.

Theory does not always appear in a separate section in the research report but should be an integral part of the way the problem is set up. Theory helps determine the research question (or questions), will be visible in the literature review, and helps define the hypotheses if the study is deductive rather than inductive.

FINDING RESOURCES AND DATA FOR YOUR PROJECT

You have chosen a general topic and a specific research question, determined what literature is available, thought about what kind of theory is most applicable, and possibly even developed some hypotheses if you have chosen to do a deductive study. Now there is a new group of practical questions to consider. First of all, what resources are available to you for data collection? Many beginning researchers in media studies choose to do content studies; others might reanalyze available opinion data; some might choose to take the extra steps required to gather original data from people or organizations. Although, in an ideal world, your research question would be completely settled, and then you would gather the best data you can to answer it, in practice the logistics of gathering the data often dictate further refinement of the question.

Resources for Media Content

Even though a media content study is probably the most practical for a beginner, you still have to solve the problem of what material to use and where to find it. If you're thinking of doing a magazine study, for example, which magazines will you choose, and for what period? Are copies even available to you?

Not all libraries archive old publications, particularly popular ones, so your study is likely to be limited to what's currently available (recent publications). On the other hand, perhaps your aunt or grandmother has a collection of pre-1950s women's magazines stashed away in her attic. Such things can be valuable resources if your local public or academic library cannot help. (Public libraries sometimes have a wider selection of popular, as opposed to academic, publications—but may have no space to archive them.)

If you decide to study how broadcast content has changed, where will you get data for previous years? The Vanderbilt Television News Archive, with indexes and abstracts in most major university libraries, contains some of this information, although it is largely limited to news and documentary presentations. Some projects can be done using the abstracts alone, but these are an incomplete substitute for copies of the original broadcasts—which are also available but too expensive for most students on a budget.

Some cable or satellite systems broadcast reruns from the early years of TV, although this limits your study to what happens to be currently available. You might choose to focus on current content and rely on your literature review to tell you what things were like in past decades. In this case, be prepared to record the material you want to use so you can examine it closely.

Video or DVD rental businesses have prerecorded episodes from some television shows. Your choices will be limited to what's on their shelves, but perhaps you will find just the ones you want there. Of course, you can also make use of this resource if you decide to study film content. Quite a number of film review compilations should be available for reference in your library in order to help you narrow down your selection to material most relevant to your research question.

Because of the rapid evolution of the Internet as a major source of news, entertainment, and information for a large chunk of the population, various forms of Internet content are popular choices for student research, but this presents logistical difficulties of another kind because of the ephemeral nature of the content. While newspapers and magazines may archive their past stories on their Web sites—extremely convenient for researchers interested in print or Web news—most Internet content appears and disappears rapidly, making its capture for research purposes a challenge. Plan ahead.

Electronic archives that include a wide variety of print news material from both papers and magazines—often global in nature—should be available in your university library. One of the most popular is the LexisNexis database. This type of resource has become increasingly comprehensive and allows ready access to material over a fairly long time range (although the further back the year, the less certain you can be that the collection is complete). Comparative studies of the news coverage created in different parts of the world are also possible using this type of resource—something that was extraordinarily difficult just 15 or 20 years ago.

Using Data From Existing Studies

Sometimes it is possible to do original research using data that have already been gathered by others. Given the cost and complexity of conducting a major public opinion survey, for example, beginning researchers interested in opinion formation or opinion trends should consider using data that have been gathered by others. Of course, if you use data someone else has gathered, he or she may not have studied the population you are most interested in, and he or she probably did not ask exactly the questions that you would most like to have had answered for your particular research problem. However, on practical grounds, reanalysis is becoming a more common and more broadly accepted alternative.

Depending on your research question, one way to use opinion data in a research study is simply to compile published information from a number of surveys. They can be examined for trends on a given issue. The results can be compared to trends in the amount and type of news coverage the issue has received. This type of research is almost always exploratory rather than hypothesis testing but can nevertheless yield important insights. Big commercial survey firms like Gallup, Roper, and Yankelovich offer some results to the public for free, either through their Web sites or a publication you might find in your library; you can also find newspaper or news magazine articles that incorporate opinion data. Be wary of the source; local newspapers may publish "fun polls" that don't yield good data. However, many larger media organizations do their own polls, sometimes in cooperation with a professional polling firm, and these can be rigorous and reliable. Good advice on evaluating poll data is available from the American Association for Public Opinion Research at http://www.aapor.org.

The Pew Foundation provides funding for a number of different opinion and media use studies; one of the best known is the Pew Internet & American Life Project at http://www.pewinternet.org. Pew and other not-for-profit foundations usually publish their studies for free on the Web, often in user-friendly form. Many colleges and universities belong to the Inter-university Consortium for Political and Social Research at the University of Michigan. The consortium's site at http://www.icpsr.umich.edu has archives of raw data available for reanalysis, as well as links to reports others have written using those data.

ICPSR also sponsors an undergraduate research paper competition for student papers that use data from its archive. If your university is a member, this is an excellent resource, although using the archive is likely to require access to, and knowledge of, sophisticated statistical software packages.

Sometimes it is possible to yield new results by compiling data from previously published experiments. This is called **meta-analysis** and is not always practical for beginners. Many published reports contain only summary statistics and not enough detail to be useful; the raw, unprocessed data may need to be requested from the author, and it may or may not be available or in a form that is ready for use by someone else. However, if you are strongly interested in a research question on which quite a number of studies have already been published, and if you are comfortable with statistical analysis, this is an alternative to think about.

Gathering New Data From People

Gathering new data from people is the alternative most people think of when they consider social science research. The researcher has control of the data collection (whether quantitative or qualitative, whether involving surveys, experiments, interviews, focus groups, or observations) and can collect exactly the data that he or she most wants in light of the research question guiding the study. Two big disadvantages include (a) the necessity to complete extra paperwork and allow extra time for human subjects (IRB) approval if required for class projects at your university and (b) the necessity to recruit volunteers to participate in the research. As you have already learned, getting a truly random sample for a survey is becoming increasingly difficult. Getting volunteers to participate in a focus group or an experiment or getting access to an organization you would like to study through participant observation is not easy either—but if you are motivated, it can often be done.

If your research question involves what people think or feel or how they act, and if you are willing to work through these hurdles, you will have the reward of being able to produce an original study that may add something truly new to our understanding of human social behavior. Most original data collection from people involves some level of compromise, so try not to be discouraged if you cannot get exactly the people you want to participate in your project.

One common alternative is to use your own classmates or other students at your university as study participants. This is easier for faculty who may be able to offer extra-credit incentives or even small cash payments or prizes to participants than it is for student researchers. Also, a student sample of volunteers is not random or representative of people who are not students. However, perhaps your research question is specifically about student behavior—for example, how is the current generation using portable communication media like text messaging on cell phones or instant messaging programs on wireless-enabled laptops? In this case, using a student sample is ideal (even though it still won't be random because it will consist of volunteers willing to answer your questions or fill out your survey form).

In some cases, you might already work in a media organization, such as a television station, a newspaper, an advertising or public relations agency, or a Web design firm—even a student one—that would be an ideal site for participant observation. The permissions issue here is tricky; you might be required to get the approval of everyone with whom you work. But the rewards could be worth the trouble.

While big surveys are expensive, small local ones you can carry out yourself can be much less expensive yet be worth doing—again, depending on your research question. Since response rates on phone surveys are falling, going back to mail surveys or even door-to-door, in-person surveys might be an option, especially on a small-scale project. Market researchers often approach shoppers with their questions, which makes sense in a study of consumer choices. (Make sure the store or mall involved knows and approves of what you are doing, of course. You'll be on store or mall property.)

In the next chapters, you'll learn more about making and carrying out these important decisions. For now, the important point is that, as you work through and refine your research question, you should be thinking ahead as to what kind of data you might use to answer it and where this might come from. All quantitative studies (and some qualitative studies) make use of **variables**.

DEFINING AND MEASURING VARIABLES

The goal of all quantitative research is to measure something (whether opinions, knowledge or beliefs, attitudes, or media content) as precisely as possible, for purposes of answering a research question and perhaps testing hypotheses. A "variable" is any item whose value varies and that the researcher attempts to count or measure, whether for purposes of description or exploration or to test a formal hypothesis. Theory is generally what dictates which variables should be considered. Variables can have as few as two values; for example, gender is usually recorded as male or female. Or they can have many values; for example, your score on an exam can range from 0% to 100%. Qualitative studies are not concerned with measurement and do not always use variables; however, some qualitative studies are concerned with identifying elements, such as themes, or descriptive variables, such as the demographic backgrounds of research participants (for example, focus group members).

Variables are usually intended to measure an underlying concept that may be more complex; such a variable is an **index** of the concept. Your score on an exam is supposed to represent your knowledge of the material, but your instructor usually cannot ask you about every item considered in the class, so he or she chooses some items to "stand in for" all of the others as an index of your knowledge. A **scale** is a type of measurement where the intervals between numbers are known to be the same, like length or weight measured by a ruler or household scale.

Up to this point, little has been said in this book about actually measuring variables. Some variables are straightforward. We are all familiar with miles per gallon as a variable describing the underlying fuel efficiency of a car. Worker productivity in an office can be measured in terms of the number of pages keyboarded, forms completed, telephone calls answered, products sold or distributed, or whatever the day-to-day activities of that particular office are. Other variables, such as attitudes, beliefs, or reasons, that may be of great theoretical interest may be much more difficult to conceptualize and to assess or measure. Media researchers are often interested in variables regarding media content, such as themes (which can also be assessed qualitatively), tone, and length.

Sometimes demographic variables, like gender, age, or income, have no special theoretical significance but are collected anyway to make certain that the respondents or subjects in the study are approximately as diverse as the population being studied. For example, if all of the volunteers for an experiment with college students were journalism majors, the results might not apply to those majoring in other fields.

In human subjects studies, it is also common to use demographic variables as **control variables** to rule out the possibility that differences observed in a survey or an experiment are really the result of a hypothesized relationship and not just a chance characteristic of particular groups of people. For example, let's say your hypothesis states that the more video games a high school student plays, the lower his or her standardized test score on reading. Let's also suppose that boys spend more time playing video games, on average, and girls have higher reading scores, on average. We wouldn't know whether it was gender or playing time that was causing this difference. To find out, we might want to look at the relationship between video game playing and reading scores just for boys and just for girls.

Reliability and Validity

Whether collected by means of a survey, an experiment, or a content analysis, quantitative data must be as reliable and valid as possible.

Reliability means that repeating the same procedure would be highly likely to generate nearly the same result. If a survey question is so ambiguous that the same person might answer it differently at different times, or if content analysis uses categories that mean entirely different things to different people, the results lack reliability. Sometimes reliability is explained by analogy to a simple and familiar measurement instrument—a ruler. Using an unreliable measure is like using a ruler that stretches, shrinks, or otherwise changes shape when you're not looking. The results have little meaning.

Validity refers to whether you are measuring the things you think you're measuring—those that interest you on a theoretical level. If you are interested in violence in children's television but measure only the number of screams you hear on the soundtrack, your measurement could be invalid (even if reliable) because some could be screams of excitement, and some violence might be silent. If you use a number of different survey questions to measure the same underlying concept, the answers from individual respondents should be interrelated. Otherwise, it may be that the different questions are measuring different things.

Reliability and validity are extremely important measurement concepts for all quantitative studies; they take many forms, and advanced texts often discuss several different kinds. Although different experts emphasize slightly different aspects of these concepts, all agree that they are critical to meaningful measurement. The more abstract a concept, the more difficult it is to achieve a reliable and valid measure. Social psychologists who are interested in attitudinal research or other complex quantitative studies involving abstract variables often spend large amounts of their effort on measurement issues.

Qualitative studies may also be concerned with reliability and validity but in somewhat different ways. For qualitative researchers, reliability means that an observation is not so unique to the individual researcher that someone else would not see the same thing, and this is sometimes assessed numerically. Validity rests primarily in whether the researcher's descriptions are legitimate ones that adequately capture the nature of a social setting.

Independent and Dependent Variables

In experimental design, the independent variable is a variable whose value determines (partly or completely) the value of a dependent variable. The independent variable can generally be changed or manipulated by the experimenter, whereas the dependent (or outcome) variable cannot. For example, if we want to see which of three advertising messages is more persuasive in terms of our subjects being willing to buy the advertised product, the message would be the independent variable, and willingness to buy would be the dependent variable. We would probably set up three **treatment groups** of subjects—one that saw message A, one message B, and one message C—and then ask each group how likely its members were to buy. We would also want to have a fourth group, called a **control group**, that didn't see any of the messages for comparison.

Although easiest to understand in the context of an experimental design, where they originated, the concepts of independent and dependent variable also apply in survey research and in content analysis. In survey research, we may ask one group of questions about political affiliation and another about voting intention. Logically, political affiliation would be considered the independent variable, and voting intention the dependent variable, because we would expect the affiliation to influence the intention rather than the other way around. However, in survey work, we cannot rule out that relationships may go in a different direction than we predict. Voters, for example, might change their sense of affiliation if they decide they like the other party's candidate better. Now affiliation has become a dependent variable, and intention is the independent variable.

In content analysis, we might hypothesize (for example) that small-town newspapers are less likely to report controversies involving local government than are big-city papers. Size of community is the independent variable, and frequency with which controversy is reported is the dependent variable. In this situation, however, we could also have a problem with a **confounding variable** that confuses our results. Perhaps big-city governments actually have more controversy than small-town governments, which means that any difference observed might not be due to reporting styles but to external events. In this case, we would have to find some way to "control for" the actual occurrence of controversies. This might turn out to be difficult. Our design may have a built-in limitation that we cannot remove.

Operationalization and Levels of Measurement

Defining a variable in a way that allows it to be measured is called **operationalization**. Sometimes this is fairly straightforward; for example, time spent watching television can be operationalized as the number of minutes per day spent in the same room with a television set that is turned on. Note that even in this simple example, the operationalization is not perfect, however. Someone could be in the room with the TV on and not be watching, but as a practical matter, we might decide to ignore this possibility because of the complexities of measurement it introduces.

Once again, the more abstract the concept, the more challenging the operationalization can become. The term *social presence* is being used in new media studies to indicate the degree to which a person might feel he or she is "really there" in an online environment or "really" connected to other people in the same environment. This has implications for the effectiveness of distance education or marketing strategies that rely on online interaction, for example. But how is a feeling of "social presence" best operationalized? There is no one immediate answer to this question.

When a researcher makes a decision about how to measure a variable, he or she should also consider what **level of measurement** is involved with a particular operationalization. Some "measures," such as gender or the network affiliation of a TV station, are simple categories. Others are true numerical scales that more precisely measure the degree of presence or absence of certain properties, such as personality characteristics or positive versus negative attitudes. More about levels of measurement is presented in a later chapter. However, even in the design stage, it is important to think ahead about this, because the level of measurement determines the types of statistical analysis that can be used with the data.

Important Terms and Concepts

Academic journal	Peer review
Blind review	Reliability
Confounding variable	Research question
Control group	Scale
Control variable	Theoretical concept
Index	Treatment group
Level of measurement	Validity
Meta-analysis	Variable
Operationalization	

Exercise

Whether or not your instructor requires you to complete a small-scale research project in this class, reviewing the literature on a research question that interests you will improve your understanding of how theory and methods are actually used in research. This exercise is designed to get you started, not produce a complete review.

1. Write a tentative research question within the general area of media studies that interests you. It is important to actually write the question down. Be as specific as possible.

2. Using the language of your question, identify at least three keywords that you might use to search library databases for published research articles in the media studies or communication literature.

3. Either online or in person, use these keywords in at least two library databases listed as either "general" or "communications" indexes. How many publications do you turn up?

4. Try the same keywords under at least one library database in another related field, like psychology, sociology, or engineering. How many publications turn up this time?

5. From the three searches, select, locate, and read at least three articles that you believe would definitely help you in refining your research question and designing a study to answer it. Summarize each in your own words in a couple of sentences, stressing the points of intersection with your own ideas.

6. Your instructor may want you to submit a short report, including your research question, keywords, and summaries, for course credit.

CHAPTER 5

Designing Quantitative Research

Surveys, Experiments, and Quantitative Content Analysis

While any research question can be approached more than one way, most of the time the best general method will be partially determined by the kind of question being asked, the nature of the theory or theoretical concepts behind it, and the research that has gone before. This chapter concerns design issues that confront researchers who have chosen to collect new quantitative data, whether from people or from media content. Quantitative studies can be surveys, experiments, or quantitative content analyses. They can sometimes involve reanalysis of survey data or a meta-analysis of previously published experiments rather than the gathering of entirely new data, and although these options are not specifically covered here, a good understanding of the logic of the original research would be essential to such projects.

In this chapter, you'll learn some of the basic "tricks of the trade" that will help you get started writing survey questions, designing experiments, and doing content analysis. Numerous books have been written on each of these alternatives; this chapter provides only the basics—the minimum you need (along with common sense and careful planning) to successfully design a meaningful small-scale research project.

SURVEY DESIGN BASICS

Perhaps because everyone is fairly familiar with answering **surveys**, the methodology seems easy and straightforward. Yet writing good survey questions is extraordinarily difficult. Interpreting the results is also not as easy as it seems, especially if the questions are hard for respondents to grasp, are ambiguous in meaning, or ask things respondents cannot answer in a meaningful way.

Writing Survey Questions

Many factors influence the results of a survey; one of the most important is having a clear idea of what the survey form, or survey **instrument**, is intended to uncover. Many people start out by making a list of "interesting" questions they would like to have answers to. However, what exactly you should ask to get the most valuable answers takes a lot of thought. Applying the concepts of a theoretically based research question involving relationships among variables should give you a much better start. Then questions related to these concepts need to be refined to the point that they are as clear and as unambiguous as possible.

As an example, let's say you want to know why the typical college-age student is attracted to a social networking site like MySpace. Your first instinct might be to ask respondents a direct question, but do you believe most people can really explain *why* they use a particular medium? They are likely to say things like "because I like it," "because it's fun," or "because I meet interesting people that way." This is a start, especially the answer about interesting people, but this kind of questioning will probably yield only partial answers without further development. You might use the theoretical concept of uses and gratifications to help you create your survey and refine your question list.

One of your final questions might be something like this: "Do you agree or disagree with this statement: I meet more interesting people on MySpace than I do in real life." Another might be "Do you agree or disagree with this statement: On MySpace, I feel like I can reveal my real self better than I can in real life." Implied here are the ideas that "meeting interesting people" and "revealing my real self" are valuable rewards (gratifications) that users might get from frequenting this site and that they do *not* get elsewhere—that is, they might represent otherwise unmet needs. To take the measurement one step further, you might ask your respondents to answer on a 5-point scale where 1 means *completely disagree* and 5 means *completely agree*. This will add precision to your results and will make it easier to determine which gratifications are stronger draws.

Of course, a longer qualitative interview might well yield some of the same information. The choice is often a matter of researcher preference, in consideration of the goals of the project. Another great option is to use depth interviews at the beginning of the project to help identify, develop, and refine the questions for a quantitative study.

Whatever questions you choose, be ready to administer several rounds of questionnaire testing using respondents similar to those you will actually use in your study. This is designed to identify ambiguous questions or those respondents might find hard to answer, for whatever reason. Watch out for "loaded" questions: "Are you in favor of increased federal regulation of broadcasting, or would you rather see children's television deteriorate even further?" Don't ask them. And don't ask "double" ones: "Are you in favor of increased federal regulation of broadcasting, *including* increased congressional involvement in PBS?" This is really two questions in one.

Finally, surveys (however administered) usually include a short introduction explaining the purpose of the research, reminding participants that they are volunteers, and explaining how the answers will be treated in terms of anonymity (the researcher will not know who completed the questions in each case) or confidentiality (the researcher may know but agrees to keep the answers confidential and not reveal them to others). They also include a statement at the end thanking the respondent and offering contact information for the researcher and, if required, for your institutional human subjects board (IRB) in case there are questions. For mail or e-mail surveys, this information is typically included in a separate cover letter. To simplify IRB requirements, avoid surveying people under 18 years of age.

Question Order, Wording, and Timing

Even small changes in question wording can have big, often unanticipated impacts on how people answer the question. Consider this example: Asking people whether they are "pro-choice" with respect to abortion decisions might produce results that are quite different from those that might be obtained by asking them whether they are "in favor of" abortions. No wonder abortion opinion surveys produce such contradictory results! But the differences in wording don't have to be this dramatic. Any small variation can produce an unexpectedly large effect. Also, your own biases can creep in very easily, producing questions almost certain to generate predictable answers without your even being aware of your influence on the results. Get other people to read your questions to help you spot this.

Remember that your survey respondents may include people of different ethnicity, nationality, or other factors related to cultural background. In short, different respondents may interpret the questions differently. You can't eliminate this factor, so strive to make the questions as unambiguous as possible. Multiple interpretations are likely for even the most carefully worded question. Occasionally, researchers overlook the cultural and social diversity characteristic of most modern nations. Asking questions that assume that all respondents are part of the college-educated middle class is an example; another is trying to survey respondents in English when it is not their first or native language.

The order of the questions is also very important. One question can suggest a context for interpreting the next in a pattern that is quite leading, even though the researcher may not intend it to be. For example, a survey on foreign policy might ask a question like this: "Do you believe that world trade has an important influence on the domestic economy?" If the next question asks whether international trade policy is an important national issue, the answers might be quite different than if the question order here was reversed. Respondents will have been introduced by the first question to the idea that international trade might have something to do with the local economy. Perhaps they had never thought of this before or wouldn't otherwise have considered this argument in answering the second question.

Timing of a survey with respect to critical events is also important. Imagine the differences that might occur if some of the same questions about U.S. policy with respect to the Middle East were asked of Americans before and immediately after the 2001 World Trade Center attacks.

Alternative Response Formats

Survey questions can be **forced-choice** or **open-ended**. A question that requires the respondent to select an answer from those provided by the researcher is called a forced-choice question, and this is the usual approach in survey research. Answers can be in the form of numerical rating scales (say, from 1 for *strongly disagree* to 5 for *strongly agree*, a common choice), or simpler verbal categories (yes, no, undecided) may be used. Which is better?

Generally speaking, rating scales produce more precise results, and more can be done with them statistically, as you'll see later in this book. The arguments against their use are that they are less meaningful for some respondents and more difficult and time-consuming to convey in a telephone survey. Yes-or-no questions can be preferable, especially for a phone survey. Scales may be better when data are being collected for a more complex analysis of, say, what factors might be influencing this opinion. In such cases, some argue that a

1 through 5 scale is not enough to constitute a true measurement; a 1 through 7 scale might be better. Researchers disagree about whether answering questions on a scale of 1 to 10 actually produces meaningful distinctions.

Some researchers prefer an odd number of choices on this kind of scale so respondents can choose a neutral answer in the middle. Some prefer an even number so respondents have to indicate which way they lean. However, a 10-point scale can be misleading in this regard, because people with no opinion or who feel neutral may choose 5. "Don't know" can be an explicit choice listed on the questionnaire, or it can be recorded only if the respondent offers this answer spontaneously. The results will differ. Some researchers believe very strongly in the need to include screening questions to suggest whether the respondent has had a chance to form an opinion at all ("Have you heard about this issue before?"). Others do not consider this essential.

Some survey questions give respondents a choice of answers—not just "agree" or "disagree." For example, respondents could be asked to choose from a list of adjectives which ones most closely describe an advertised product or to choose among a list of reasons for feelings about a given issue. Lists of choices should always be as exhaustive as possible of all of the answers that might be offered, even though "other" is also generally included as a choice. Here extensive pretesting or the use of interview data is almost essential to developing the choices. A technique sometimes called a **semantic differential** scale asks respondents to rate items (often consumer products or political candidates) on a scale between two adjectives that are polar opposites. For example, respondents might be asked to rate a political figure on a scale in which 1 represents *dishonest* and 7 represents *honest*.

A question that has no predetermined list of possible answers is called an open-ended question. While common in survey work, this is actually a form of qualitative research. These questions are used when the researcher cannot easily (or does not want to) "prejudge" what respondents' possible answers will be. They can also be used to give respondents the opportunity to elaborate on the reasons for other answers or comment on the survey as a whole. These data should be handled in the same way as other qualitative data are handled, which you'll learn about in more detail a bit later on.

Watch out for questions that may induce what is called **response bias**, meaning questions that imply a right answer. "Do you believe immigrants should be given fair treatment?" is an example of a question with an implied right answer; of course people will be reluctant to state that they oppose "fair treatment" under any circumstances. Survey respondents may also be reluctant to admit wrongdoing. For example, the question "Did you give correct information on your income tax form?" will put pressure on respondents to stretch or even edit the truth, even if they are assured their answers will be confidential.

Occasionally, respondents may make up answers arbitrarily to finish the survey in a hurry. On a series of scale questions, someone who always answers with the same number is probably not paying much attention to the questions, and most researchers would consider discarding these responses.

In using a series of agree/disagree scale questions, it is a good idea to mix questions where the more positive answer is *strongly agree* with questions where the more positive answer is *strongly disagree*. For example, on a political candidate survey, a positively worded question like "Candidate Smith seems very honest" might be followed by a negatively worded question like "Candidate Smith does not have enough experience."

Which Demographics?

Questions on **demographics** are often saved for the end of the survey because respondents might resent answering questions about personal matters, such as their ethnicity, income, or religious beliefs. This resentment may be less after the researcher and respondent have had a short history of interaction in the process of completing the survey, even if this is over the phone. Also, if the respondent refuses these questions, the researcher may still be able to make use of the rest of the survey. Even for mail surveys, demographic questions put at the end of the survey form and described in a neutral way as necessary "to make sure we have reached people from all walks of life" or something similar may be less likely to discourage someone who has just invested time in completing the rest of the questionnaire than someone who is still deciding whether it should go in the trash. Including a "decline to answer" category for all demographic questions can help.

What demographic questions should be asked? Age, gender, ethnicity, and income are standard, although all can be sensitive; choosing among categories for age and income may be less threatening than having to fill in a blank. For income, include a low option, such as "less than $10,000," as an income choice so that lower-income respondents will be less likely to be forced to choose the bottom category. The terms *gender* and *ethnicity* are generally preferred to *sex* (which is a physical rather than a social characteristic) and *race* (which has no standard accepted definition and may be especially problematic for mixed-race individuals).

Ethnic categorizations are especially challenging. Some people in the United States who are of African descent prefer to think of themselves as "African American," while others prefer "Black." People with Spanish-speaking family backgrounds might not like having to choose between calling themselves "White" and calling themselves "Hispanic"—many may consider themselves both. It is becoming more common to ask about having a Spanish-speaking family background as a separate question. Some Native Americans have returned to a preference for the word *Indian,* although survey forms nevertheless avoid this term because others might find it offensive. One simple solution may be to leave ethnicity as an open-ended category and let respondents suggest for themselves how they should be described. Whatever you choose, it is best to leave a category for "other." The main thing is to be sensitive to how the full range of individuals in the population under study will react to your choices.

Gender can also be a problem; gays, lesbians, bisexuals, and transsexuals may resent being forced to choose one of only two categories. It's best to provide a "decline to answer" category for gender, as well as for age, ethnicity, and income. Even if completely inadvertent, offending part of your sample can ruin your survey results.

For some surveys, such factors as political or religious affiliation, marital status, occupation, education, and where a respondent was raised may also be important on theoretical grounds and should be included as needed. However, please resist the temptation to always ask everything you can think of about your respondents. Ask yourself what's minimally necessary to ensure that your sample is reasonably representative of the population of interest—usually, age, gender, ethnicity, and income are sufficient. Add only those questions that are important in terms of your particular research question. Every question on the survey should have a purpose.

How Many People, and Where to Get Them?

With survey research, the primary goal is to have a **representative sample**—that is, the group of people who actually respond to the survey must be as much like the population of interest as possible. The goal of saying something about the larger group from which your respondents have been drawn can only be achieved if this condition is met—increasingly difficult to accomplish because people have been surveyed so often that many refuse to respond. Occasionally, survey work can use a **census** rather than a sample—that is, everyone in the population can be included, which eliminates issues of representativeness altogether. However, for large groups of people, only major national efforts like the U.S. Census that takes place every 10 years are organized as censuses because of the huge logistical challenges and major expense.

How many people should be included? A typical professional telephone survey published in a good academic journal or high-quality news medium will often contain information from 1,000 or more respondents. Such surveys may use such techniques as **multistage sampling**, which involves first choosing a representative sample of cities or counties, for example, and then choosing a sample of individuals who live in the chosen geographic areas. However, this practical approach increases the statistical complexity of the interpretation, and a good statistician will be needed. Fortunately, student surveys can achieve good results with smaller groups.

A good rule of thumb for a simple survey using only one "level" or stage of sampling from a single **sampling frame,** or list of possible respondents (for example, everyone listed in the Chicago phone book, all registered voters in Smith County, or whoever answers the phone at any household that has a sixth grader enrolled in a particular school district), is that a minimum of between 200 and 400 responses is needed, which often means that at least 400 to 800 surveys must be mailed or phone calls made. Smaller numbers may work, especially for exploratory research; however, the smaller the sample, the harder it can be to draw definite statistical conclusions. Student research may get by with smaller numbers, as long as it is acceptable for the conclusions of the study to be tentative rather than definitive.

Samples drawn from lists, such as phone books or other directories, are commonly determined by **systematic random sampling.** Typically, the researcher chooses a random starting point (usually by consulting a random number table or by using a calculator or computer program that will generate a random number on demand), then skips a certain number of names and takes the next one, then skips the same number and takes the next one, and so on. The number to be skipped is determined by the number of names in the sampling frame divided by the number the researcher wants in the sample.

Ideally, the sampling frame should include everyone in the population, or the group to which you hope to generalize your conclusions. Remember, however, there is no master list of the population of an entire country. Phone books that include addresses are available for almost all areas, but it's not always easy to separate businesses from individual home numbers, unlisted numbers are not included, and people can choose not to list their address. For phone surveys, computer programs are now in common use that generate random telephone numbers reflecting the distribution of area codes and local prefixes among the population of interest. With the increasing use of cell phones in place of land lines, even this approach now appears more limited. An unknown number of people do not have a conventional land-line telephone at all.

Internet survey procedures are being developed to fill the gap, but until everyone is Internet connected, these will introduce a new bias—the "digital divide" that separates the information rich from the information poor. In some states, voter registration information and other official records are publicly available; survey firms may collect and use this information, but this practice raises important issues about the confidentiality of personal information.

Many other sampling schemes are used. The goal is always to get an unbiased, representative sample of the population, but given all the complexities of developing a truly random sample, the practical goals of the research often dictate a different choice. **Quota sampling** adds respondents who fit certain characteristics until the proportions in the sample resemble those of the population in terms of age, gender, ethnicity, or other demographic factors of particular interest—in fact, this choice is common for market researchers. Market researchers collecting data in malls and other public places may even pick particular respondents because they match a target group that is of interest for the study at hand—such as women shopping with small children.

Surveys designed specifically to understand differences among ethnic groups may deliberately oversample particular minority groups that would otherwise make up only a small percentage of the respondents. For practical reasons, your own first survey may rely on a **convenience sample** of a readily available group, such as the members of your research class. If your research question is about college students, this is a more reasonable choice than if you are trying to draw conclusions about the general population.

No matter how large the sample or how it is created, applying conclusions beyond the population actually included in the sampling frame (to other cities or states, student groups, and so on) is a risky business—and, technically speaking, *never* fully justified on statistical grounds. On the other hand, if your study is about a defined group, such as members of a particular profession or organization, you might be able to get a complete (or nearly complete) listing from which to draw your sample. Some groups maintain e-mail lists for members; if your purpose appeals to the group's leadership, you might gain access this way.

Regardless of what sampling technique is used, there is always the possibility that your sample may include more of those who agree to participate because they are especially interested in your issue; because they have extra time on their hands; because they are easy to persuade, bored, or want attention; or because they just like to give their opinions. No scheme can eliminate these kinds of problems. The main concern is avoiding systematic biases that collect disproportionate numbers from different groups of people.

Internet samples consisting entirely of volunteers are becoming more common. It is easy to post an Internet survey using software that is readily available commercially and at most universities. You should be particularly wary of these, however. Out of millions of Internet users, the few that happen to find and fill out a particular survey are unlikely to be representative of any larger group.

Which Survey Method Is Best?

Should surveys be conducted in person (door-to-door) or by Internet, mail, or telephone—or by quota sampling on campus or in the local shopping mall? Each method has its advantages and disadvantages. Door-to-door surveys are relatively rare these days; obviously, they are more expensive, and a possible disadvantage is that a person appearing on the doorstep might get turned down in this era of high crime rates and fear of strangers. Mail surveys are easily tossed in the trash with all the other junk mail. And telephone surveys increasingly get low numbers of responses. Telephone survey workers must be carefully trained to administer surveys appropriately; for beginners, there are powerful arguments for paper surveys (whether handed out to a group you have access to, such as your class, or mailed) or Internet surveys that can control question wording and order without having to worry about these problems.

An important goal is to achieve the highest-possible **response rate,** or percentage of acceptances among those asked to participate in a survey. A low response rate means the sample could be biased. But there's no easy rule of thumb about what an acceptable response rate should be. Some marketing surveys achieve very low response rates, perhaps less than 10%. People are a bit more willing to participate in surveys when the purpose is identified as academic research, but the old goal of having a response rate of 60% or 70% is not realistic anymore. Between 40% and 50% is more typical, even for a well-presented and carefully conducted survey. Surveys that try to reach groups of experts, such as doctors or scientists, are more likely to reach response rates 30% or below.

Experienced survey researchers have a lot of tricks to increase response rates. Providing mail-survey respondents with stamp-affixed return envelopes rather than business-reply envelopes may increase response rates because people are believed to be less likely to throw a stamped envelope away. Sometimes, a token payment is added as an incentive. Respondents might be offered a chance to be included in a free drawing—although this could bias the sample in unknown ways. Unfortunately, some of these are expensive choices from the point of view of student researchers.

In mail surveys, a carefully designed cover letter and a questionnaire that looks perfectly professional can help response rates. Your human subjects board (IRB) may require you to submit these for its review. Polite follow-up reminders are also important.

DESIGNING BASIC EXPERIMENTS

Like survey researchers, experimental researchers also want their subjects to be as representative as possible; however, this is even more difficult because a participant's involvement in an experiment usually takes more time and is more of an interruption of daily life than involvement in a survey. On the other hand, many researchers argue that as long as the characteristics of experimental subjects are known and there are not major differences between the characteristics of the treatment group and those of the control group (which is often achieved by random or systematic random assignment of subjects to the groups), the experiment is still valid, with the limitation that the conclusions may only apply to people like those included.

Most commonly, experimental research gets more human subjects board (IRB) scrutiny than does survey research, partly because participants may find it more psychologically difficult to withdraw from an experiment once it's started—whereas with a survey, especially one done over the phone, on the Internet, or through the mail, they are probably going to be comfortable just stopping if something concerns them. In addition, some experiments may pose a risk of embarrassing a subject, or the researcher may provide subjects with false information in order to judge their reactions. IRBs look for safeguards that any such elements are fully justified and properly managed. Experimental subjects are usually required to sign a separate legal statement giving their informed consent. As with surveys, it is best for student researchers to avoid using subjects under 18 years of age.

The simplest kind of experiment involves just two groups: a single treatment group and a control group. The treatment group is exposed to some experience, whereas the control group is not (or is exposed to a similar experience that lacks key elements), and some measurement is then made of both groups for comparison (such as what they know, how they feel, or what their attitudes are toward something). The options and requirements for how to construct the questions are similar to those for surveys; questions must be unambiguous, either categorical or scaled answers might be used, and demographic questions must be carefully chosen. If the groups are indeed equivalent, any differences measured between the groups at the end of the experiment can reasonably be attributed to differences in their experience during the course of the experiment—the treatment variable. This is called a **posttest**-only control group design.

For example, the researcher might be interested in the effects of an educational video on global warming on attitudes toward energy conservation. Subjects assigned to the treatment group would watch the film. Subjects in the control group would not, but to make the experience equivalent, the researcher might ask them to watch some other film on an unrelated subject of about the same length and general style.

To make sure that the groups are actually equivalent, the researcher may add other variables (both demographics, such as gender and age, and other important characteristics that might be particularly relevant to the research purpose, such as—in this case—general orientation toward environmental issues). Data considerations involving recording of age, gender, ethnicity, income, and so on are similar to those for surveys. The number of subjects is more variable than with survey research; sometimes a carefully controlled experiment can produce interesting results with only a limited number of people (perhaps even as few as 20 or 30 for exploratory research). However, this depends entirely on the magnitude of the differences being tested, which is not always known ahead of time. Larger numbers will be required to pick up small differences.

More Complex Designs

In the above example about global warming, what if, despite great care on the researcher's part to achieve equivalence, a larger number of subjects who are already concerned about energy conservation end up in the treatment group instead of the control group? This could easily happen by chance, especially in a small-scale experiment, and would confound the results. One solution is to **pretest** subjects on the important dependent variables (in this case, attitudes toward energy conservation). This serves as a check against the possibility that the groups are unbalanced. The scores at two different times on such a measure might not come out exactly the same even with no treatment; the procedure provides a "baseline" measurement for each group so that the researcher can judge the exact amount of change in the treatment group in comparison to any change in the control group. This is called, simply enough, a **pretest-posttest design**. Sometimes a pretest-posttest design can be used with a single group (no control group). As a practical matter, perhaps this experiment is taking place in a large class in which the educational video is being shown, and the researcher has no practical opportunity to divide the class in two. However, if a control group is included, this is then called a pretest-posttest control group design.

A disadvantage of the pretest-posttest design is that giving subjects a pretest focuses their attention on the subject of the experiment (energy conservation), so they could become especially sensitive to information related to this subject that is presented to them shortly thereafter. This could change their responses on the posttest. Here there are a variety of solutions. The pretest might include a battery of questions on a wide range of subjects so that the key questions about the subject of the experiment (the questions about energy conservation) are "buried" in a host of others. However, this means the experiment will take more time and be more complicated to develop. Use of a control group would also help here, but another alternative is to give the pretest to only *half* of the subjects. The researcher should then be able to judge whether the pretest experience is changing the results.

Sometimes there is more than one treatment variable. For example, say you want to compare newscasts, newspapers, and interactive video as alternative media for conveying important health information and then measure your subjects' knowledge gain on a particular topic (say, cancer prevention). Here there are three different treatment conditions. You would also want a control group that was not exposed to any of these (but, perhaps, might be given something else to read or watch on a different topic). This is called a **multifactorial** design and involves more subjects and a more complex statistical analysis of the results, but the principle is the same. The challenge of this design for media studies researchers is that it is difficult to ensure that the three treatments actually contain identical information.

Two somewhat related variations on experimental design are commonly used in media studies. One is the **quasi-experiment,** and the other is the **field experiment.** A quasi-experiment is used to study real-world processes that cannot be easily duplicated in the laboratory, by making some use of the logic of experimental methods but without all elements of a controlled experiment. For example, a researcher might want to study which of two approaches to teaching journalistic writing is more effective. He or she could do this by evaluating the writing of two classes taught by different instructors using the two approaches. However, this is a quasi-experiment, not a true controlled experiment, unless students who registered for the classes were randomly assigned to one class or another. Perhaps this would involve a pretest-posttest design, which would be especially helpful in this case. A field experiment is a study carried out under field conditions—that is, it looks at some kind of real-world change process (such as the introduction of new technology into a newsroom) as a natural experiment. The researcher can gather useful insights by documenting the apparent effects of the change in technology but may have no control group for comparison.

As a beginning researcher, you should be able to do most of your work with these simple designs. Advanced methods texts will suggest many more approaches that can be useful under special circumstances or for more complex problems.

CONTENT ANALYSIS

Content analysis is the research method of choice for answering many questions about the mass media. Is the news actually biased against female politicians? How many of the models used in advertising are actually too thin? Has a health communication campaign about smoking cessation gotten any news coverage, and what kind? Are the local news anchors in major markets ethnically representative of the populations that they serve? What kind of material is most commonly posted on Internet blogs? How often are "green" appeals used in advertising? How much violence actually appears in children's cartoons? How does the nature of war news coverage vary from community to community, and what community characteristics seem to determine this? Sometimes we want questions like these answered for practical reasons; sometimes they are related to important criticisms of media performance. Media content analysis can help evaluate and sometimes improve media performance, provide input that is relevant to media policy decisions, and help assess the effectiveness of information or advertising campaigns.

Although content analysis by itself can say little or nothing about influences or effects on people, we need to be able to produce accurate characterizations of media content in order to draw conclusions about problems that might need to be addressed (for example, a lack of minority characters in television dramas or one-sided news coverage of political issues), as well as to think clearly and argue effectively about the possible influences of that content. Information from content analytic studies is sometimes combined with public opinion polls to test hypotheses about media influence on opinion. We may also need this information to assess how well a publicity campaign is working or what messages audiences that interest us might be consuming.

Content analysis is the systematic study of what is actually contained in media messages, whether news or entertainment. Mass communication research as a scholarly field has led the development of content analysis methodology and is the research method most closely associated with media research. It can be primarily qualitative or primarily quantitative. Content analysis is a practical choice for answering many questions about the mass media, and it is also popular with student researchers partly because it does not add the complications associated with research on human subjects, such as recruiting volunteers and securing official permissions. Purely qualitative content analysis is considered in a later chapter; this chapter is concerned primarily with quantitative content analysis techniques, but the line between them is not always distinct.

Simply measuring the actual amount of space or time given to particular topics is one simple form of media content analysis. Agenda-setting theory tells us that this matters. More often, the purpose of content analysis is to go further to classify certain elements of media material (whether this consists of news stories or soap operas) in a particular way, in order to answer a particular research question that the researcher has posed.

Sometimes this classification is straightforward. For example, content analysis of news stories might involve identifying the types of sources used in direct quotes according to a predetermined list of roles or occupations, such as politician, ordinary citizen, businessperson, and so on, in an exploration of source diversity. We might count how many representatives of particular political parties are included, as a check for news bias. Research on media representations of scientists on television dramas can reliably count how many women versus men there are or evaluate the ethnic composition of this group. However, content analysis is often concerned with less clear-cut categorizations, such as the presence or absence of particular themes (subtopics) or frames (alternative forms of story emphasis).

Some texts refer to the more apparent or literal elements of media content as "manifest" content, meaning content that is reasonably obvious on the surface of things, while other content is called "latent," something under the surface that we can only identify through a process of interpretation that may have subjective elements. Themes and frames are latent to some degree; that is, they really cannot be directly measured but represent categories that researchers apply by exercising judgments that are partially subjective.

Studies of latent elements inevitably blur any absolute distinction between quantitative and qualitative approaches. Yet we may want to treat this kind of content data as quantitative, whether for the purpose of constructing accurate (and persuasive) descriptive summaries, for comparing content in one medium (or location or time) to that in another, or even for testing hypotheses. For example, we might hypothesize that the presence of certain types of sources in a news story is associated with particular types of news frames. The presence of news frames, however, cannot be directly measured. Different researchers might describe these using different words and different categories, and they certainly might disagree about what frames are present—or dominant—in a particular case. Clearly, some element of subjective judgment begins to appear that might threaten our ability to use this kind of content data in a quantitative analysis.

As a result, a variety of techniques are used to evaluate whether different researchers reach the same conclusions, producing what are called **intercoder reliability** estimates. These are designed to help compensate for the subjectivity of any one person helping classify the material under study (that is, any single "coder"; see discussion that follows), which makes the use of the resulting data in quantitative analyses more legitimate. The argument is that if different researchers identify the same elements in the material most of the time, the subjective element is small enough that it can reasonably be ignored. More information about reliability calculations is included in the next section.

A different approach to studying media content might involve judgments expressed in terms of ranked categories or scale scores. For example, an Internet site might be rated as to how easily users are able to access its information, using such categories as "very easy to access," "accessibility about average," and "very difficult to access." Here again, intercoder reliability estimates could be used. Or, to increase precision, we might employ an actual numerical scale, similar to an agree/disagree scale in survey work (see discussion earlier in this chapter), in which 1 represents a site that is the most easy to access and 7 represents the most difficult. The researcher might indicate on such a scale where, in his or her judgment, the site in question falls. Note that this is still a judgment, but expressing the judgment in numerical terms makes it easier to compare judgments across sites—as well as those made by different raters. If we had a number of different raters participate, we might choose to simply average the results and take the averaged scale score as our best estimate of the actual difficulty.

A similar approach is often used by political scientists and others who are primarily interested in the "tone" of a news story, most often expressed as "positive," "neutral," or "negative" but sometimes converted to a rating on a numerical scale. However, from a media research perspective, judgments about "tone" alone generally fail to capture the nuances of media representation of an issue in which we are most interested. Generally, media researchers are also interested in evaluating the presence or absence of specific elements (whether sources, narrative structures, arguments, statements, story lines, characters, frames, or themes) that we believe are also important. In media research, content analysis most often tries to classify specific elements like these from a body of media content into categories, rather than producing overall ratings along single dimensions.

Organizing a Content Study

Conceptually, the design of a quantitative content analysis borrows much from survey research. The project has to begin with a well-defined research question, just as a survey has to be designed on the basis of interest in a specific topic. Neither can go forward without a good sense of what kind of information it is most important to have. Then, just as in survey research a limited sample of people is most commonly included in order to represent the opinions of a larger group (or population), in content analysis a smaller subset or sample of the media content related to the question at hand is typically used to represent the content of a larger body of media data. In both cases, the relationship between the sample and the larger population is a crucial consideration; the sample has to be representative of the population, usually established by choosing a probability sample—one in which every population member has an equal chance of appearing—although there are many variations on this theme.

Content analysis, like survey research, occasionally uses a census in which all of the elements in an entire population are included. For example, a researcher might have access to an archive of every e-mail that has been sent in a given organization over the past year and might decide to study the entire group of messages. More commonly, exactly like survey researchers, content analysts rely on sampling.

Content analysis takes many forms, and no one study is designed to investigate every element of content. The researcher with a well-defined research question that helps define the measurable elements (or variables) that are of primary interest has the easiest task. For example, if a research question regarding agenda setting asks how much front-page space in major national newspapers is typically devoted to coverage of political events, you could actually use a ruler to check column inches. On the other hand, as discussed in the previous section, your research question may be broader and require you to view or read each message included in the study and classify it, using an element of judgment, into somewhat fuzzier categories. These categories can be topics, themes, frames, or any other elements that are considered important from the researcher's point of view; multiple elements are almost always coded in the same study, but which ones these are will vary.

Given that most content analysis involves this kind of classification exercise rather than pure measurement, here is a major decision point. Should you begin your classification project with a predetermined list of categories? Or should you just start looking at the messages and make up categories as you go along? Quantitative content analysis often begins with a predetermined list of categories in cases where the same or a similar problem has been researched before, as uncovered in the literature review. There is some advantage to using a scheme that has been developed by someone else, because it has been tested and because your new results can be compared to those already available.

However, if the research question of primary interest is not answered by the list of categories someone else developed, a new list should be constructed. This could be done by logical reasoning and common sense, based on the nature of your research question, or you might choose an inductive approach to category development that is sometimes referred to as **grounded theory** (but is actually a method rather than a theory). Grounded theory analysis is a qualitative method, so it will be discussed in more detail in a later chapter. In a quantitative study, grounded theory analysis might be used in an exploratory phase to develop categories that are then applied to a separate body of material in a quantitative procedure, complete with intercoder reliability checks. This is exactly parallel to the development of survey questions using depth interviews and then to the administration of survey questions using a forced-choice survey instrument.

The purpose of quantitative content analysis is to identify and document consistent patterns, often those occurring in a vast sea of media data. This requires a consistent approach throughout the study.

Unit-of-Analysis Considerations

In one respect, content analysis is much messier than survey research, however. This concerns the unit of analysis. When we conduct an opinion survey or poll, we are almost always concerned with the answers given by individuals. Each individual's answers are counted just once, exactly as if each was voting. All of the demographic data we collect describe the individual. All of the data are organized by respondent and are interpreted and analyzed in terms of individuals. The individual person is the unit of analysis, in other words. This is such a taken-for-granted fact that it might be difficult to think of it as a choice, but there are other ways to organize a survey.

For example, some types of surveys may be interested in the household rather than the individual as the unit of analysis. Consider a marketing survey about laundry detergent use. Chances are everyone in a given household most often uses the same box or bottle of detergent; typically, one person might do the majority of the household's shopping. So a survey about laundry detergent use would be conceptualized and organized quite differently from the typical opinion survey. Questions about the numbers of household members and their ages and genders might be asked, but the purpose is to characterize the household as a unit. Someone responding to the researcher's request for information would be speaking on behalf of the household. The unit of analysis for this survey is the household, not the individual. The U.S. Census is generally organized this way as well.

We can imagine other surveys concerned with groups or organizations rather than either individual people or households. For example, we might conduct a survey of a sample of public relations firms in New York City, asking questions about the business, such as numbers of employees and clients, or we might do a survey involving the circulation, readership, or advertising revenue of various newspapers or the public information activities of different universities. We are, in a way, still studying people—but not individuals. We do not really need—or want—to ask each group member the same questions in these cases; one knowledgeable person can answer on behalf of the entire company or organization. Here the organization, not the individual or the household, is the unit of analysis.

For media content analysis, the choice of unit of analysis gets much more complex. To start with a simple example, suppose we want to study the advertising content of a new magazine that has suddenly become very popular among teenagers. Perhaps we are concerned with the gender stereotypes this influential publication might be encouraging. Our unit of analysis might be the individual advertisement. But what about ads that take an entire page—wouldn't these be more important than smaller ads because they would be more eye-catching and more young people would see them? What do we do when we have units of different size, whether advertisements, chat room posts, or news articles? All advertisements are not equal. Most likely we would solve this problem by making size or length a variable in our analysis.

However, if our research question concerns gender stereotypes, perhaps our unit of analysis should be the individual represented in an advertisement, whether an individual ad contains 1 person or 20. Or perhaps we want to compare entire issues to see if there are changes over time. Then the unit of analysis becomes an entire issue. We could even make all issues of an *entire magazine* the unit of analysis, in order to compare all of the ads in the magazine we are studying to all of the ads in competing magazines, magazines targeted toward different age groups, or those published in different countries.

In other words, the question of unit of analysis is much more of a problem in content analysis than it typically is in survey work, where the choice is most often an obvious one. We can also use multiple different units of analysis in the same study. In the previous section, we discussed the option of identifying particular themes in news stories. Subsequent analysis might use the individual theme, rather than the entire news article, as the unit of analysis. We might want to count how many themes fall into each of several categories, regardless of whether a given article in our original had 1 theme or 10.

More About Sampling in Content Analysis

The purpose of sampling in content analytic studies is exactly the same as for surveys. We usually cannot analyze, investigate, or test every single example of what we are trying to study, whether we are talking about newspaper stories in a major daily or text messages in a college dorm. Content researchers usually do not attempt to create census data but instead will generally try to choose a reasonably representative sample to examine in further detail. A project's organizers need to settle on a unit of analysis (or perhaps decide to use a more complex strategy involving more than one unit of analysis) before they can think clearly about sampling. Most content studies are guided by an interest in a particular type of programming and limited in important ways by practical considerations. Most studies are limited to a particular time, although many of the most insightful of these incorporate a comparison to help us understand how media treatment of images and issues might change over time. Even so, truly random sampling is often challenging.

As is the case for surveys, a true random sample (or "probability sample") meets the condition that every individual unit has exactly the same chance of being included in the sample, whether the unit is a person or a page. But truly random sampling of the stream of media content is not easily accomplished. First, it's hard to decide what to include in the population. This is not as intuitively obvious for media studies as it is for survey work. For example, in studying available television programming in a given community, would we include all options available on cable or by satellite or just network programming available over the air? The answer might depend on how many people in the community receive which kinds of programming. Once this is decided, should our study focus on the most popular programming or treat every available series equally? We might choose to use a limited number of the more popular programs as case studies, to make our project more manageable. Researchers use the logic of random sampling but rarely achieve it in its ideal form.

Then there's the logistics of the sampling itself. Capturing every prime-time ad (for example) that appears on several different channels for a given time period can take a lot of recording and a lot of time—and it may require as many sets and recorders as there are channels if the goal is to get everything available during a specified period. For historical studies, you have already read that collections of many media materials that extend back in time are rare and may be difficult to access. As a practical matter, truly random sampling of the stream of media material, especially broadcast and Internet material, is almost impossible. If we are interested in studying media communication over e-mail, cell phones, or instant message systems, we would have an even more challenging problem with sampling (and we might have new human subjects issues as well, since these are private, personal communication media).

One common sampling technique used for sampling daily newspapers' content employs what is called a "constructed week" to improve the representativeness of a sample. While a truly random sample should end up including about the same amount of material from each day of the week, on average, it is possible for a given sample to include (say) too many Wednesdays or not enough Saturdays, just by chance. This matters because the type of news published on each day varies in a systematic way, with less breaking news likely on Saturdays and perhaps a smaller news hole on Wednesdays. Some researchers will begin sampling on a random day—let's say it turns out to be a Tuesday—and then choose the Wednesday paper from the following week, the Thursday paper from the next week, and so on, ensuring that the data coming from the sample will be equally distributed across possible days.

Coding

Assigning content (at whatever unit of analysis) to categories (whether or not predetermined), as well as collecting data on other variables that might be included in a content study, such as "tone," is usually called **coding**. This is simply because various content elements and other items are generally identified by numerical codes when they are put into computer files later on. As explained in an earlier section, in quantitative content analysis, various measures of intercoder reliability are used to ensure that everyone involved in the research (everyone, that is, who is "coding" data by assigning them to categories with numerical labels) is using the categories in the same way. Intercoder reliability is checked by having different researchers code the same body of data. Sometimes an entire study's coding might be repeated by a second coder, but more commonly, only a predetermined proportion of the data (perhaps 10%) is coded two or more times by different people. How this is organized depends on the size of the project and how many people are available to work on it.

In its simplest form, intercoder reliability can be expressed as the percentage of instances in which two coders or researchers agree on the appropriate classification or classifications to be used. The result is easy to interpret, even for inexperienced researchers, although some methods experts consider this simple approach misleading and more sophisticated approaches are gaining in popularity. A number of more complex indexes are readily available that compensate for the proportion of agreement that can occur by chance, and some of these can deal with results from more than two coders. The most commonly used today are probably Cohen's kappa, Scott's pi, and Krippendorff's alpha; there is not yet complete consensus on which is best in all circumstances. These generally produce lower indexes of agreement than simple percentage calculations because they compensate for agreements that occur by chance. Whether thinking in terms of percentages or more rigorous indexes of agreement, higher is better. Any number below 0.70 certainly means that the data are suspect, and some researchers are not completely satisfied at this level.

If there is only one person involved in coding the data, intercoder reliability is not actually a factor; however, as the use of intercoder checks is becoming more standard, one-coder studies are less common, except as exploratory research. Sometimes a code-recode procedure is used to assess reliability in cases where there is only one coder. For a small-scale study in an introductory class, this is probably sufficient.

To keep track of what the categories mean, and to make sure everyone is using the same definition, researchers often create a **codebook** that describes as simply and specifically as possible the meaning assigned to each category of a content analytic study. (Codebooks are also commonly used in survey research.) The codebook is where the researcher records exactly how the categories (whether source types, themes, frames, or other characteristics) used in his or her study were identified in the media content used. The larger the study and the more coders involved, the more important the codebook becomes.

Each individual category choice should be defined as succinctly as possible but in enough detail that a coder new to the project will have all the information needed to match what previous coders have done.

Sometimes coder differences are resolved by discussion among the different coders and result in a codebook revision and a new intercoder reliability check.

Special Challenges in Content Analysis

A discussion of content analysis, the most widely used methodological approach associated specifically with mass communication research, would not be complete without some frank discussion of its problems and limitations. It is much easier and cheaper to do content analysis than it is to do survey research or to conduct experiments. Many content analytic studies are purely descriptive, recording how often certain themes emerge but with little consideration for why this might be important, either for theoretical reasons or from the point of view of practitioners. Perhaps the contemporary emphasis on intercoder reliability springs in part from such problems, but perfect reliability does not turn every content analysis into a meaningful piece of research. Simply categorizing various forms of content is not enough. Good content analysis work, like all research, follows well-defined research questions and, where appropriate, hypotheses.

Many times, beginning researchers are tempted to make cause-and-effect assumptions on the basis of content data. If children's television is full of advertisements for unhealthy foods, this must be the cause of the so-called obesity epidemic. Maybe, but perhaps the real problem is too much time spent watching TV, regardless of content. If the Internet is full of misleading "facts," democracy will necessarily be harmed rather than hurt by its growth. Maybe, but under what circumstances are people's information-processing or information-seeking skills able to compensate, and what can be done to improve these skills? If images of men as well as women in advertising overemphasize physical perfection, this will cause young people to lose their self-esteem. Maybe, but how important is this factor in comparison to the influence of familial approval and support? Too often, the conclusions drawn from content data rest on unstated assumptions that may not hold up when more is known.

Content analysis is important and has given us important insights, especially into how media content has changed with society. However, it is a limited tool that may be most useful when its results can be combined with those of other forms of research, such as surveys, experiments, and ethnographic and other qualitative approaches.

Figure 5.1   Measuring the important things about media content isn't easy.

Important Terms and Concepts

Census

Codebook

Coding

Convenience sample

Demographics

Field experiment

Forced-choice question

Grounded theory

Instrument

Intercoder reliability

Multifactorial

Multistage sampling

Open-ended question

Pretest

Posttest

Pretest-posttest design

Quasi-experiment

Quota sampling

Representative sample   Semantic differential

Response bias   Survey

Response rate   Systematic random sampling

Sampling frame

Exercise

Media content analysis is the research method most unique to mass communication studies, but a number of problems with it are still to be worked out, including the best way to ensure a high degree of intercoder reliability. As a class exercise (or by dividing into pairs to work outside of class), experiment with content analysis as described below.

1. In groups or pairs, using today's issue of your local newspaper, develop a list of theme categories you would like to use to classify the content on the front page. You will want to consult the paper in order to do this, because your theme category choices might depend on the types of articles that appear on this particular day.

2. As a team, develop a simple codebook that defines each theme category as clearly as possible. Then have each person separately code the front-page article themes according to the definitions in the codebook. Note that individual articles may have just one theme or several different ones. Calculate your intercoder reliability as a simple percentage agreement.

3. If time permits, your instructor may ask you to exchange codebooks with another team. Recode the page using the codebook developed by the other team. Does your intercoder reliability change? If different teams are using different materials, exchange materials at this step as well.

4. Your instructor may also want you to discuss, as a class, the similarities and the differences in the different codebooks.

CHAPTER 6

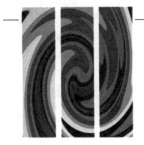

Designing Qualitative Studies

Participant Observation, Interviews, Focus Groups, and Qualitative Content Analysis

The challenge of qualitative studies may be less in preplanned technical elements of design, as it is with quantitative studies, and more in the researcher's ability to make the most of the opportunity at hand. This means recognizing the uniqueness of the setting, people, or material under study; keeping good records, including detailed notes (and/or audio recordings of interactions, as appropriate); being sensitive and receptive to the experience by setting aside preconceptions; making sense of what is learned and seeing the patterns within it; allowing conclusions to emerge from the data; and then being able to capture those conclusions in a written product that makes them vivid—and therefore convincing, without the benefit of tables, charts, and statistics—to the reader. However, qualitative research (just like quantitative research) also has technical elements; it requires strong analytical skills and a highly systematic approach, not just good intuition and flexibility. Qualitative research is no less difficult than quantitative research—it may be more difficult, done well—but it is different, even though there can be a great deal of synergy between the two. Doing qualitative analysis well is a bit like cooking a gourmet meal without a recipe; it requires a lot of practice, and even then, there will probably be some minor adjustments as the project moves along.

This chapter discusses participant observation first. All qualitative research in some ways follows the model of participant observation. The common goal is an act of interpretation that may be best exemplified by the participant observer experience in trying to understand the "insider" viewpoint of members of a social group to which the researcher usually does not belong. Interviews and focus groups, like participant observation, also try to capture someone else's point of view but in somewhat less natural circumstances; qualitative content analysis is more dependent on the researcher's own reactions than anyone else's but involves the same spirit of setting aside preconceptions and asking what is actually being communicated—what deeper meanings does the material in question offer?

PARTICIPANT OBSERVATION

Participant observation has its formal origins in the attempts of early-20th-century researchers to make sense of previously unknown and unexplored cultures that must have seemed to them to be vastly different from their own. Informally, it mirrors the experience of other travelers trying to make sense of another culture, whether in today's world or an earlier one. How does anyone try to make sense of an unfamiliar cultural reality, especially someone left to his or her own devices in a foreign land? The participant observation pioneers did their best to fit in with other cultures in order to understand what was going on, in the process helping elevate ethnographic study to a recognized and legitimate strategy for understanding social settings, including those close to home as well as those in exotic locales.

Research using participant observation and other qualitative techniques is rarely guided by formal hypotheses. However, the researcher still needs to have a general research question or goal in mind to make the best use of the experience. Early ethnographers were often prepared to spend a year or more making sense of an unfamiliar culture. We usually do not have that much time, so the effort needs to be more focused. Fortunately, the settings we are likely to have opportunities to observe are often not so completely unknown. This makes the task easier in many respects, though it creates a stronger mandate to consciously set aside preconceived expectations, especially if we are already a member of the group we propose to study.

What does it mean to be a participant observer? Unlike unobtrusive observation, where the researcher strives to be either invisible or as much as possible like a quiet mouse in the corner, the key to *participant* observation is to become a "regular" member of the group under study. The researcher's own feelings, reactions, and mistakes provide important data. As noted in Chapter 2, participant observation has been used to study media organizations for about as long as mass communication research has existed. If you work (either as a regular employee, a volunteer, or an intern), you can use the method of participant observation to gain meaningful research experience at the same time, simply by paying attention in a systematic way to your surroundings.[1] If this work is in a communication or media organization, so much the better. You can also be a participant observer in other readily available settings; for example, if you are on a college campus, potential projects include observing life in a college dormitory, recording interactions at meetings of a student organization, or documenting what it means to leave home and become a college freshman.

In workplaces and other formal organizational settings, observe what important divisions of labor or work roles there are in the organization and how these seem to be thought of in terms of relative status and leadership. How are decisions actually made? How do members talk about their work, and what else do they talk about? Who is really in charge, and how is his, her, or their influence communicated? Sometimes complex organizations are characterized by powerful informal lines of communication and control that may be quite different from the formal hierarchy. Think about what new informal, as well as formal, rules you may need to learn in order to "fit in" smoothly with the organization's expectations and routines. How are people supposed to dress, for example? How important is it to arrive exactly on time? What seems to be most valued? Many of these questions also translate well to less formal settings outside of workplaces and formal organizations; prescribed social roles and patterns of leadership are important everywhere.

What kind of research question might such a study be designed to answer? For example, let's assume you want to know how today's community newspapers are actually organized and what their work is like, and you have the opportunity to observe one. In recent years, community newspapers in many areas have been purchased by larger companies that own whole chains of small papers. It is widely believed (by both journalists and scholars) that this is changing the way that these local news organizations operate, so such a study would have some theoretical foundation. But what is today's community newspaper actually like? With limited resources, how much news is written locally, how much is repackaged from wire reports, and how are these decisions made?

What are the different work roles, and how are other editorial decisions made? What seems to be important to the employees? Are they conscious of pressures from outside (e.g., from a chain owner), or not? You will get a more *holistic* picture by doing participant observation, and probably an answer that is more true to life, by observing what is actually going on than through any other approach.

Studying a single organization like this in depth is one kind of case study. Although its results aren't always perfectly generalizable to other, similar organizations, the data obtained are still valuable beyond the specific organization or case. We can expect that *some* elements we observe will indeed be characteristic of other organizations or institutions, especially those with much the same role. At a minimum, such a study could guide someone else doing another case study of a similar organization; with information from multiple cases, the existence of patterns would become clearer. Human activity is patterned, and different social groups engaged in the same kind of activity generally have much in common.

While quite a ways from its original uses, participant observation is also a good way to study the social meaning of the mass media—the role media play in everyday life. For example, sports fans seem to agree that watching a game "live" on television (that is, at the time it is actually being played in real life) adds a great deal to the experience. For many, watching it with a group of fellow fans is also important, but even when the event is observed alone, the viewer may *imagine* the existence of other fans elsewhere who are watching at the same time. Whether in a sports bar or at home on a holiday, you don't have to be a sports fan to realize how dedicated fans are to this ritual of game watching or how important it is in their lives. Friends or family members who don't otherwise spend much time together get a chance to rekindle the bond between them on such occasions—in the United States, televised Thanksgiving football games serve exactly this purpose and have become something of a cultural ritual.

Similarly, college students (and others) may make a regular event of watching television soap operas as a group. Like sports fans, they may record the shows to save them for a time when the group can get together. Sometimes this becomes one of the most important events of the day for some people. The group character of these experiences is important. What's going on here? What's different about watching with a group as opposed to watching alone? What do group members seem to get out of the experience? How do they talk about what they're watching, and how does their interaction with one another seem to be influenced by the "presence" of a mass medium? Of course, millions of other audience members watch the soaps alone. If we were from an entirely different culture, what would our reaction be to such a phenomenon—how would we make sense of the role of these televised dramas in the lives of their viewers? How would we explain it to a visitor from a distant land?

Getting Started and Taking Notes

As either an honorary or an actual member of a social group, you have decided it would be important or interesting to study that group. You have obtained permission from the members of the group and (if required) your university human subjects board (IRB) to use the experience for your own research. If the group is not one you are already involved with, you have made arrangements to attend its meetings or sit in on its events on a regular basis. What next?

If engaged in a formal study, it is essential to be honest and open with the group being studied about why you are there, but you also want the group to forget to the extent possible that you are there as a researcher. So your first objective is to just blend in. Relax and try to be as natural a group member as possible, but without being so obtrusive that you might have too much influence on the group dynamics. A reality of ethnography is that you *will* change the social setting to some extent by your presence. This cannot be avoided, only minimized.

As a practical matter, you may not be able to take notes visibly, especially at first—an activity likely to make your informants self-conscious (although in some settings, like a public reception area, writing on a clipboard might go completely unnoticed). So plan on remembering as much as possible and save your note taking for later on, as soon as possible. You may be studying a one-time event, whether a press conference or a shared meal, or you may be following a group over a period of days, weeks, or months. Either way, be scrupulous about recording your observations as soon as possible after leaving the setting. This is important. Otherwise, it can be remarkably difficult to reconstruct what you learned and observed and how you reacted even after very few days have passed. Perhaps it is a characteristic of the human mind, but our initial observations seem to fade very quickly, becoming replaced with whatever general impressions or conclusions we take away. It is those initial observations that our notes are designed to capture.

What, exactly, do you take notes *about?* Observe who's present, what they do, and what they say—including their nonverbal communication or "body language." Write down as much detail as possible; don't do too much prescreening or filtering of what seems important and what doesn't. But pay special attention to things that seem confusing, surprising, interesting, or novel to you as an outsider—even if you don't especially understand *why* something strikes you as significant at this stage. Even notes about how people dress, what they eat or drink, and when they come and go might also be important— if only as memory aids for other sequences of events. What seems to be important about what they are doing, from your respondents' own points of view? How do you know? Above all, don't overlook the apparently obvious.

More on Choosing a Setting and Making It Work

You want to begin, as always, with a clearly defined research problem—and, for participant observation, a carefully chosen setting. However, you also have to be an opportunist on the lookout for a chance to do this kind of project if you want to succeed, because not all organizations or groups are going to grant you access. And once you are there, you want to be alert to interesting events that may not fit your original idea about what you thought would be most interesting.

If you're trying to locate a setting for this type of study, be alert to groups where you already have an "inside track" that will make it easier for you to get permission to do your study, as well as easier for you to be accepted as a member. Perhaps a family member or close friend works in a media organization of a type that interests you and can help arrange permission for you to observe it. Maybe you know someone who is a bit of a video game addict and will let you into his or her world. We live in a media-saturated society; opportunities to study the relationship between media and everyday life are everywhere around us.

Participant observation is not as easy as it might sound, though. This section will probably generate more questions than answers, but that is the nature of this kind of naturalistic inquiry. An abiding curiosity about all aspects of human interaction will serve you in good stead. Remember, though, that you are in the setting you are studying as a guest—and, in the end, an outsider. Try to suspend judgment, and try to avoid playing too active a role. It is also good practice to avoid making records of things that might actually embarrass or offend someone.

INTERVIEWS

Some aspects of the social world are not readily visible to researchers as observers, however. Perhaps your research question concerns individual use of media rather than group use or the structure of media organizations. Or perhaps you do not have an opportunity to do participant observation, or your research question requires information from a number of people who are not necessarily members of a single group or organization. The goal of understanding the "insider's" perspective can be met in another way. Either as the primary "stand-alone" method for a particular study, a supplement to participant observation, or a complement to a quantitative approach like a survey, the use of the depth interview (or semistructured interview) is an equally important qualitative approach.

In many ways, depth interviews are more practical than participant observation; you can schedule these interviews at a time of mutual convenience, you will not have to worry about getting permission from an entire group but only from those who agree to be interviewed, and you can manage the way the conversation proceeds rather than being dependent on naturally occurring events to demonstrate what is going on. Interviews allow you to use your time more efficiently, especially if you have a subject area for your research that is well defined. The depth interview is much more flexible than survey research because it can go in different directions depending on what the interviewee has to say; it is also more flexible than participant observation because you have more control over the structure of the interaction.

Qualitative interviews begin with something called an **interview schedule** (or interview guide) that lists the most important topics to be covered—perhaps with tentative question wording suggested but not intended to be administered word-for-word like a survey questionnaire. This guide is designed to make sure you remember to cover all the topic areas that are important but also allows you to probe certain areas for more information or pursue an entirely different topic that might come up and that appears worth exploring. Let the research question guide the construction of the interview schedule. (Good feature reporters often employ a similar interview style to that used in the social scientific depth interview.) If depth interviews are being used as part of a larger study based on participant observation, results from the observation (unanswered questions or things that need to be clarified) will, of course, contribute to the list. Interviews can also be used to add perspective to survey responses, probing why respondents might have chosen particular answers to close-ended survey questions.

Recruiting interviewees can take many paths. Random sampling is usually not the goal; although it might be useful in some studies, it is very difficult to get a randomly chosen stranger to agree to a lengthy interview for research purposes. One good strategy is to use a **snowball technique**. In this procedure, you let each interviewee suggest two or three other people for your study. For example, let's say you've decided to interview women communication professionals in your community about their career paths. Your research question concerns the particular barriers they may have experienced and what factors they believe made them successful anyway. If you can identify just one or two such people by word of mouth, they will be able to suggest others.

Sometimes it is necessary or especially important to interview only a few people, as in a case study of a small media organization where the interviews are being used to supplement participant observation work. You can interview a handful of individuals in some cases and still come away with important information from a social scientific point of view, especially when the research goal is to understand the world from another's vantage point—and a "handful" is a practical size for a student project. Just one interview with a homeless person, for example, would give you a lot of rich information about what this way of life—very different from, say, that of the average person reading this book—involves. Of course, it would be better to have interviews with several, even though the sampling considerations typical of quantitative studies do not apply to qualitative interviews.

For some studies, more interviews are required. There is no upper limit; on the other hand, for most studies of particular groups, a couple of dozen interviews, at most, should suffice. Some more complex studies may use 80 to 100 or more, especially if the goals of the research require the inclusion of a broad range of viewpoints.

Conducting an Effective Interview

It does take skill to keep the depth interview focused while also keeping alert to new directions you might want to follow. Make this easier by choosing a relaxed and quiet location. If you are interviewing someone you do not know well, a coffee shop is a good neutral location. If you interview someone in his or her office, which may be necessary for some busy interviewees, remember that this will change the character of the interaction. You'll be on the interviewee's territory, so to speak, and the person controlling the territory usually has a stronger sense of control.

Some people are much easier to interview than others. In some cases, you will need to work hard to get the person talking and keep the flow going. A good interview should take at least three fourths of an hour, but some people just will not talk that much. Others are hard to stop and will want to tell you many interesting stories that do not seem particularly relevant. In these cases, you may need to delicately push the conversation back on track. Remember, when you express a sincere interest in how people think or what's important to them, and when you've been successful in making them relax and trust you a little bit, most are more than happy to talk.

Eye contact and other body language should indicate to the interviewee that you are interested in what he or she is saying. Resist the temptation to fill awkward silences by talking too much yourself. If the person you are interviewing is on the quiet side, you will need to make use of follow-up probes like "Tell me more about that" or "That is very interesting; can you explain a bit more?" to keep the conversation going. As natural a conversational flow as possible is what you want to achieve, without your slipping out of the role of interviewer. Let your informants know you are listening and care about what they have to say; offer them some neutral feedback ("I see" or "All right") from time to time.

Pay particular attention to specialized terms, whether professional vocabulary, slang words or phrases, or special uses of everyday language. Ask for definitions or clarification: "What do you mean by that?" "Why is that important?" "What's the difference?" As with participant observation, pay attention to things that you don't understand, and when an answer or an anecdote puzzles you, don't be afraid to ask for a clarification. Tailor your language to the respondent. If you're interviewing a professional, it helps to sound as professional as possible, but if you're interviewing a child, use simple language. Be patient, and don't be satisfied with one-word answers. Be ready to shift the line of questioning if the answers you are receiving don't seem to be helping, but don't give up on trying to understand the informant's perspective.

Try to be sensitive to the same kinds of differences of perspective you'd be looking for as a participant observer. Chances are, your informant's response makes sense from his or her point of view, but you may need to follow up to understand this. Try very hard to avoid making assumptions about how your informant looks at things; keep your questions as neutral as possible—for example, "Can you tell me a little bit more about that? It sounds interesting, but I don't quite understand it." It can also help to repeat back the answers you receive in different words (for example, "So you are saying that the managing editor doesn't make that kind of decision?").

Depending on whom you are interviewing and what he or she knows about you, you may need to make a point of making it clear that you are not interviewing him or her as a journalist for a story but as a research student for a paper. In some cases, this may make the interviewee less nervous about being interviewed, as well as about the interview being recorded if you decide to propose that; it is common courtesy to be clear about your role, in any event.

As with journalistic interviews, using an audio recorder has advantages and disadvantages. Most people who agree to be interviewed will probably agree to be recorded, and they'll soon forget that the recorder is running. Then you don't have to be distracted by the necessity of getting everything down in your notes and can concentrate on listening and understanding. But it's still helpful to take at least some notes, especially on points that you want to follow up on later in the interview or that seem especially important. This may prevent your having to sift through a half-hour's recording to find a particular bit that you want to hear again word for word.

FOCUS GROUPS

Focus groups assess the responses of a group of individuals and can actually be designed in many ways. As you'll recall, the advantage of a focus group over an individual depth interview is that the respondents or informants involved (let's just call them focus group participants here) can react to one another, as well as to the interviewer. In interview situations, the relationship between the interviewer and the interviewee can be a bit unnatural and one way, which intimidates some participants. The researcher may be perceived as powerful, and the informant may feel pressured to give a certain kind of answer. In a focus group situation, the participants are likely to relax and interact more naturally. Furthermore, they have the opportunity to "pick up on" and react to one another's comments and responses, which creates a richer set of data for many purposes than can result from a single interviewer's interaction with a single respondent.

In market research, focus groups made up of consumers are often used to assess reactions to a new product, service, program, candidate, or advertisement. Focus groups can also be used to identify the problems that exist among various professional groups within a complex organization or to study how public opinion on important social or political issues is beginning to form. Focus groups that assess reactions to emerging issues may be given background information ahead of time to provide them a basic orientation to the topic; this needs to be done with caution, of course—both to provide enough information (but not so much that the participants will not read it) and to provide balanced information that will not influence the discussion in a particular direction.

Those who study small-group interaction and communication patterns may also use focus group data to study such things as how leadership patterns emerge and how "body language" contributes to group interactions, regardless of the actual subject of the discussion.

Logistics

Recruiting subjects for focus groups is a special problem, however. Usually, there is at least some intent to produce results that apply beyond the group of individuals who actually participate in the study. But it's not practical to try to create a random sample for the purpose. Most people who are asked to participate in a focus group are going to refuse because they must disrupt their normal, daily routine—and perhaps lose part of a paycheck in the process. Even when the available research funding permits paying focus group participants for their cooperation, many potential participants will simply not have time. Most of us have full days as it is. Those who accept may be less busy, more cooperative, and perhaps poorer (where financial incentives are offered) than the population from which they are drawn. This needs to be considered when interpreting the data.

However, a researcher doing focus group work as part of a case study of an organization can solicit the organization's cooperation in recruiting a good mix of participants. Sometimes, outside organizations, such as a local civic group, can be persuaded to recruit participants from among their members; volunteers pool their earnings as a fund-raiser for the organization even where they would not have been induced to participate for the small amount they could have earned individually. If the group is not too atypical in terms of its political orientation or social makeup, this probably produces a more nearly representative group than an attempt—inevitably flawed—at truly random sampling.

Elaborate physical facilities are often used for focus group work, especially when this method is used for market research in which clients must be impressed. Video cameras allow participants' body language as well as their comments to be recorded; one-way glass allows others interested in the research to observe participants' reactions directly. But analyzing the rich visual data recorded on videotape in a meaningful way is difficult and time-consuming and may not yield definite conclusions. In fact, a general danger of using focus groups in market research is that too much faith is invested in the conclusions without consideration of whether the participants constitute a representative sample of the general population. For example, consumers who are especially fond of a company's line of products—the most likely focus group volunteers—may be wildly enthusiastic about the latest ad campaign but highly unrepresentative of the potential general consumer market for the product!

Audio recording focus group discussions is certainly much easier and cheaper than videotaping, though using both is ideal when resources permit. Most of the analysis will probably focus on the verbal statements of the participant, even if videotape is available. However, videotape is worth having if it is reasonably convenient to arrange. Market research firms often maintain files of people who are willing to participate in focus group research, but it's hard to argue that these individuals are representative of a larger population. When focus group work is designed to find out what members of a particular group think or feel—for example, if a government agency is studying the needs and concerns of farmers so as to design a better communication campaign aimed at them—the membership of organizations within the group of interest is the logical place to turn for focus group recruits.

Sometimes, several different groups are chosen to represent various groups or points of view; for example, separate groups might be created to represent student, faculty, and staff points of view on university communication issues. In this type of case, it is especially important not to mix the participants, not only because their separate points of view are being sought but also because having groups involving participants of mixed status may put a "damper" on the discussion of some members. Students might not speak as freely in front of faculty, for example, as they would in a group composed only of their peers (other students).

Similarly, any group composed of people with widely varying educational and occupational types can be a problem. Some group members will tend to defer to those they consider more authoritative. In fact, some authorities recommend that focus groups contain participants who are as much alike as possible, although the best solution always depends on the purpose of the groups.

Conducting the Group

Leading a focus group discussion is an art—like conducting a depth interview, only much more complex. As with surveys, it's often considered important to introduce the question, problem, product, or message that the group will consider in a consistent way. Even though focus group research is a qualitative technique, the direction of the discussion may be very heavily influenced by the way the problem is presented, so it's important to use a carefully worded introduction that is the same for each group. Some specially designed focus groups assign a mock task to the group. For example, group members might be told to imagine they are being asked to act as a citizens' advisory board on an important planning issue. Other studies might simply seek reactions in a more open-ended way: "Tell us how this product (or message or issue) makes you feel" or "What do you think about when you see this ad?"

The most difficult thing for the focus group leader is to keep discussion going as long as possible without directing the discussion in ways that will too heavily influence the responses that the research is designed to uncover. For example, say a group is asked for its reaction to a front-page newspaper story on local government corruption. Above all, the focus group leader should remain neutral and not argue with the respondents or reveal too much about

Figure 6.1   Leading an effective focus group discussion requires skillful orchestration.

his or her own point of view. Even if a focus group participant appears to be incorrect about a factual issue, any additional information should be introduced tactfully and certainly not in an argumentative way. As with response bias in surveys, it is natural for focus group participants to want to please the researcher or group leader, and they may try hard to come up with the kinds of arguments they think are desired without even realizing it. Instead, the leader should stick to neutral questions like "Is there anything else anyone would like to say?" or "Are those all of the things that come to mind?" without in any way directing the discussion.

Remember that the leader's tone of voice or facial expression can also influence participants, so this person needs to appear pleasant, friendly, interested, professional, and objective. An important advantage of having at least a tape recording of the discussion is that the focus group leader's performance and use of probes can be reviewed.

These discussions typically take an hour or more, depending on the size of the group. However, taking much longer than that is usually not advisable. People get tired and tend to lose their focus after about an hour's intense discussion. Data from these discussions can be categorized and summarized numerically. Mechanically, this process is more or less similar to the quantitative analysis of media content data. However, the results should be interpreted somewhat differently, keeping the structure of the focus group discussion in mind as context for what was said. This introduces a qualitative element, even if there is an attempt at quantitative analysis.

Using Quantitative Pretests and Posttests

Sometimes, focus group participants are asked to fill out attitudinal or other survey questionnaires before and/or after participating. As with experimental designs in general, pretesting participants' opinions should be done with caution because it can have a sensitizing effect; however, posttesting tells us nothing about the perspectives or opinions the group members might have had coming in—which could also be important clues to understanding group dynamics. Some research designs may explicitly concentrate on the effect of the discussion on attitude change, in which case pre- and posttests are probably essential.

Pretesting might also be used to rule out the possibility that participants hold extreme views on the subject under discussion or to place them in groups with similar views. At a minimum, demographic data should be collected to ensure the participants are at least roughly representative of the population of interest, whether a target population intended to be reached with a particular communication campaign, "ordinary people" who do not yet have strong opinions on an emerging issue or political contest, or the likely target group for marketing a new product.

QUALITATIVE CONTENT STUDIES

In the previous chapter, the discussion of quantitative content analysis introduced the distinction between "manifest," or relatively superficial, and "latent," or deeper symbolic, content. Even quantitative content analysis typically deals with the latent as well as the manifest. Qualitative content studies are much more focused on latent content, however, and can better take into account subtleties of the structure of arguments and narratives not easily captured by quantitative summaries.

Content analysis can be purely qualitative, purely quantitative, or partly quantitative and partly qualitative. Just as in observing social settings or interviewing individuals in an exploratory way, a purely qualitative approach is preferable in cases where the particular aspects of content being studied are difficult to capture in quantitative analysis schemes or are simply not definable with certainty in advance of conducting the study. Sometimes, the main interest is in the nuances suggested by the "gestalt" of particular narrative forms, not isolated elements that can be weighed, evaluated, or measured item by item, as in quantitative approaches.

The qualitative methods used in such cases are sometimes referred to as **discourse analysis**, textual analysis, or rhetorical analysis. All of these distinct approaches share certain elements. They are holistic, like ethnography, and they attempt to deal with messages and meanings in cultural context rather than as isolated elements. Different scholarly traditions think of these alternatives in different ways. Faculty and students in university departments of speech communication and literature (representing humanities approaches) are often the experts in these techniques, as they may draw from the same intellectual traditions underlying the analysis of literary fiction and public speech, respectively. These more interpretive traditions often provide a very different "lens" than the traditions of social science with which this book is primarily concerned and that underlie all quantitative and many qualitative but empirical approaches.

The social science norm of being rigorously systematic in procedures for sampling content, for example, may not be relevant to these studies, in which subtleties of message structure and the culturally shared rhetorical resources on which they draw may be more at issue. Many things can be interpreted as "texts" whose narrative structures are worthy of examination—not just media messages but architecture, art, and the whole range of popular culture forms are "in the business" (sometimes quite literally) of sending messages to audiences.

Although a few researchers originally trained in the social sciences still tend to discount textual, rhetorical, or discourse-analytic studies, these qualitative means of assessing content can be just as rigorous as, say, ethnographers' qualitative methods of studying people—and just as carefully grounded in the evidence at hand. And although interpretive methods cannot directly answer questions about cause and effect, the mutual influence of social scientific and humanities approaches is increasingly apparent in cutting-edge media studies thinking.

Rhetorical and literary theory can help guide the researcher in deciding what to look for, just as social science theory is needed to help guide the construction of other types of studies. Sometimes both are used: A conflict theorist may use discourse analysis to suggest how power relationships within society are reflected in the way the mass media portray certain issues. However, as in all interdisciplinary work, the researcher who is interested in such questions sometimes navigates uncharted waters, with little in the way of methodological precepts to provide a guide.

Sampling in the statistical sense is not necessarily an important consideration for qualitative media content studies, just as it is not an important consideration for some ethnographic studies; rather, the intent is to gain a "window" on a particular worldview, whether represented by one or a few human informants or by a limited set of media messages selected purposively (that is, with a purpose in mind) by the researcher. Nevertheless, the selection should make sense. The material should be representative—not in the sense that the sample used in a survey is statistically representative of a larger population but in the sense that the material reflects important culture values and iconography that are relevant to the study. Key texts may offer particular clues to the cultural significance of message elements that is independent of statistical representativeness.

Some qualitative researchers talk about using the feelings and reactions of the researcher as a tool of content analysis just as ethnographers have historically used their own feelings and reactions as tools to discover what other cultures are like and how they are different from the researcher's own culture. This element of reflexivity (or awareness of one's own interpretation and influence on the social construction of events) is part of what is meant by a "close" (or "ethnographic") "reading" of a mass media (or other) text. Just as the ethnographer observes and interprets events within a particular social setting, the ethnographic approach to analyzing media content considers the cultural significance of particular media texts.

Without a full awareness of the nature of humanistic methods, it can be hard to distinguish opinionated essays illustrated with selected examples from more rigorous, yet still qualitative, scholarship. Essays may make interesting and persuasive reading, but they are not always scholarly "research," which should always represent something beyond personal opinion even if qualitative methods underlie them. Excellence in qualitative content analysis requires not only an open-minded researcher but also a reasonably specific research question and a systematic way of looking at whatever content is chosen—even if only a relatively small, selected set of messages is used in the analysis. The trade-off between using small message samples and analyzing them in depth versus analyzing larger samples quantitatively is similar to the trade-off involved in doing a limited number of depth interviews versus achieving the generalizable results that characterize survey research. Both approaches have value, and triangulated studies that use both are often the most persuasive.

It is important to remember that qualitative content studies can follow the basic principles of social science—a systematic approach grounded in the evidence at hand—and are not "unscientific" just because they are more interpretive than positivistic in their approach. Generalizability in these studies lies in the observation of patterns and relationships that appear to be relevant beyond the case or example under study, just as generalizability for the cultural anthropologist lies in discovering universal patterns in social organization that seem to extend beyond the case at hand. This is very different from the statistical concept of generalizability but no less valid. Nevertheless, this is not an excuse for being less than completely rigorous in looking for— and describing—these patterns! The main criticism of purely qualitative research lies in the free rein given to the researcher's own interpretation. Thus, a main goal of summarizing such a study in a paper or an article should be to demonstrate that this interpretation has cultural foundations worth attending to.

What guidance do these generalities provide to the student researcher setting off in these uncharted waters? Alas, not much! No formulas or doctrines predict success. However, some principles are worth reinforcing. A *systematic* approach is more defensible. Choosing examples that fit a predetermined argument is generally not as effective, or as revealing, as setting aside preconceptions and trying to understand the underlying structures of messages and associated arguments. Like an ethnographer on an adventure in a foreign land, *look at things afresh*. What exactly does a message reveal about the cultural context in which it was created or the assumptions members of that culture might make? Whether analyzing a science documentary, a television sitcom, or a Hollywood film, what are audiences expected to bring to the interpretive task? This type of analysis is what the anthropologist Clifford Geertz (1973) has called "thick description," or the analysis—and documentation (i.e., description)—of the cultural baggage the viewer (who may also be the researcher) must bring to bear on the culturally relevant interpretation of the message at hand. What do we *need to know* to make sense of a particular mediated reality?

Important Terms and Concepts

Discourse analysis

Interview schedule

Snowball technique

Exercise

This chapter presents participant observation as a sort of model for other types of qualitative research, such as depth interviews, observation, and qualitative content analysis. Participant observation can be applied in everyday social settings in which the researcher is already a participant.

1. Choose a setting (a workplace, an organization or a club, a group event, or another social situation) in which you are a member and have the opportunity to observe characteristic activities.

2. Practice the skills of keen observation and careful note taking presented in this chapter for at least an hour—the typical duration of an organization meeting or, in the case of a work setting, a reasonably large chunk of a typical workday.

3. Prepare a two- to three-page written report about what you observe. Remember that articulating your observations is an important part of qualitative research. Your instructor will decide whether this report will be turned in for course credit, used as the basis of class discussion, or both.

Note

1. University IRBs differ greatly in how they respond to participant observation in organization studies. However, notes kept for private use and not intended to produce a research report would not be defined as research by the U.S. National Institutes of Health guidelines that cover human subjects research. If part of a formal research project, the requirements could be different, even if the observations take place in a public location.

PART III

Approaches to
Data Analysis

Basic Tools

CHAPTER 7

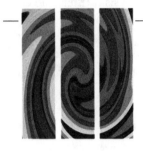

Describing a Numerical Data Set and Making Inferences

Y ou've learned about samples and populations, independent and dependent variables, the basics of research design, and something about the challenges of measurement in previous chapters. Quantitative studies, in a nutshell, measure variables in a sample, usually in order to draw conclusions about a population and, especially in the case of studies based on cause-and-effect hypotheses, about the relationships between independent and dependent variables. **Descriptive statistics** summarize sets of numerical observations so they are easier to conceptualize and communicate. Reasoning from available data to estimate the values in a population is the fundamental purpose of **inferential statistics**. This reasoning is also necessary for the testing of hypotheses because it allows estimation of the accuracy of variable measurements. What tests are appropriate depend on the type or level of measurement of the variables involved; for more about this, see below.

This chapter is intended to give you some idea of what to do with quantitative data once you have them (which, for many researchers, is really the fun part!) and to look briefly at a few more advanced techniques for both variable measurement and statistical analysis that you might want to use later on. You'll work through details of the arithmetic and algebra involved only for a few of the most simple cases, as illustrations of what these calculations are all about. This book *does not* assume that you have had a beginning course in statistics; if you have, some of the material in this chapter should serve as a helpful review. Many excellent textbooks and more advanced courses are available to help you pursue this type of analysis further, and computer programs like the SPSS package (see Box 7.1) will usually do most of the complex arithmetic for you—and even help walk you through some of the decision making involved. The goal of this chapter is to get you started thinking about the potential uses of statistical analysis and to give you some of the conceptual and analytical tools needed to get started.

BOX 7.1

Statistical Software

Recent generations of research students have little notion how much more tedious and time-consuming it was to calculate statistics by hand. Many advanced analyses that can be done today in minutes took weeks or months with pencil and paper. Of course, most numerical data today are analyzed by computer, a significant advantage. The major drawbacks are probably that the ready availability of statistical software tempts researchers at all levels to generate statistics that they don't fully understand or that overwhelm them to the point it is difficult to decide what is important. Sometimes the search for a solution to a social scientific problem benefits more by clear thinking and simple statistics than by mountains of calculations. But there is no doubt that on balance, statistical software development has been crucial to the advancement of the social sciences.

For quantitative analysis of social science data, SPSS (Statistical Package for the Social Sciences) is probably the best-known computer software used in mass communication studies, as in many of the other social sciences. This software is often available for free use or discounted purchase to students and others affiliated with a university. Today SPSS runs on most personal computers and is set up much like an ordinary spreadsheet, but it is much more powerful. It is useful to realize that it organizes data by unit of analysis (whether person or household, article or theme, and so on), with variable names listed on a single line along the top and each case with its corresponding variables' values listed on a horizontal line. Most of the common data management and analysis tools it contains are controlled by a set of user-friendly drop-down boxes—another big change from when these programs ran on big mainframes and required, in essence, their own programming language.

For more advanced students, software is also available that provides specialized tools for everything from certain kinds of high-level quantitative analysis to the collection of experimental data via networked personal computers. Other commercially available software products provide tools some researchers find useful for qualitative analysis.

LEVELS OF MEASUREMENT

A wide variety of variables and statistical analysis techniques is used in mass communication studies. Some variables, such as the presence or absence of certain themes or the use of certain kinds of sources in a news story, are assessed using simple counts. Others, such as the length of a story in inches or many types of questions used to assess opinions or attitudes, are represented by scales. Statisticians use the term *level of measurement,* initially introduced in Chapter 4, to capture these distinctions. Knowing what level of measurement applies in the case of each variable helps researchers decide what kinds of statistical tools can be used. Most commonly, these are divided into two **categorical** or "counting" levels and two **continuous** or "scaled measurement" levels.

Categorical Variables

Nominal variables are categorical variables in which measurement consists simply of assigning each case to a named category. For example, in a study of children's television programming, we might classify some programs as "educational" while others are "entertainment." This would be an example of a nominal variable with just two values. Perhaps we are also interested in the ethnicity and gender of the people who appear on these shows. Ethnicity and gender are also examples of nominal variables, as are eye color and hair color. These variables can have any number of values; for example, university officials often need to count the number of students following different majors, which can involve many dozens of possible choices. No matter how many majors are available, this is still a nominal variable (a simple category, not a scale measurement).

An **ordinal** variable is another kind of categorical variable in which the different categories can be ranked by being put in some sort of logical order. To follow the example of children's television further, the researchers might categorize some programs as "low educational value," others "medium educational value," and yet others "high educational value." The different items (programs) are still being placed into different categories, but the categories can be arranged in a logical sequence from low to medium to high. Similarly, university officials may need to find out how many students are freshmen, sophomores, juniors, or seniors. This is another example of a ranked or "ordinal" classification that goes from those who are just beginning college through those who are in their last year; it but is not a true scale measurement.

Using categorical data, whether nominal or ordinal, it is not possible to calculate a meaningful average. For example, it is not possible to state an "average" major for a particular college campus. We can identify which major is most popular, and we can calculate the average number of students in each major, but the idea of averaging major itself simply makes no sense. Sometimes, for convenience, numbers are assigned to the values of categorical variables. We could assign the number 1 to represent African Americans, the number 2 to represent Asian Americans, the number 3 to represent European Americans, and so on. But that does not make it possible to average all these numbers and come up with a meaningful figure called "average ethnicity."

With ordinal data, practice varies. If the children's television researchers assigned the number 1 to "low educational value" programming, the number 2 to "medium educational value" programming, and the number 3 to "high educational value" programming, they might be tempted to try to find the mean figure for educational value among all the children's programs they evaluated. While common and convenient, technically speaking this would be incorrect, because these values do not represent a true scale. The definition of a scale is that the distance between each point is the same. We have no way of knowing that the distance between "low" and "medium" is the same as the distance between "medium" and "high"; the fact that we used the numbers 1, 2, and 3 to represent these categories does not really change that.

On the other hand, if we recorded the total number of credit hours completed instead of the class level of students (freshman, sophomore, and so on), or if we recorded the exact number of informational statements per episode instead of making a general judgment about "level of educational value," we would jump up to a higher level of measurement—continuous—in which true scales are used.

Continuous Variables

In contrast, such everyday items as weight, height, and temperature are usually measured on continuous scales in which the distance between one number and the next has a consistent meaning. A 150-lb. person is 5 lb. heavier than a 145-lb. person, just as a 105-lb. person is 5 lb. heavier than a 100-lb. person. Similarly, a 5-ft., 6-in. person is 2 in. shorter than a 5-ft., 8-in. person and 2 in. taller than a 5-ft., 4-in. person. A full flour canister that holds 6 cups of flour has 2 more cups than a flour canister holding 4 cups of flour. A temperature of 80 °F is 5 degrees above 75, exactly the same amount as 65 °F is above 60. Number of credit hours completed and number of informational statements made behave similarly. Each 3-hour course completed adds the same amount to total credit hours completed, and each statement would be counted as exactly one unit.

Two different kinds of continuous variables are available, those measured by **interval** scales and those measured by **ratio** scales. Ratio scales are probably the easiest to understand because they are the most common. Ratio scales allow the calculation of ratios by dividing one value into another. A cook knows that 6 cups of flour will make twice as many cookies as 3 cups. Someone who has completed 75 credit hours of college coursework has completed exactly three times as many credit hours as someone who has only completed 25. A program containing 24 informational statements has four times as many of these statements as a program containing only 6. In each case, the ratio comparison is possible because the scale begins at a true zero point—a flour canister that is empty (with 0 cups of flour), a person who has completed no credit hours at all, and a program containing no informational statements all make sense. These are all ratio scales.

But temperature doesn't seem to act the same way. If it is 40°F outside, is it twice as warm as if it is 20°F? Not really, because degrees on a Fahrenheit scale do not begin at a true zero point. Even in degrees Celsius, in which the freezing point of water is assigned a scale value of 0, this is a completely arbitrary choice. You still cannot divide one temperature point by another and get a meaningful ratio. This is true even though each point along these temperature scales is the same distance from the next point (a one-degree rise from 35°C to 36°C represents exactly the same amount of change as a one-degree rise from 90°C to 91°C)—that is, even though temperature scales are true scales, they do not always have meaningful zero points. Only degrees Kelvin, used by scientists and beginning at a point called absolute zero where there is no heat present (273°C below the freezing point of water) has a true zero point. Temperature scales without a true zero point are interval scales—each degree is the same "size" as the next degree—but not ratio scales.

Interval scales may be uncommon in everyday life, temperature measurements aside, but they are very common in social science research. Anytime you are asked to indicate, on a scale of 1 to 10 (called a 10-point scale), how much you agree with a particular statement, the result is likely to be considered an interval scale score. The assumption is made that the "distance" between any two points on this scale is the same. This assumption might be misleading; some researchers argue that it is false because people might conceptualize these scales in different ways. Some people might find it more difficult to choose one of the endpoints (1 or 10), for example, creating a greater psychological distance between 1 and 2 and between 9 and 10 than exists between other adjacent pairs of numbers. This is sometimes thought of as a "rubber ruler" problem, akin to using a ruler that is stretched out along different parts of its length.

However, it is common practice to treat scores on these scales as interval data. (The alternative would be to treat them as ordinal data, ranked but not representing exactly equal units.) They are *not* ratio scales, however; there is no zero point. Someone who chooses the number 8 on one of these scales *is not* necessarily indicating "twice as much" agreement as someone who chooses the number 4.

Because of the common practice of treating data from this type of scale as interval-level, researchers are able to calculate summary statistics such as "average level of agreement" and do many other statistical manipulations that would not be appropriate for ordinal data. This is extremely useful for comparing levels of agreement for different statements, for example, and for testing hypotheses about them. Scholars sometimes disagree about how much of a problem it is to treat 5-point-scale data as interval. This uncertainty needs to be weighed against the amount of uncertainty introduced by presenting respondents with a 7- or 10-point scale, where the fine distinctions may not be completely consistent or even meaningful, defeating the purpose of using a more accurate scale. A 3-point scale, such as the low-medium-high scale used to rate the educational value of children's programs in the example above, would typically be treated as ordinal only.

Choosing a Level of Measurement

In the early stage of designing a research project, decisions must often be made between one level of measurement and another—what type of categories to offer in a forced-choice questionnaire, for example. Experienced researchers think ahead and generally choose the scale that will give them the most flexibility later on. However, there are exceptions.

One important set of exceptions reflects respondent sensitivity to being asked personal questions. Income in actual dollars and age in actual years are both continuous (ratio) measurements; income or age chosen from a list of equal categories (1 to 10, 11 to 20, and so on) is still continuous but less precise, and such a question may yield only ordinal data if categories such as "over ___" or "less than ___" are used. But such categories are often offered anyway on practical grounds. It is generally believed that respondents are less embarrassed, threatened, or offended by having to choose from a list of categories than by having to state their income in dollars or their age in years, as introduced in Chapter 5. As always, this type of research decision involves a trade-off between the ideal world and the practical constraints of gathering data from real people whose goodwill is important.

Other exceptions involve judgments about the meaningfulness of different levels of measurement in particular circumstances. For example, political scientists may categorize the tone of news stories about an issue using ordinal categories such as positive, negative, and neutral. While it might be better from a statistical analysis point of view to use a scale score for tone ranging from (say) −3 to +3, this presumes that a coder's judgment about the appropriate score would be reliable enough across the entire group of stories being coded to make these fine distinctions valuable. Would having the coder recode the data produce different scores? Using a smaller number of broader categories might improve intercoder or code-recode reliability.

IDENTIFYING AND SUMMARIZING PATTERNS

A common place to begin a data analysis that can be used with categorical (nominal and ordinal) as well as continuous data is by examining a **frequency distribution** showing how many cases fall into each of a number of categories, often with percentages. Data can also be presented in what are sometimes called **cross-tabs** or cross-tabulation tables. Cross-tab tables are especially useful for the analysis and presentation of categorical data where the number of other options can be limited; however, they can also be used to observe patterns in continuous data. To construct a cross-tabs table for two variables, one variable's values are listed across the top, and the other's values are listed down the side. For example, a cross-tabs table showing categories of student majors by year of graduation for a particular college or university might look like Table 7.1.

Table 7.1   Student Majors by Year of Graduation for a Hypothetical College in Five Most Recent Years

Year	Major				
	Journalism and Communication	Social Sciences and Humanities	Engineering and Science	Fine Arts and Music	Total
2004	500	250	200	100	1,050
2005	400	220	180	90	890
2006	450	260	150	60	920
2007	550	210	140	30	930
2008	800	270	100	20	1,190
Total	2,700	1,210	770	300	4,980

This simple cross-tabs example tells us a lot of information quickly for nearly 5,000 students. While the number of social science and humanities majors have changed over the years, steady declines are more apparent in engineering and science and especially in fine arts and music, where an 80% drop in majors occurred between 2004 and 2008. Journalism and communication majors—always the most popular choice—accounted for the great majority of the 2008 graduates, despite a drop in 2005 followed initially by a more gradual gain and then a huge one in 2008.

This table tells us nothing about why journalism and communication has become more popular than engineering and science or fine arts and music at this college. However, cross-tabs tables can also give us some preliminary ideas about causation in some cases. For example, a different cross-tabs table showing only women might reveal that they are increasingly less likely to choose engineering and science majors, even though the college might do a good job recruiting excellent woman students. This could call into question the effectiveness of recruiting strategies being used by those particular departments. Of course, caution is in order; there would be many other competing explanations for such a pattern.

However, the use of descriptive statistics goes beyond looking at frequency distributions and cross-tabs tables, whether for categorical or continuous data, to provide "shorthand" numerical characterizations of key features of data distributions.

Simple Descriptive Statistics

Descriptive statistics allow you to summarize a set of numerical data in a meaningful way. If your study has collected dozens of measurements for dozens of cases, as is very commonly the case, you will need to find ways to simplify your results so both you and, ultimately, the readers of your research report can make sense of them.

Statistics that measure the tendency of data to cluster together toward a central point are called **measures of central tendency**. In many (but not all) distributions, extremely high or low scores are less common than those closer to the middle. While measures of central tendency are available for all levels of measurement, the **mean** or arithmetic average—the sum of all of the data points divided by the total number of scores—is the most common and familiar, although it can be used only with continuous (interval or ratio) data. The mean score on a test, the mean price of a gallon of gasoline, and the mean number of minutes of advertising in a half hour of prime-time TV are all familiar examples. The **median** score, or the middle score if all of the scores are ranked from lowest to highest, is another measure of central tendency that can be used with continuous or ordinal data. The **mode** or most common category is the only measure of central tendency that can be used with nominal data. In the example in Table 7.1, journalism and communications is the most common, or modal, category of major for all years shown for this hypothetical college.

A second very common type of descriptive statistic is the **measure of dispersion**. While not quite as ubiquitous as measures of central tendency, many examples of measures of dispersion are familiar to us. Such measures are shorthand ways of capturing whether a set of scores or other data points cluster closely around a central point or are more spread out. The simplest measure of dispersion is the **range**, the distance between the highest and the lowest scores. Let's say we ask a group of 10 Internet users to keep track of the number of hours they spend on the Internet in a typical day and report them to us. The answers might vary anywhere from 1 to (say) 15, so the range is 14. But range doesn't tell you as much as you might like to know about the variation in a data set; it takes into account only the two most extreme scores. We might like to know whether most people are around the average for the group, while the scores of 1 and 15 are rather unusual, or whether the answers are more spread out.

For any continuous data, we can use the **variance** statistic to tell us more. Variance measures dispersion by calculating the amount that *each score* differs from the mean, squaring that difference, and dividing the total of the squared differences by the total number of scores *minus 1*. Algebraically, this is written as

$$S^2 = \frac{\Sigma(X - \bar{X})^2}{N-1},$$

where S^2 stands for variance, Σ means "summation" (the total for all cases of the expression that follows), X stands for an individual score, $\bar{X}$ is the mean score, and N is the total *number* of scores. Whether a score is greater than the mean or less than the mean, the farther away it is from the mean, the higher its contribution to the overall variance. (You'll remember from high school that two negative numbers multiplied together produce a positive result, so whether an individual score is greater than or less than the mean score does not matter to this calculation.) Using the *square* of differences from the mean also gives additional weight to extreme scores. Statisticians consider a calculation that is sensitive to extremes in this way to be a better representation (or description) of the total variation in the data than a calculation without this property.

Another even more common measure of dispersion for the distribution of a continuous variable is called the **standard deviation**, which is simply the square root of the variance. It is typically symbolized as S, whereas variance is S^2. Because the standard deviation is expressed in units equivalent to the units of the original measure (whether scores on a test, number of hours spent on the Internet, or advertising minutes in a block of prime-time TV), it is easier for many people to grasp.

Relationships Between Variables

To describe the statistical relationship between two variables—that is, the degree to which a change in one variable is related to a change in the other—a statistic called the **correlation coefficient** is commonly used. There are many kinds of correlation coefficients appropriate for use with various levels of measurement. However, regardless of what measure is used, it is absolutely crucial to remember that a correlation coefficient is only a descriptive tool. If there is no correlation (or a low correlation) between two variables, there is probably no simple relationship between them. But the existence of a nonzero correlation is *not* proof of causation, and very often the *direction* of causation is especially unclear. *This point cannot be over-stressed: Correlation does not imply causation.* This is often a particular problem for media research.

To take a very simple example about direction of causation, let's assume we found a close statistical relationship (correlation) between people's degree of preference for elite national newspapers (versus, say, popular tabloids or local newspapers) and their knowledge of current events. It is quite inviting to conclude that reading elite newspapers *causes* people to become better informed. However, it's also very likely that people who are better informed in the first place are the ones who prefer the elite papers. They may also be people with higher levels of education, and some of them may have a professional interest in national news (if they are stockbrokers, businesspeople, government officials, professors, or journalists, for instance).

A slightly more complex example is found in the perennial debate about media effects. Some research suggests that young people who watch a great deal of violent television in their early years are more likely to become criminal or violent later in life, as young adults. But by itself, this line of reasoning cannot prove that TV violence is the culprit. Various other possibilities cannot be ruled out, including the possibility that individuals who select a disproportionate amount of violent television are already being influenced by their own personality characteristics or by family or community dynamics in the direction of those choices. The fact that other research supports the same conclusion is an important argument, but clear cause-and-effect proof is not available from these correlational studies.

A somewhat more subtle example is found in research that has attempted to prove that any media coverage of technology-related controversies, whether positive or negative, always "results in" negative public opinion, based largely on correlational data. However, media generally do not provide controversy-oriented coverage of noncontroversial technologies. Rather, operating as they ideally should, journalists provide an "early warning system" about controversies on the horizon. The fact that they are often right about the existence of an emerging technological controversy does not mean that they created it—or "caused" public opinion to shift. Such ideas must be tested with additional analysis. All of these examples are intended to reinforce the point that *correlation is not causation.*

Many different types of correlation coefficients are used with different types of data measured at different levels. A standard convention across all of them is that they all range from -1 to $+1$, with 0 indicating no relationship whatsoever, $+1$ indicating a perfect **positive correlation** (every time one variable increases, there's a known *increase* in the value of the other variable, too), and -1 indicating a perfect **negative correlation** (an increase in one variable is always associated with a predictable *decrease* in the other variable).

By far, the most commonly used correlation coefficient is **Pearson's r**. This statistic is used for measuring a **linear relationship** between two continuous variables. (Many other correlation coefficients are available to assess relationships even when variables are not measured on a continuous scale, but Pearson's r is the one most commonly in use and will serve as our example here.) In practice, correlation coefficients are almost always less than perfect ones; the meaning or importance of a less-than-perfect correlation is a matter of judgment and depends on the research question and how it is understood theoretically. Calculating r by hand is not actually difficult, but it is tedious and the formula is a bit cumbersome; all standard statistical software can handle it with ease, however.

Linear and Nonlinear Relationships

What is a linear relationship? This is a relationship that's essentially the same along the whole range of values of both variables. Visual inspection helps assess the shape of a relationship. If you graph two variables that have a linear relationship and a perfect positive correlation (unlikely in practice), the graph would look like Figure 7.1.

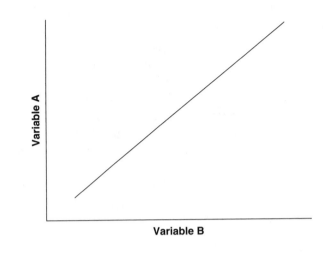

Figure 7.1   Perfect Positive Relationship

This relationship can reasonably be described as a straight line. (Incidentally, the algebraically minded may be interested to know that Pearson's *r* also describes the *slope* of the graph line. The line is steeper when the correlation is high and nearer to flat when the correlation is low.) A perfect negative correlation for two variables that are linearly related, on the other hand, would look like Figure 7.2.

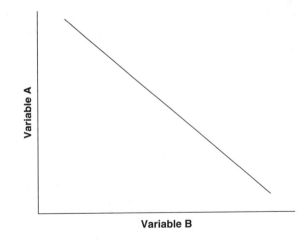

Figure 7.2   Perfect Negative Relationship

However, not all strong relationships between variables are linear. A nonlinear relationship might look like Figure 7.3 or even like Figure 7.4. What is a nonlinear relationship? A nonlinear relationship can consist of *anything other than a straight line*. This situation is complicated by the fact that actual data never fall as nicely and neatly on *any* line (straight or curved) as these exam-

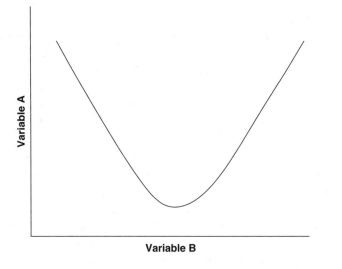

Figure 7.3   One Example of a Nonlinear Relationship

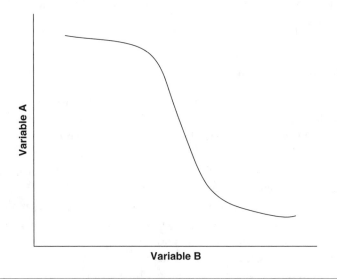

Figure 7.4   Another Example of a Nonlinear Relationship

ples suggest. Always graph the data you are concerned with to be sure it seems reasonable to make an assumption of linearity. Otherwise, a correlation coefficient may give very misleading results; it will miss most nonlinear relationships altogether, leading you to overlook an important part of the picture, and it may understate others.

Two variables can be related less than perfectly in either a negative or a positive direction; in other words, a correlation coefficient such as Pearson's r can take any value between -1 and $+1$. Very small correlations may or may not mean much; it depends on the purpose of the study and the theoretical significance of the variables, as well as the sample size. Even high correlations may not mean as much as they appear to. If two attitudinal items turn out to be highly correlated, you must decide (on the basis of theory and common sense) whether an interesting new discovery has been made or if the two items are actually just measuring the same underlying idea using slightly different wording.

Another way of thinking about Pearson's r is that its *square* (r^2) tells you the proportion of the variance in one variable that can be predicted on the basis of the other. This is sometimes called a **coefficient of determination**. If there's a high correlation between two variables and you know the value of the first variable, you can make a good prediction of the second—the value of the first variable partially "determines" the value of the second. The higher the correlation, the better your prediction—whether the relationship is negative or positive. If the correlation between two variables is (say) 0.50, then the coefficient of determination—the proportion of variance in the second variable that can be determined if you know the value of the first—is 0.25 or 25%.

Other Possible Relationships

Ordinary linear and nonlinear relationships do not exhaust the possibilities for how variables may be related. Sometimes the relationship between two variables may involve an **interaction effect**. This means that two or more independent variables interact to produce an effect on a dependent variable. For example, perhaps reliance on social networking sites for interpersonal interaction might further limit social engagement for people who already have problems making friends; for others, it is a helpful complement to face-to-face interaction that acts in a positive direction. A correlational study might not reveal any particular relationship between use of social networking sites and level of face-to-face social engagement with others, when in fact, there is a negative effect for those who are socially disadvantaged and a positive effect for those who are not.

An **intervening variable** is one that is believed to further explain or mediate a relationship between an independent and a dependent variable. For example, perhaps media literacy education reduces some negative effects of the media on young people. The negative effects in question might involve modeling one's own behavior with respect to driving after drinking alcohol on negative examples in films. But how exactly does the education work? Increased media literacy might result in changes in the perception that films mirror the normative expectations of real life. This kind of indirect effect can be studied by looking at the correlation between media literacy education and this perception and between the perception and personal behavior, separately.

REASONING FROM SAMPLE TO POPULATION

Often, the main objective in working with descriptive statistics about *sample* values is to make reasonable, well-supported guesses about the actual value of a *population* **parameter**, or characteristic (in this case, the true value of a population variable). Accuracy here is defined in terms of the probability that you are wrong. Generally speaking, researchers aim for at least a 95% probability that their results from a sample actually represent the population accurately. The greater the sample size, and the better understood the problem, the more reasonable it is to aim for a 99% probability of accuracy, so larger studies on well-understood problems routinely aim for this higher level. Conversely, for exploratory research—perhaps a smaller **pilot study**, aimed at gaining some initial understanding of a new problem—a 90% level may be considered quite satisfactory, suggesting a finding worth pursuing with further research. There is nothing "magical" about the 95% or 99% levels; these represent only agreed-on researcher conventions.

Naturally, it's easier to be confident that a population parameter is *close* to a sample value—within some range—than it is to be confident that a particular sample measurement represents *exactly* what the population value would be. The only way you could be completely certain that you really know exactly what the population value would be involves surveying everyone in the population, involving a census rather than a sample.

The objective of inferential statistics is to be able to determine, with a known degree of confidence (probability of being right), what range the true value of the population parameter is likely to be within. When survey results are reported in the mass media, stories often use language like "results are accurate to within 3 percentage points"—language often found in the fine print in the corner of a graph or in the closing paragraphs of a news story, although sometimes it is omitted. So, if, for example, 25% of the survey sample agrees with a certain statement, the researchers are stating in this hypothetical case that they are reasonably (perhaps 95%) confident that the true population value for that parameter is between 22% and 28%.

Because such a statement is an assertion about the likelihood that the true value of a population parameter lies within a given range, or interval, with a known degree of confidence, that range is sometimes called a **confidence interval**.

Relevance of a "Normal" Distribution

One theoretical way to determine the accuracy of a survey result is to repeat the survey many times and examine the variation in your results. Let's say the true population parameter for an agree/disagree judgment on a 5-point scale is *exactly* 2.6. (In reality, we never know this when evaluating sample means, of course—this is a very hypothetical situation.) Sometimes, your sample value might turn out be 2.5, 2.6, or 2.7, and so on. Occasionally, if you kept running the experiment on various random samples, you might come up with—by chance—a sample value as low as 1.0 or as high as 5.0. (Remember, this question used a 5-point scale, so 1.0 is the lowest— and 5.0 the highest— possible value for the sample result.) If you did repeat a survey like this many times, you'd have a distribution of different results that should look like Figure 7.5. Since the true population value (hypothetically) is 2.6, the mean of all the various samples you attempted should converge on 2.6, the "0" point in the figure (meaning zero deviation from the population mean).

This basic shape is called a **normal distribution**, sometimes referred to as a **bell curve**. Bell curves can be pinched or stretched horizontally in shape and can lean to the left or right, but they are a very typical shape for all kinds of naturally occurring continuous (interval or ratio) variables, including the weight and height of human beings, for example. It is the shape that educational psychologists aim for when they design intelligence, aptitude, and achievement tests. The mathematical properties of normal distributions are very well understood by statisticians. Fortunately for your purposes, this is often the shape taken by the distribution of possible sample-based measurements of a population mean, called the **sampling distribution of means**. Usually, although not always, the shape of this distribution is "normal" regardless of the shape of the distribution of the actual individual values. Most of the mean values in our example would cluster around a middle point, but a very few could be as low as 1.0 or as high as 5.0.

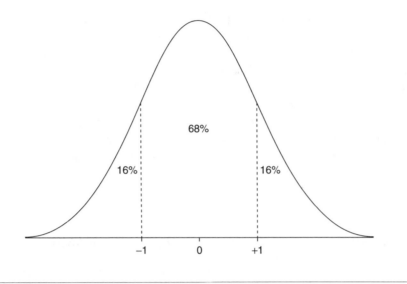

Figure 7.5   Normal Distribution

Note that the *area under* such a curve represents the probability that results within a certain range will be obtained. It is more likely that your sample results, by chance, will be somewhere around the true value of 2.6 than that they would be at one of the extreme ends. One of the things known about the normal distribution of possible means in such a case is that if you go out exactly one standard deviation from the mean of the sampling distribution of the means in either direction, you will be including just over two thirds of the area, or 68%. If you go out just about two standard deviations from the mean in each direction (the exact number is 1.96 standard deviations), you will include 95% of the area. And if you go out about another half standard deviation in either direction (actually to 2.58 standard deviations in either direction), you'll have included 99% of the area under the curve. Going out just 1.65 standard deviations in either direction, on the other hand, would take in 90% of the area under the curve. So you know a lot about what a distribution of possible sample results would be likely to look like, if only you had one!

In practice, of course, we don't repeat our sample measurement zillions of times to explore the nature of this distribution. A "best guess" about the mean of the sampling distribution of possible sample mean values is based on the information available. Let's suppose that the mean value for a sample is 2.7. There's no way of knowing whether it's higher or lower than the population value (which is the same as the mean of all possible sample values), so 2.7 is going to be our best guess of the mean of all possible such values—since that's our only available information.

What is the standard deviation of this distribution (the sampling distribution of means with an unknown-to-us actual mean of 2.6 but an estimated mean of 2.7, an estimate based on a single sample)? Logically, you'd probably want to use the amount of variance in the sample as the basis for an estimate of the amount of variance in the sampling distribution of means. This would give you some idea of how the answers on our 5-point scale varied from person to person. The larger the sample size, the more certain you can be of the accuracy of both the sample mean and the sample variance with respect to the values that really exist in the entire population. But if the answers in our sample were all over the board, we might be less sure of the population mean than if the answers in our sample were mostly within a narrow range.

Standard Deviation of the Sampling Distribution of Means

For reasonably large samples (samples of, say, 100 or more; Minium, 1970), the formula for the standard deviation of the sampling distribution of means—also called **standard error**—turns out to be the standard deviation of the sample, divided by the square root of the sample size. However, the smaller the sample, the less accurate you can assume your population estimate to be, so you must adjust your estimate of standard error accordingly. Unfortunately, the shape of the curve on which your adjusted estimate will be based is not exactly the well-known normal curve and is slightly different for every possible sample size. Actually, this forms a whole family of distribution curves (one for each possible sample size) of the statistic known as Student's t. (The mathematician who first described these distributions wrote under the pseudonym "Student.")

Most advanced statistics or quantitative methods texts will give the values for Student's t for various **degrees of freedom**. This term reflects sample size and refers to the number of scores in the sample that could be assigned any arbitrary value (that's the "freedom" part—they are "free" to vary) and still come up with the same mean. Both the distribution of t and the number of degrees of freedom are automatically taken into account by statistical analysis programs. For our simple problem of measurement of a single parameter, degrees of freedom (often abbreviated df) would be 1 less than the sample size (that is, for a sample of—say—15, your df would be 14).

Let's assume our hypothetical variable, based on 15 scores, which has a sample mean of 2.7, also has a sample standard deviation of 0.96. So our best guess regarding the sampling distribution of the mean of all possible such results is that it would have a mean of 2.7 and a standard deviation of 0.96 divided by the square root of 15, or 0.96/3.9, or 0.25.

Now, if the sampling distribution of means were a normal "bell curve" distribution, you could begin to draw some useful conclusions. You know that 95% of the area under a normal curve is between −1.96 standard deviations and +1.96 standard deviations from the mean. But your sample size is *not* 100 or more—it is only 15. So the sampling distribution of means is not normally distributed. Instead, you must substitute the shape of the distribution of Student's *t* when $df = 14$.

In *that* distribution, 95% of the area under the curve falls in the range of ±2.15 standard deviations from the mean. As a result, you can estimate the population value of your variable as $2.7 \pm (2.15 \times 0.25)$, or 2.7 ± 0.54, or the range from 2.15 to 3.24. Notice that this is not too terribly far from the range you would have estimated assuming a normal sampling distribution ($\pm 1.96 \times 0.25$ from 2.7). Logically, it should by now make sense that the precision of your estimate is a bit less than it would have been if your sample had been larger. At any rate, you can now state, with good justification, that you believe there's a 95% probability that the population value of your variable is between 2.2 and 3.2. In reporting statistical research results, this is often abbreviated to something like 2.7 ± 0.5 (95% confidence).

Fortunately, in today's world, we don't have to go through this complicated reasoning every time. Statistical software generally reports the estimated accuracy of our results automatically, although in slightly different formats depending on the software we are using. However, the sampling distribution of the means is, alas, *not* always normally distributed, even for large samples. A statistician can help you figure out how to test for this and can suggest necessary corrections if your results cannot be treated as described above.

Media Reports of Survey Error Margins

The preceding discussion may remind you of the typical survey research reports in the media in which the results are said to reflect a **margin of error** of so many percentage points. The idea is exactly the same. Actually, big national surveys often use rather complicated sampling schemes, not just simple random sampling, and their statistical analysis can sometimes be much more complex than the example used here. But the principle is the same, except that survey data are usually reported in the form of proportions or percentages, not mean values. The reported margin of error reflects the estimated accuracy of these proportional results, based on a certain confidence level.

Surveys are often based on agree/disagree or yes/no questions—questions with answers that fall into **dichotomous** (or two-valued) **categories** rather than continuous scale measurements. Under these circumstances there's a reasonably simple procedure for calculating the standard error of the percentages. This procedure produces different answers depending on the proportions of the respondents in each of the two categories for a given question, but the largest error exists when the proportions are 50–50, with half the respondents in each group. So making the assumption that respondents' answers are divided equally will produce the largest estimate of error, minimizing the chances of overstating accuracy. The error estimate based on this assumption is the one generally used to suggest a margin of error for an entire set of survey data in which the results are expressed as percentages.

Using the large-sample assumption that the sampling distribution of means is normal and choosing a 95% confidence interval, this formula is $\pm 1.96 \times \sqrt{0.25/N}$. (A 99% confidence interval would use $\pm 2.58 \times \sqrt{0.25/N}$, and so on.) For a random sample of 500 respondents, then, the margin of error would be stated as $\pm 1.96 \times \sqrt{0.25/500}$ or ± 0.044 (4 percentage points) using a 95% confidence interval; it would be $\pm 2.58 \times \sqrt{0.25/500} = \pm 0.058$ (6 percentage points) using a 99% confidence interval.

All survey results reported to the public should include a margin of error. This has substantial real-world significance. In the case of political races, a candidate with a 52% "lead" in the polls is not necessarily on track to win. If the sampling error (or margin of error) is 2% or more, it's a toss-up, even if the election were held immediately and everyone voted exactly the same way he or she answered the survey questions. And regardless of the size of the sampling error, there's always a chance that the results reported are more inaccurate than the range suggested by the error term. How big a chance? This depends on the confidence interval chosen. With a 95% confidence interval, for example, there's still a 5% (or 1-in-20) chance that the sample misrepresents the population value by an amount greater than the range specified. With a 99% confidence interval, there's a 1% chance of greater error, and so on. So confidence level must also be reported.

The Significance of Correlation Coefficients

Confidence intervals can be calculated for any population parameter, not just for means but for variances, standard deviations, and any other population statistics, including correlation coefficients. The procedure's logic is the same; a sampling distribution of the possible values of the statistic in question is the basis of the inference in each case, just as it was for estimating a mean. However, the sampling distribution of Pearson's r is a nonnormal distribution with a shape that varies depending on both the size of r and the size of the sample. So calculating confidence intervals for a correlation coefficient is not so straightforward.

Fortunately, researchers are usually most interested in the question of whether a relationship does or does not exist in the population between two variables that (in your sample) are correlated. In other words, you want to know whether the population value for r could reasonably be assumed to be zero or whether your sample r is so large (either in a positive or a negative direction) that this would not be a reasonable assumption. In this case, the standard procedure is to test the hypothesis that there is no correlation. If you can't support it because your value of r is too far from zero to be reasonably attributed to chance variation, you can reasonably assert that the correlation has **statistical significance**.

If you assume that the true (population) correlation is zero, you can calculate a value from your sample r that turns out to have a distribution just like Student's t. The relevant degrees of freedom are defined as $n - 2$, where n is the number of score pairs. Say you have a sample consisting of 30 subjects, and you've measured both level of interest in current events and years of education for each of them. There are 28 degrees of freedom $(30 - 2)$. You calculate a correlation of 0.60 between the two variables. The formula for calculating t from r is $r \div \sqrt{(1 - r^2/(n - 2)}$ and in this case gives you a value for t of 3.97.

You decide on an acceptable **confidence level** (probability that your result was not obtained by chance variation) of 99%. A t-value table (from a statistics or quantitative methods text) tells you that for $df = 28$, you need to go out to a value of 2.76 in either direction from the mean to include 99% of the area under the curve. Because your t value of 3.97 exceeds that value, you can reasonably reject the assertion that there is no actual correlation between interest and education in the population you've sampled and conclude instead that there probably is (with a 99% or better confidence level). The likely range of the population value of r does *not* include zero.

Today's statistical software will report the statistical significance of a correlation as effortlessly as it calculates the correlation itself, so you probably won't actually have to follow these steps in most cases. The logic is parallel to the logic of estimating any other population parameter: You are still reasoning from the correlation within a sample to the likely correlation in the entire population.

Interpreting Correlations' Significance

A very small correlation (say, less than 0.10) can have high statistical significance if it is based on a large enough sample. That is, you can be almost completely certain that there's some correlation, which sounds impressive. But even a significant 0.10 correlation means that a proportion of just 0.01 (only 1%) of the variance (change or variation) in one variable can most likely be predicted on the basis of the other. Shouldn't you be more concerned about the other 99%? It is important not to overrate the real-world significance of statistically significant correlations, especially those obtained from large data sets. Sometimes the interpretation of results like these can have important societal implications.

It is always possible, and even likely, when working with very large samples that even very small correlations will be statistically significant. But with low correlations, this does not necessarily translate into significance in the real world because factors *not* represented in the correlation are likely to be much more important influences. So use these statistics with caution and common sense.

Important Terms and Concepts

Bell curve	Margin of error
Categorical	Mean
Coefficient of determination	Measure of central tendency
Confidence interval	Measure of dispersion
Confidence level	Median
Continuous	Mode
Correlation coefficient	Negative correlation
Cross-tabs	Nominal
Degrees of freedom	Normal distribution
Descriptive statistics	Ordinal
Dichotomous categories	Parameter
Frequency distribution	Pearson's *r*
Inferential statistics	Pilot study
Interaction effect	Positive correlation
Interval	Range
Intervening variable	Ratio
Linear relationship	Sampling distribution of means

Standard deviation Statistical significance

Standard error Variance

Exercise

The following list represents 15 people's estimates of the amount of time they spend on a typical weekday watching television and the amount of time they spend on a typical weekday using the Internet. Since there are only so many free hours in a day, some researchers have argued that time spent with a new medium (Internet) will reduce the time spent with an older medium (television). These data allow us to test this idea, at least in part.

Respondent	Hours Spent With TV	Hours Spent With Internet
John	1.0	1.5
Jane	2.0	4.0
Mary	2.5	0.5
Bill	0.5	0.0
Susan	3.0	0.5
Carol	2.0	2.0
Frank	1.0	4.0
George	1.5	3.0
Mike	4.0	2.0
Beverly	2.5	1.0
Tricia	6.0	1.0
Deborah	1.0	5.0
Bob	1.5	3.5
Rick	3.0	2.0
Louise	4.0	2.0

The data presented above are only hypothetical. Your instructor may want to take the time to substitute actual values from the students in your class for this exercise. If so, you could base your estimates on your results from the exercise in Chapter 3. However, remember that unless you happen to have exactly 15 students in your class, you will also need the distribution of Student's t for the appropriate number of degrees of freedom (one less than the number of respondents) to answer Question 2, so your instructor may also need to provide this.

1. Calculate the mean estimated time spent with each of the two media for all individuals combined, plus the variance and the standard deviation for each of these statistics.

2. If this group were a random sample of the population of your college or university, what would be your best estimate of the means and standard deviations of these figures for the entire student body, at a 95% confidence level?

3. Graph the relationship between television use and Internet use (use individual points, called a "scatter diagram," rather than trying to connect them with a line). What does the result tell you about this relationship? Is it linear or nonlinear? Does it seem to show a positive correlation, a negative correlation, or no correlation at all?

   An optional next step would be to calculate the actual correlation coefficient. While this book does not present the details (for the sake of simplicity), you can find them in most statistics texts, or you can use many spreadsheet programs (including Microsoft Excel) or any statistical software (including SPSS) to do this. Does the result confirm what you suspected?

CHAPTER 8

Testing Hypotheses and Exploring Other Relationships

S tatistical techniques allow estimation of population parameters from samples, as you have seen through the examples in Chapter 7. By reasoning from the confidence intervals surrounding population value estimates, we are also able to test many sorts of hypotheses about whether variables are related; which **statistical tests** are available in a given case generally depends on the levels of measurement involved for our independent and dependent variables. Other statistical techniques allow further exploration of more complex relationships involving multiple variables. This chapter introduces the basics of hypothesis testing and provides a conceptual explanation of many common techniques for **multivariate analysis**, the analysis of complex relationships among multiple variables.

TESTING SIMPLE HYPOTHESES

A statistical test helps you determine whether *conclusions* based on sample data are warranted. While confidence intervals tell us what our sample predicts is the likely population value for a variable, with a known probability of being correct, confidence levels tell us the probability that a hypothesis tested on our sample data and either accepted or rejected would actually be accepted or rejected if we had the entire population to work with. This is another very powerful form of inference. Of course, if we really did have data for the entire population of interest, no probability estimates would be necessary. Just as a census gives an exact value for a population variable so confidence intervals aren't necessary, statements about differences in subpopulations are absolute and don't need to be qualified with confidence levels.

For example, if we knew the income of every man and every woman in the United States and calculated the mean income for each group, we could make an unqualified statement about the difference between them. Confidence levels, like confidence intervals, are used because we rarely have census data for the questions we are trying to answer; we are more commonly working from samples rather than populations. Typical values for confidence levels are the same as those for confidence intervals: 99%, 95%, or in some cases of small-scale exploratory research, 90%.

Understanding the Limitations of Hypothesis Testing

Just as population parameters (by the chance variation that occurs in sampling) may not fall exactly within our specified confidence intervals, a test of a hypothesis may sometimes (by chance) provide false results. There are two ways this can happen. The probability that a hypothesis will be found to be true when it is actually false is called **Type I error**. Type I error is the complement of the confidence level (one minus the level, expressed as a proportion). At a confidence level of 95%, there is a 5% chance of this type of error. If the experiment were repeated 10 or 100 or 1,000 times, then 5% of the time, on average, this kind of false result would occur.

To minimize the chance of Type I error, the researcher sets the confidence level as high as possible. But if it is set *too* high, the test may miss important inferences. This is the reason why confidence levels of 99% or even 99.9% are not universally the rule of thumb. Missing the opportunity to establish the existence of a hypothesized relationship, even if the relationship may actually exist in the population, would happen too often. This other type of error (obtaining results that dismiss the existence of a relationship when they should not have) is called **Type II error**. Although other factors are involved, in general, the lower the probability of Type I error, the higher the probability of Type II error.

One way to think of this is that a higher confidence level makes it more difficult for a hypothesis to "pass" a statistical test. This seems more rigorous, but in exploratory research where measures are still being refined and relationships are not completely understood, or when using smaller sample sizes for whatever reason, setting the confidence level too high may mean that even correct hypotheses fail to "pass." For well-understood problems being investigated with larger-scale data sets, a high confidence level (typically 99%) is appropriate. In other cases, research may progress faster with lower confidence levels as the standard (typically 95% or even 90%). Future research, using larger samples and better-developed measures, can confirm these results at a higher level.

If a researcher sets a confidence level of 99.9%, any result obtained would have only a 1-in-1,000 chance of being wrong. This is powerful evidence. However, important conclusions that might otherwise have been drawn could be overlooked. Perhaps someday other researchers will serendipitously rediscover the relationship you've accidentally overlooked. But perhaps not.

Type II error is harder than Type I error to control or assess. But there are steps you can take way back in the beginning of your research design to minimize the possibility of Type II error (that is, of overlooking a potentially important correct result because your test does not achieve statistical significance). Measuring accurately, controlling experiments carefully, following the principles of randomization scrupulously, using adequate sample sizes, and choosing an appropriate confidence level (not always 99%, especially for early research into a new problem) all help ensure you'll find what you're looking for if it is represented in the measurements you make.

The bottom line is that just because an individual experiment doesn't support your hypothesis, *you never have absolute proof that your hypothesis is wrong.* There is always some chance of Type II error, even if it is a small one.

The Logic of Hypothesis Testing

In Chapter 7, you briefly encountered the idea of testing a hypothesis about a correlation coefficient being nonzero—that is, testing whether some statistical relationship might actually exist between two variables, such as television viewing and Internet use. In the case of a correlation hypothesis, we are actually looking at whether the confidence interval for the correlation statistic would include a possible value of zero or not. In essence, the question we ask is the *opposite* of the question we want to know. We want to know if a correlation is other than zero. We do this by finding out if a value of zero is consistent with the data in hand.

The assertion that the correlation might, after all, be zero in such a case is referred to as the **null hypothesis**. A null hypothesis is what is true *if the hypothesis itself is not true.* Statistical tests then allow you to evaluate whether the evidence supports your null hypothesis as true or whether your data force you to abandon this assumption. It is actually the null hypothesis that is tested.

Similar logic is used in all statistical tests, whether or not they involve testing correlations. Only if the evidence you've gathered is strongly inconsistent with the null hypothesis, based on a given confidence level (that is, based on an acceptable probability of Type I error), are you in a position to advance your hypothesis as the alternative explanation.

This is easier to understand with an example. Let's say that your hypothesis is that "20-something" women *are more likely than men* to rate magazines highly as a source of information about nutrition and fitness. You've observed both groups standing in line at the grocery store, and you believe that only women seem to gravitate toward this type of magazine. You therefore expect that they will rate magazines higher as a source. The null hypothesis would be that women *are equally or less likely than men* to rate magazines highly as a source in this area. You test the null hypothesis, by asking (in essence) if the data at hand are consistent with that idea.

Assuming that you have asked your respondents about this by using a question that yields continuous data (a scale), the type of statistical test you are likely to use in this case is a test for the difference between two means. Your null hypothesis is that either the mean for men and the mean for women in the age group in question is the same or the mean for men is actually higher than that for women. If the test shows, with a specified level of confidence, that this is not true—that the null hypothesis of men's ratings being equal or higher must be rejected—then your hypothesis is supported, leading to the conclusion that women's ratings are indeed higher.

What if the test does not show a difference strong enough to force you to abandon your null hypothesis? It is still possible that Type II error has produced a false result. It is also possible, however, that your original observation was misleading or misinterpreted. Perhaps men do not like to be seen in public reading about nutrition and fitness, for example, but still rate magazines about as highly as a source for this information as women do. Perhaps men are less likely to be doing family shopping and, with smaller numbers of purchases, spend less time in line reading *any* magazine. Perhaps women read these magazines for reasons other than as a source of high-quality information. Typically, when a hypothesis is not supported, it is appropriate to look for alternative explanations, even though Type II error may actually be to blame for the result.

Directional and Nondirectional Hypotheses

A **directional hypothesis** incorporates an assertion about the direction of an inequality; that is, it suggests which of two values should be higher. In the example above, the hypothesis is a directional one. The researcher in this case is not just proposing that men and women are different with respect to how they rate magazines as a source of nutrition and fitness information, but he or she has a specific idea which group (women) will rate the magazines higher. A statement that two values are simply different, but without specifying which will be higher or lower, is called a *nondirectional* hypothesis.

An example of a nondirectional hypothesis would be the assertion that one group (let's say recent U.S. immigrants) might have different opinions from another (let's say native-born U.S. citizens) about current U.S. immigration policy. It is logical to think that these two groups might have different perspectives on this issue; however, the researcher might not have strong reason to suggest which group would be more positive. Nondirectional hypotheses are more common in exploratory research and should be the default choice when there is no strong reason to say in which direction a difference might be found.

A directional hypothesis is tested by what's called a **one-tailed test**, whereas a nondirectional one uses a **two-tailed test**. This seemingly small distinction can be quite important for some types of statistical tests. We return to this point later in the chapter.

Parametric and Nonparametric Tests

Statistical tests for examining hypotheses are generally divided into **parametric** and **nonparametric** tests. The distinction has to do with the assumptions that are made about the data. Parametric tests are used with continuous (interval or ratio) data; the term *parametric* derives from the idea that these tests rest on specific assumptions about population parameters that are generally only valid for continuous data. The test for significance of a Pearson's r correlation (a statistic used with continuous data only) presented in Chapter 7 is one example of a parametric test; the test for the difference between men's and women's mean ratings of magazines as sources for information presented above would be another.

Nonparametric tests are very important in media research because many variables of interest—especially those derived from content analysis, which typically classifies media content into nominal categories—are not measured on continuous scales. Content analysis often yields numerical data, but not in the form of continuous (interval or ratio) measurements. For example, if we did a content analysis of the proportional amount and type of nutrition and fitness information in magazines targeted at women versus magazines targeted at men, we would most likely be working with categorical data and nonparametric statistics.

Of the dozens of nonparametric statistics and statistical tests that have been developed (see, for example, Siegal, 1956), the one most commonly used in mass communication research is the **chi-square test**, which simply determines whether two or more simple frequency distributions are proportionately alike (the null hypothesis) or different to a greater degree than chance alone can be expected to account for.

UNDERSTANDING CHI-SQUARE

This chapter presents the chi-square (or χ^2) test in some detail not only because it is commonly used and helpful in many media research projects but also because the algebra and arithmetic that underlie it are much simpler than for many other tests. Understanding this one, relatively simple test is therefore a good foundation for understanding the basic logic of many other types of statistical tests. All of them depend on comparing some observed value or values to what would be expected if a null hypothesis were true. Chi-square does this for categorical frequency data, asking whether two or more distributions differ from one another in a statistically significant way.

The distributions in question are often frequency distributions of answers to a survey question or other demographic information. The content analysis of men's and women's magazines described in the previous section would likely yield counts of how many articles in each type of magazine were on one topic, another example of a pair of frequency distributions we might want to compare using chi-square. Another example would be the choices of major previously presented in Table 7.1. Here there are four separate frequency distributions. It seems obvious that the four groups of majors presented are showing different trends, but for statistical confirmation, we could use chi-square.

Sometimes chi-square is also used to compare a single frequency distribution based on empirical data to a second frequency distribution that reflects a theoretical assumption, often an assumption of equivalent distribution. For example, we might ask 60 Republicans and 40 Democrats about whether they believe energy independence for the United States is going to be very important in the next presidential campaign or not. This yes-or-no question yields categorical data.

Making the assumption of equivalent distribution—that is, that there is no important difference between Republicans and Democrats on their answers to this question—each group should be distributed about the same way as the entire 100 people. If 30 out of the 100 people answer this question "yes," then about 30% of the Republicans (or 18 out of the 60) and about 30% of the Democrats (or 12 out of the 40) should answer "yes." A chi-square test could tell us whether our actual results (unlikely to be *exactly* 18 Republican "yes" answers and 12 Democratic "yes" answers) differ from the expected proportions in a statistically significant way.

Note that in the above case the chi-square test is an alternative to the calculation of a margin of error as presented in Chapter 7. However, margin-of-error calculations suggest where the population values might be expected to fall, whereas technically speaking the results of a chi-square test apply only to the sample data being analyzed and (like other nonparametric results) are not generalizable beyond them. The null hypothesis for a test of this type is always that the distributions are the same; directionality is not a consideration.

Another example is presented in Table 8.1, which presents hypothetical data comparing intended college major for high school students versus that for college freshmen. From Table 8.1, it looks as though there might be some differences between the preferences of the two groups, which could be explained by shifts that tend to occur after high school graduates enter college, by the existence of differences of some sort between the two groups or by random chance in terms of respondent selection from larger populations.

Table 8.1   Intended Major for High School Students Versus College Freshmen

	Student Group	
Intended Major	*High School*	*College*
Mass communication	20	20
Other social science	11	22
Humanities	29	22
Biology/geology/natural science	10	20
Physics/chemistry/mathematics	16	21

One way to clarify how these data should be interpreted, especially as the number of high school students in the study is not the same as the number of college students, is to calculate the total number in each group and then the proportions (or percentages) for the two frequency distributions, as shown in Table 8.2, which is easier to interpret. For example, in this table it is more obvious that proportionately more college students intend to major in "other social science" (21% vs. 13%) and lots fewer in humanities (21% vs. 34%), in comparison to the high school students. But is this really a "big" (statistically significant) difference or just a "little" (random) fluctuation?

Table 8.2   Intended Major for High School Students Versus College Freshmen by Number and Percentage

| | Student Group | | | |
| | High School | | College | |
Intended Major	Number	%	Number	%
Mass communication	20	23	20	19
Other social science	11	13	22	21
Humanities	29	34	22	21
Biology/geology/natural science	10	12	20	19
Physics/chemistry/mathematics	16	19	21	20
Total	86	101	105	100

Chi-square tests use the same general rules of thumb that you've seen for making descriptive inferences about populations based on sample data. If there's a 95% (or 99%, or 90%) probability that the two distributions are different due to something other than random chance, then you have sufficient evidence to reject the null hypothesis of no difference between the two distributions and conclude that something potentially interesting is going on. You still would not know whether the difference is attributable to changes in student preferences after entering college or unknown differences between the two groups (for example, in demographic makeup), but it should be possible to rule out random chance as the explanation.

Like Table 7.1, the tables above are of a type sometimes referred to as "crosstabs" or cross-tabulation tables, meaning the results are tabulated "across" two variables. Another name for one of these is a **contingency table** because the table gives values of one variable *contingent on* the value of another. (If more than two variables are involved, multiple tables need to be constructed.) The space that each individual value occupies on the table is referred to as a **cell**; the cells are arranged in rows and columns. There will be as many columns as there are values of one variable (in this case, student group) and as many rows as there are values of the others (in this case, intended major).

Chi-square calculations involve comparing the observed frequencies with the ones that we would expect *on the basis of the null hypothesis*. If there were no important differences between high school students and college students in terms of their intended majors, you'd expect *each* of these distributions to be about the same as the *total* distribution for *all* students (just as in the case of Republican and Democratic opinion among 100 people described in the previous section). To see this more clearly, we can calculate the total distribution of intended majors for both student groups combined (in numbers and percentages) and add it to our contingency table, as shown in Table 8.3.

Table 8.3 Intended Major for High School Students, College Freshmen, and Both Groups Combined by Number and Percentage

| | Student Group | | | | | |
| | High School | | College | | Combined | |
Intended Major	Number	%	Number	%	Number	%
Mass communication	20	23	20	19	40	21
Other social science	11	13	22	21	33	17
Humanities	29	34	22	21	51	27
Biology/geology/natural science	10	12	20	19	30	16
Physics/chemistry/mathematics	16	19	21	20	37	19
Total	86	101	105	100	191	100

If there were no real differences between the two groups (high school vs. college students), and if (as shown) 21% of all the students combined chose mass communication as their intended major, you'd expect about 21% of the high school students *and* about 21% of the college students to indicate an intention to major in mass communication. Instead, 23% of the high school students and only 19% of the college students indicated this intention. (The number of intended mass communication majors is the same in each group, but this is misleading because there are more college students in this analysis than there are high school students.)

Exactly how many high school students would we expect to indicate an intention to major in mass communication, if our null hypothesis of equivalent distribution is correct? This is easy, if a little confusing, to calculate. Note that 45% of the students in the sample are in high school (86 out of 191), while 55% are in college (105 out of 191). The *expected value* for the number of high school students intending to major in mass communication would be 45% (the proportion of high school students in the entire sample) times 21% (the proportion of people in the entire sample who intend to major in mass communication) times the number of people in the sample, which is 191. This is 0.45 × 0.21 × 191, or 18. Instead, the actual value observed is 20, which reflects that a slightly higher proportion of high school students are intending to choose a mass communication major, in comparison to students already in college.

In order to complete the chi-square calculations, an expected value must be calculated in this same way for each of the cells in Table 8.3. Fortunately, there is a shorthand way to do this that may not make quite as much intuitive sense but that gives exactly the same result. For each cell, take the total number in the whole row, multiply it by the total number in the whole column, and divide by the total number in the whole sample. Using the high school example cell worked out on the basis of percentages above, this would be (40 × 86)/191, or (again) 18. It's useful to write this *expected* value (perhaps in a different color of ink) beside each *observed* value in each cell.

The actual formula for the value of the chi-square statistic is based on comparing expected and observed values and looks like this:

$$\chi^2 = \Sigma \frac{(O - E)^2}{E}.$$

Here χ is the Greek letter *chi*. As before, Σ means summation (total of all cases) for whatever follows. O means observed value, and E means expected value. For each cell, the difference between O and E is squared, always resulting—of course—in a positive value. These results are added up and then divided by the expected value. (Some texts use the symbols f_O and f_E, respectively, for observed and expected frequencies.)

In the student-major example, there are 10 cells, so the procedure is repeated 10 times, and the results are added together. For the first cell, with its expected value of 18 and its observed value of 20, this works out to $2^2/18$, or 0.22. Try it for the other 9 cells. If your arithmetic is correct, you should get a value for chi-square of 7.47.

Now, count the rows and columns. You also need (just as for Student's *t*) to calculate a value for degrees of freedom or *df*. For this type of problem *df* is defined as one less than the number of rows (R) times one less than the number of columns (C), or (R − 1) × (C − 1). In the example, this is (5 − 1) × (2 − 1), or 4. As was true of degrees of freedom in other types of problems considered earlier, you may find it helpful to think of this number as the number of cells that are hypothetically "free" to vary, as opposed to being "fixed" by the values of previously determined cells.

Chi-square is not a normally distributed statistic, and the shape of the distribution of possible values of chi-square depends on the degrees of freedom involved. However, as with t, statistics books and advanced methods texts provide tables of the distributions of chi-square for each possible number of degrees of freedom for reference purposes. The appendix to this book provides most of the chi-square values you are ever likely to need (see Table A1). One entry in that chi-square table covers the situation in this student-major example (note that "level of significance" is based on the confidence level but is expressed as its complement, the acceptable probability of Type I error):

df	Level of Significance		
	0.10	0.05	0.01
4	7.78	9.49	13.28

The chi-square value for our example, 7.47, is not quite high enough to allow you to reject the assumption of equivalent distribution and conclude instead that there is a statistically significant difference in the choices made by high school and college students. We would have needed a chi-square value of 7.78 to assert, at a 90% confidence level, that there was a difference; 9.49 to make this assertion at a 95% confidence level; or 13.28 to make this assertion at a 99% confidence level. Note that, in line with the discussion of Type II error earlier in this chapter, *this doesn't mean that there are no meaningful differences,* but you simply don't have enough evidence to assert that this is the most likely explanation. Perhaps a larger study (or a differently designed one) would yield a different answer.

In interpreting results from a chi-square test, it is also important to recognize that even a statistically significant chi-square does not identify *which* differences within the two distributions are important; it only establishes that the two distributions *as a whole* are significantly different. A few other special cautions apply to the use of chi-square tests.

A special correction called **Yates's correction** (calculated automatically by most statistical software) is required when the degrees of freedom for a chi-square test are equal to 1—that is, in a two-row by two-column (2 × 2) table. This correction reduces the magnitude of the difference between the expected and obtained frequency for each cell by 0.5, regardless of the sign, before squaring.

Also, chi-square tests are not reliable when the expected frequencies are quite small. Any time that *all* of the expected frequencies have values of 5 or more, however, there is no problem. Some researchers routinely combine or "collapse" categories before completing the analysis to ensure that this condition is met; in our example, if we had any expected frequencies below 5, we might have combined the two science choices together, and so on. Others point to statistical opinion that suggests that if no more than *one fifth* of the cells have expected frequencies below 5 there should be no problem, except in the special case of 2 × 2 tables where *all* cells must have expected frequencies of 5 or more. Although statisticians vary in their recommendations, it is certainly best to avoid *any* expected frequencies less than 5 whenever reasonably possible.

Again, remember as well that the results of chi-square tests cannot be generalized to the population from which the sample was drawn.

COMPARING TWO MEANS

This section considers a typical example of a statistical test for use with continuous (interval or ratio) data. The *t test* for comparison of two means is a very common, relatively simple, and extremely useful statistical test of this type. This test is based on the same *t* statistic you have already encountered. It is an option widely available in standard statistical packages. We won't go through the calculations for it here, which are a bit more complex than those for a chi-square test, but the underlying logic of all statistical tests is very similar. This particular statistic, which allowed us to use the sampling distribution of the mean to estimate confidence intervals for population values, also allows us to use the sampling distribution of the *differences* between two means to set confidence levels for whether the population values are actually *different*.

A simple *t* test is valid only for comparing *two* means. If you have multiple means—say, for example, if you've calculated separate scores on an attitudinal scale for four different ethnic groups—you cannot compare all the different possible combinations just by using a series of repeated *t* tests. This limitation is related to a more general problem of statistical inference. Whenever you make multiple statistical tests on the same set of data, you risk violating the key assumption on which confidence levels are based. Recall that if you are working with a 95% confidence level, there is a 1-in-20 chance of Type I error. So if you were to run 20 different statistical tests on the same set of data, odds are that, on average, 1 of the 20 will turn up "proof" of a hypothesis just by chance, regardless of the population values.

This is not so bad in exploratory research, where the researcher is trying to generate new hypotheses inductively that he or she expects to test later on new data, but it is not acceptable in true hypothesis-testing research. Technically speaking, researchers need to retest any ideas derived from running multiple statistical tests on the same data set (as when reanalyzing preexisting survey data, for example) with a new sample for the results to be completely valid. Applied to the *t*-test situation, this means that comparing the mean of some variable for Group A with the mean of that for Group B and then comparing that Group B variable mean with the mean of the same variable for Group C violates the assumption underlying the estimate of Type I error.

Fortunately, special modifications of the basic *t* test are available (and usually included in statistical packages) that enable comparing multiple means *simultaneously,* much like a chi-square test compares two or more whole frequency distributions. A positive result from a multiple-mean *t* test doesn't tell you which means are responsible but does indicate that there is too much variance among them for the researcher to decide that it was produced by chance.

Applying the t Test

As an example of what *t* tests can tell us, let's suppose that you work for an advertising agency that is developing an advertising campaign for a new multi-function cell phone. Your client company's product line has historically done much better with male customers than female ones, and the company wants to change this, so it is particularly interested in developing advertising that will appeal to women as well as men. You hire a market research firm to try out a television ad you've developed; the firm tests the ad with a group of 50 men and 50 women. Each of these 100 subjects is asked to rate the level of his or her "willingness to buy" after viewing the ad on a 7-point scale ranging from *not at all willing to buy* to *very much willing to buy* the new model cell phone.

Suppose you get a mean score on this scale for the women in the sample of 5.1, whereas for men, it's 4.8. These numbers are not too far apart. How do you decide if this is just sampling error (a random result due to exactly which women and which men you have, by chance, included in your sample) or likely to be indicative of a real difference between men and women generally in terms of the extent to which they have a positive reaction to the advertisement? Clearly, the difference is not great, but you are under some pressure to be able to prove to your client's satisfaction that it is not a meaningful difference.

The *t* test comes to the rescue in situations of this type. It uses the same kind of logic as other hypothesis tests do. Your null hypothesis is that there is *no difference* between the two means, that for men and that for women. Sample results are compared to the theoretical sampling distribution of *possible differences between two means* (the distribution of possible differences you might have observed had you done this experiment over and over) to determine whether your null hypothesis should be rejected at whatever confidence level you've chosen. Your mean difference is 0.3 (5.1 minus 4.8). Is this far enough away from a measured difference of zero that it can safely be ignored, or not?

Statistical software such as SPSS can carry out this sort of test very easily. The procedure uses the variance in the two samples to estimate the population variance, just as for setting up confidence intervals around a single mean. One decision you may have to make is whether or not to assume the two sample variances are equal, which allows the data from the two samples to be combined for a better estimate of the population variance. Unless there is a statistical indication that the two variances are different, this is generally assumed to be the case.

The *t* test as described here applies only to two *independent* means; if the two measures are somehow related—for example, where the same set of subjects is asked two different survey questions—the means are *not* considered independent, and other procedures must be used. The results of *t* tests are also sensitive to large differences in the sizes of the two subsamples.

Testing Directional Versus Nondirectional Hypotheses

The hypothesis tested by a *t* test can be directional or nondirectional. In the example above, the hypothesis is that men and women are different; the null hypothesis is that they are the same. This involves a nondirectional hypothesis. But there might be good theoretical or practical justification for working with a directional hypothesis instead. In the cell phone advertisement example, perhaps the client company does not really care about men's willingness to buy the new product—it is not targeting this model to men at all. The company wants to create an ad that will persuade women more than it does men, not one that appeals to both equally. Can you prove that your ad meets the company's needs?

This kind of problem calls for a directional hypothesis and a one-tailed test. In a one-tailed test, the null hypothesis is rejected more easily. Note that statistical packages often report the confidence level reached by *t*-test data, which can in theory be anything from 0 to 1.00. You're aiming, typically, for 0.95 or better. If, in this example, a confidence level of 0.94 was achieved, you'd certainly be disappointed. But, using a directional hypothesis and a one-tailed test, your confidence level is 0.97 (exactly halfway between 0.94 and 1.00), therefore meeting the 95% criterion.

The "tail" here refers to the extended outer ends of the normal distribution of the sampling distribution of the differences between means. In a two-tailed test at a 95% confidence level, to reject the null hypothesis of no difference, the cutoff points are the point at which 2.5% of the cases fall to the left (in the left-hand tail) and the point at which 2.5% of the cases fall to the right (in the right-hand tail). If the observed difference between the means is big enough that it reaches either of these points, the null hypothesis can be rejected. However, for a one-tailed test, only one tail matters. The cutoff point is the point beyond which 5% of the cases fall in one direction or the other, depending on how the hypothesis is worded. The shape of the distribution is the same; the observed difference between the means does not have to be as extreme to reach this point in the case of a one-tailed test as for a two-tailed test.

While this may be a bit hard to visualize, clearly it is tempting to *always* use directional hypotheses and one-tailed tests, since they make it easier for an observed difference to reach statistical significance. However, you should have a very sound justification for choosing a directional hypothesis—not just a hunch or a bad case of wishful thinking. Some statisticians believe that the criteria for appropriate use of a one-tailed test are rarely, if ever, met.

WORKING WITH COMPLEX VARIABLES

So far, most of our examples have involved relatively simple variables, generally reflecting simple, **unidimensional** concepts that can be measured with a simple scale—often, for the sake of simplicity, represented by a single question. Generally, however, the accuracy of scale measurements can be increased when multiple questions are used to measure slightly different aspects of the same underlying concept.

The familiar 5-, 7-, or 10-point scales used as examples in several chapters in this book are often referred to as **Likert scales** because of a technique invented by an educational researcher with that name. Likert's original technique continues to be useful in social science research. For each unidimensional item to be scaled, this approach involves comparing the scores on individual items to the total score for that respondent. Items whose answers aren't highly correlated to the overall score are considered to be measuring something else and are eliminated. These and other scales of similar form often measure attitudes, defined as persistent positive or negative orientations toward classes of items (whether objects or ideas or people). But similar scales can also measure many other things such as credibility or believability, preferences, needs, satisfaction, and so on. Unless the scale has been developed using Likert's technique, questions of this form should be described as "Likert-like" scales.

Whatever the details of the scaling approach used, if the answers to a set of questions intended to measure the same concept are not highly correlated with one another, then it is likely that the questions are not really measuring the same thing. It may be that there are one or more poorly chosen questions in the set, that the underlying concept is not well defined, or that it is not actually unidimensional but should be broken down into different elements that are measured by separate scales or subscales. Whenever multiple questions are used to measure a single underlying concept, the validity of the resulting scale needs to be evaluated through some form of systematic analysis that considers these alternatives. (The Cronbach's α statistic is sometimes used for this purpose.)

The existence of different dimensions can be studied by looking at relationships between scores on individual questions and establishing which ones are and are not highly correlated with one another. Sometimes exploratory factor analysis is used for this purpose (see below). An example of a complex concept (sometimes called a construct) that is often used in media studies research would be the concept of media literacy. A number of books have been written about this idea, and different scholars have put forth rather different ideas as to what media literacy might encompass. Most likely, a fully developed measure of media literacy would involve several independent dimensions, such as basic knowledge of how the media industries work; the ability to identify the intent of advertising and other persuasive messages; awareness of media's potential influence on our thinking, feelings, and behavior; and the ability to understand and make use of news messages about current events.

Another example is trust. A great deal of research is being done on the relationship between trust in sources and perception of messages, especially for technically complex topics like stem cell research or nuclear power policy where most of us need to rely on experts for guidance. Which experts do we trust? However, trust is multidimensional and may involve the perception of shared values, confidence that the person will tell the truth, a belief in the person's competence with respect to the area of his or her expertise, and possibly other factors not yet identified.

A thorough examination of scaling procedures for complex concepts and constructs is well beyond the scope of this book. Often, prior research uncovered during a literature review will include studies that have developed and tested measures for complex constructs. It is usually advantageous to begin with scales that have already been validated, where these are available. Not only does this save work, but it also allows direct comparison of current research results with earlier findings. Small changes in question wording may produce very different results in both surveys and experiments. The same word may also not mean the same thing to everyone, particularly across ethnic groups. These factors complicate the development of meaningful scales for complex variables.

MULTIVARIATE TECHNIQUES FOR STATISTICAL ANALYSIS

In addition to considering primarily unidimensional concepts measured in relatively simple ways, this book has been primarily concerned up to now with simple two-variable problems. A good general introduction to systematically building more complex theories and models using quantitative variables is provided in Shoemaker, Tankard, and Lasorsa (2003). This section gives a very basic introduction to some of the most commonly used statistical techniques appropriate to studying complex sets of interrelated variables on an exploratory basis.

Analysis of Variance

In its simplest form, commonly called **one-way ANOVA,** where **ANOVA** is short for analysis of variance, this technique allows the researcher to answer questions about the relationship between a single categorical independent variable and a continuous dependent variable. For example, one-way ANOVA would allow exploration of the extent to which gender influenced attitudes toward a political candidate or type of media ownership influenced the tone of newspaper articles. When the independent variable has only two values, one-way ANOVA is similar to a *t* test.

Other ANOVA routines can assess the influence of two or more categorical independent variables simultaneously on a continuous dependent variable and search for interaction effects. For example, ANOVA would allow examination of the independent and interactive contributions of political affiliation and ethnicity to opinions on an issue such as immigration policy.

ANOVA analyzes the extent to which the dependent variable can be statistically predicted on the basis of one or more independent variables. Causation is still something the researcher can only infer, not something "proved" by a set of ANOVA data. Nevertheless, this kind of analysis can provide significant insights that can sometimes lead to the development of solid theories of causation.

Historically, equal cell sizes have been recommended for most analysis-of-variance problems; however, statistical packages have grown more sophisticated, and some programs compensate for this problem.

ANOVA is used only with categorical independent variables. Recently, however, SPSS has combined ANOVA with other approaches used with continuous independent variables (see **linear regression** below) in a new General Linear Model (or GLM) routine. Using GLM, both kinds of independent variables can be tested simultaneously.

Linear Regression

Linear regression looks for simple and complex linear relationships between continuous independent and dependent variables. Many variables can be combined in regression analysis, although the results can be challenging to interpret. A limited number of binary or two-valued variables such as gender can be incorporated into regression analysis along with truly continuous independent variables. Regression analysis is related to correlation analysis, which also uses coefficients to assess the strength of linear relationships between continuous variables.

Regression is most commonly used to try to determine which of a group of potentially important independent variables best "explain" (that is, statistically predict) variation in a dependent variable. For example, opinions on complex public policy issues may be influenced by a number of different attitudinal factors. Like ANOVA but using continuous data, regression analysis can determine which influences are most important.

"Stepwise" regression adds variables in sequence based on how much each variable improves the predictive power of the analysis. As a technique to control for demographic influences in a study of other variables, demographic variables are sometimes added first.

SPSS has recently combined multiple regression and analysis of variance into a single General Linear Model (GLM) routine that can manage both categorical and continuous independent variables (see ANOVA above).

Factor Analysis

A technique called **factor analysis**, which looks at the intercorrelations among a set of variables, can be used to explore whether a complex set of data can be reasonably well represented by a smaller number of independent underlying "factors." The output of a factor analysis includes a table of numbers that describe the strength of the relationship (positive or negative) between each of a series of continuous independent variables that are most closely related (positively or negatively) to each factor identified; these numbers are called "factor loadings." Media researchers interested in how underlying attitudes such as trust in particular spokespeople predict reactions to media content are most likely to use factor analysis.

It is customary to develop descriptive names for these factors that try to capture the commonalities among those independent variables that are most closely related to each factor. This is often more art than science, but factor analysis is a very powerful way to take a highly complex set of data (for example, attitudinal data, opinion data, or personality data) and reduce it to something more meaningful that can be used in further analysis.

Sometimes, the most closely associated items for each factor can be used to form a simpler index that can be used in future research, which reduces the number of questionnaire items that must be administered.

Factor analysis can also be used to confirm whether different subscales included in a single questionnaire actually seem to be measuring distinct concepts.

Discriminant Analysis

Discriminant analysis is used to figure out which variables among a complex set best divide (or "discriminate") one group from another. For example, a researcher might want to know which stands on issues most reliably predict, or discriminate between, U.S. Republicans and Democrats. This could be helpful in designing an effective political communication campaign.

Cluster Analysis

Cluster analysis is used to classify *cases* rather than variables. For example, audience or market segments that share similar tastes and preferences might be identified using cluster analysis. Cluster analysis can take into account categorical or continuous variables.

Unlike discriminant analysis, cluster analysis does not begin with a predetermined set of categories (such as political party affiliation) but determines the categories based on the data. In market research, cluster analysis is a valuable way to divide a population into distinct lifestyle groups, based on some combination of market preferences, demographics, and opinion or attitude variables.

Path Analysis

Path analysis is a technique used to construct causative models based on close examination of correlations in data sets, such as large surveys. Although a good prior theoretical understanding of the data relationships is absolutely critical, path analysis can help a researcher decide (on the basis of correlation strengths) what model best describes a complex sequence of influences that take place over time.

Path analysis might, for example, help to tease out the details of the relationship among personality, prior media exposure, and an outcome such as voting a particular way or becoming an activist for a particular cause. A newer, more sophisticated approach called Structural Equation Modeling, or SEM, has a similar purpose, but both are completely dependent on having a good theoretical understanding of the problem.

Time-Series Analysis

Many problems in media research involve "chicken-and-egg" questions where the sequence of events in time is a factor. For example, does the political agenda set the media agenda, or is it the media agenda that sets the political agenda? While in truth it is likely that influences exist in both directions, **time-series analysis** attempts to use data about which changes may have occurred *first* to answer these and other perennial quandaries about causation.

Important Terms and Concepts

ANOVA (analysis of variance)	One-tailed test
Cell	One-way ANOVA
Chi-square test	Parametric
Cluster analysis	Path analysis
Contingency table	Statistical test
Directional hypothesis	Time-series analysis
Discriminant analysis	*t* test
Factor analysis	Type I error
Likert scale	Type II error
Linear regression	Two-tailed test
Multivariate analysis	Unidimensional
Nonparametric	Yates's correction
Null hypothesis	

This chapter has explored a lot of territory and has left many questions about advanced statistical techniques only partially addressed. For this exercise, let's stick to basics. Your instructor might request a short written paper, for course credit, answering the following:

1. Identify a research question related to the media's influence on society that interests you and that you think might be amenable to quantitative analysis. What key independent and dependent variables are of interest? How do you propose to measure them?

2. Are your variables simple or complex? Are they well understood or still exploratory? What hypotheses can you propose about the relationships among them? Based on the material in this chapter, how would you test them?

3. Answering the above questions is a good test of your ability to translate a problem into a quantitative research design—it's not easy. What major limitations do you see in your design? Can these be resolved, or are they elements you must accept as built-in limitations of a quantitative approach?

CHAPTER 9

Qualitative Analysis

Identifying Themes and Writing Meaningful Summaries

Good qualitative research is every bit as difficult as good quantitative research; in fact, it is probably not as easy to learn or to explain. Experience is the best teacher, but an authentic sensitivity to alternative points of view is equally important. A central advantage of qualitative research strategies is their flexibility, but this means there is no rigid rulebook. Although there are general guidelines that can be offered, qualitative research always involves the exercise of good judgment and ongoing sensitivity to someone else's worldview. Nevertheless, the guiding principle of cautious, open-minded, and systematic inquiry is no different in qualitative or quantitative work. Qualitative work also demands an even stronger quality of good judgment from the researcher because most conclusions are acts of interpretation.

This chapter focuses on how to analyze qualitative data. One important challenge of the qualitative approach is that it is easy to select and report only the themes and examples that fit the researcher's preconceptions—to see what someone wants to see. Of course, some qualitative researchers might respond that the preconceptions behind quantitative research results are at least equally powerful but better disguised. However, the real response to this criticism is that good qualitative work proceeds with an open mind, takes all relevant data available into account as systematically as possible, is guided by a carefully chosen research question (or questions) rather than the impulses of the researcher, and makes a contribution to the development of theory (even on occasions when it is directed primarily toward answering a practical question, such as how well a particular advertisement is working). In other words, doing qualitative work is as rigorous and demanding as doing quantitative work—and certainly not the same as writing an opinion piece.

WORKING WITH THEORY AND IDENTIFYING THEMES

Whether qualitative data come from participant observation of institutions or organizations, qualitative analysis of a certain genre of media product, ethnographic study of large audiences or of other, more informal **social settings** in which media play a key role, focus groups conducted at a market research firm, or qualitative case studies of an important event, some elements of the researcher's task are the same. In each case, a major goal is to identify important themes in a body of qualitative data. Although qualitative work is generally inductive rather than deductive, this analysis should be guided by theory as much as possible.

Theory Testing in Qualitative Research

How is a theory "tested" by qualitative methods? The usefulness of theory is evaluated in terms of its ability to help you understand the phenomena you observe. Thinking theoretically is, in qualitative work, an integral part of the process of data analysis. If, in situation after situation, a particular explanation is a "good fit" for the data—if it is helpful in allowing researchers to improve their understanding of patterns in what is observed—then that piece of theory is confirmed. The integrity of this process depends on the researcher's alertness to information that does and does *not* fit a particular explanation, however, rather than formal tests of hypotheses. This means being open to alternative explanations.

A conflict theorist, for example, may begin with a theory about the media's role in maintaining power and be primarily interested in the media's role in furthering the interests within society of those who are already in control but, in the process of conducting a study of a particular media organization, may also note that the mass media do not always support status quo positions.

Careful observation here may show that the media can also be used to express genuine opposition and advocate for change under some circumstances. Qualitative research is rooted in—and tested by—empirical investigation no less than quantitative research. Nevertheless, it is also true that two different qualitative researchers, working from different theoretical positions, might produce analyses that emphasize quite different dimensions of the same setting or problem.

Sociologist Robert Merton (1968) called for the development of *middle-range theories* that could guide meaningful empirical inquiry, connecting grand, sweeping characterizations of the big forces at work in society with problems of a manageable size for conducting empirical studies. Useful middle-range theories do exist in mass communication research, such as agenda-setting theory, uses and gratifications theory, and theories about selective influence, about stereotyping, about violence effects, and so on. There have been attempts to connect these to form broader theoretical explanations of media phenomena (such as DeFleur and Ball-Rokeach's [1989] idea of "dependency theory" or Shoemaker and Reese's [1996] "hierarchy of influence" model). But as a field, we still have a lot of progress to make in theory building. In particular, most of our commonly cited middle-range theories, such as those listed above, have been investigated and supported primarily by quantitative data.

Qualitative analysis should always be informed by theory, but the path connecting either grand or middle-range theory, a research question appropriate to qualitative work, and a strategy for gathering relevant evidence on that question may not always be clearly marked. The traditions of qualitative research as developed in cultural anthropology and other fields, as you've learned, encourage a more holistic approach, recognizing the interconnectedness of many aspects of social and cultural life. Theory building and theory confirmation in qualitative work is more likely to be inductive or "bottom up" rather than "top down." Because of the emphasis on holism, qualitative researchers are more likely to be interested in the media's social influences—their broader relationship to society and to other social institutions—than in specific effects at the individual level.

A good example of using theory in a qualitative study is Lang and Lang's (1983) case study of how the discovery of the Watergate break-in during Richard Nixon's presidency evolved into a media event and, ultimately, a major social and political crisis. This research studied the actual sequence of events surrounding Watergate's emergence as a media story and made use of a variety of qualitative approaches such as interviews and content analysis. The research was informed by a general interest in the theoretical concept of agenda building, an extension of agenda-setting theory that emphasizes the interaction of multiple social institutions in turning events into "news" (instead of attributing this solely to media and concentrating on the specific effects of the media on individuals' perceptions of the news agenda). Lang and Lang used this interest to guide their research, which helped demonstrate the role of government agencies and political organizations in co-creating the media agenda.

One way to think about the role of theory when it comes to the analysis of qualitative data is as a source of **sensitizing concepts**, concepts that lead the researcher to pay special attention to particular dimensions even if they are not full-blown theories. For example, in a study of the ways that politicians interact with the media, a researcher particularly interested in gender as a sensitizing concept will pay special attention to elements of the interaction that seem to reflect gender-based differences.

Identifying General Themes and Patterns

Qualitative case studies oriented toward particular events may rely on a variety of data sources, and some—like the Lang and Lang (1983) Watergate study described above—may be oriented toward the reconstruction of those events. Much like investigative journalism but more systematic (and often involving reliance on a broader range of data), these studies try to identify the key elements behind a sequence of occurrences. Many other qualitative studies base their conclusions at least in part on the systematic identification of recurring themes within a body of visual, verbal, or textual material, such as interview or focus group transcripts, media texts, or notes from a participant observation. Focus groups are often video recorded to capture the "body language" of the interactions between participants, and the analysis of film, advertising, television drama, and other visual media materials often depends on subtle visual cues, not just the story line and dialogue that would be recorded in the script. For other purposes where the main mode of communication is verbal, such as when using interview data, audio recordings are usually used alone.

Visual materials (whether from focus groups or media products) are especially difficult to subject to systematic analysis, and the researcher is more dependent on his or her intuition to identify important elements. Nevertheless, they provide insights that usually go well beyond what is captured in verbal material alone. When working with visual material from the media—ranging from television advertisements to films—video recordings are almost essential. While it is both possible and desirable to take notes (similar to the notes from other forms of observation) about the material and personal reactions from watching media programming or advertisements, these are not usually a complete substitute for a video recording.

Even when the analysis is confined to verbal material such as in interview transcripts, a range of approaches is possible. At one end of a continuum, in what we might call a purely qualitative approach, the researcher relies most heavily on his or her own impressions of what the interviewee is trying to say— or what the narrative is trying to convey—but may group the themes identified into at least broadly representative categories reflecting persistent patterns. Sometimes these may involve narrative structure as well as content. At the other extreme, the analysis may develop a set of very explicitly defined coding categories in a procedure quite similar to that used for quantitative content analysis and that yields numerical results (frequency counts).

The distinction between qualitative and quantitative analysis becomes blurred at this point, and different authorities may describe similar techniques in different ways. However, quantitative content analysis and surveys (even those containing open-ended items) generally rely on sampling from a larger population, whereas qualitative work typically does not. The end result of applying a coding procedure to qualitative material can be numerical counts of categories with explicit definitions, and these can be subject to intercoder reliability checks just like material gathered for a quantitative study. However, if the data were not collected through a sampling procedure, the results are still qualitative—there is no foundation for generalizing on statistical grounds to a larger population, which is not the goal of qualitative work in any event.

Because of the persuasive power of numbers to overcome concerns about subjectivity, the numerical approach is becoming more common in situations where it is feasible. The data are still gathered using qualitative methods, but the analysis has elements of a quantitative approach. In such cases the unit of analysis becomes extremely important; for interview material, most qualitative researchers continue to use the theme as the unit of analysis, but it is also possible to imagine other choices, such as a conversational turn, a statement, an episode (say, of a television drama), and so on.

Whatever the unit of analysis, identifying themes and other patterns remains partly a matter of judgment; there is no magic formula for it. Specific projects may be designed to concentrate on specific types of themes or other responses. However, you may recall from previous chapters the discussion of the constant comparative method developed by Glaser and Strauss (1967). In cases where a systematically collected qualitative data set (whether of media content or of interview or focus group transcripts) is available and the types of themes to be identified are not prescribed by the nature of the research question, the constant comparative method is the logical choice. Glaser and Strauss also refer to their method as "grounded theory analysis." Although this type of analysis is a method, not a theory, it is an inductive approach designed to generate data that can contribute to theory building or theory refinement. We return to this approach later; first, the practical considerations involved in creating and managing a body of material for analysis deserve some discussion.

ANALYZING QUALITATIVE DATA

How do you begin to turn a pile of tapes or a notebook into a research report? The challenge depends on the size of the project; the larger the project, the more important it is to be well organized. Major projects may involve many dozens of interviews or notes from weeks or even months of observation. Working primarily with transcripts of interviews or focus group discussions rather than the tapes themselves makes it much easier to be systematic and is by far the most common choice, even though some nuances of verbal expression (such as tone) are lost, along with the nonverbal elements that would be present in a videotape. This section will concentrate primarily on analyzing transcripts of verbal material, the most common type of qualitative data media researchers are likely to encounter. However, transcribing recordings of natural conversations is much more difficult than it may appear.

Transcriptions and Field Notes

Even very articulate people do not normally speak in clear, grammatically complete sentences in ordinary conversation; this makes **transcription** more difficult. The transcriber must listen very carefully to avoid on-the-spot editing of partial or incorrect speech and resist the temptation to "fill in the blanks" where the recording isn't perfect. Regardless of the quality of the tape, there will be times when two people are speaking at once (whether in a focus group or in an interaction between a single interviewer and an interviewee) or when someone's audible speech trails off at the end of an unfinished thought. These are difficult and time-consuming to interpret. By comparison, transcribing a news broadcast where those speaking have been carefully trained to speak clearly and not interrupt one another is relatively easy.

While commercial transcription services are available, student research does not usually have access to funding for this purpose, so beginning researchers are likely to be doing all of the transcribing themselves. It is important to think about the purpose of the transcript. Resist the temptation to edit what speakers say into grammatically complete thoughts or to edit out slang. Sometimes the "mistakes" of speech convey important information about what the speaker is trying to get across or how he or she seems to be thinking. While journalistic stories often edit what someone says to eliminate these very common imperfections, research reports are anonymous and do not need to worry about "cleaning up" anyone's language. Rather, conveying the exact language someone uses—even if there are mistakes—can be important.

On the other hand, it is usually not important to record every "um" or "er" or pause, and it is usually not important to spend the effort to capture phrases that trail off, words that are mumbled, or passages in which more than one speaker is talking in a way that makes it difficult to understand what is being said. Transcript data for qualitative research should be as complete as possible, but trying to decipher speech that remains unintelligible even after being replayed several times can use up inordinate amounts of time without always—in the end—contributing any additional significant information. Sometimes recording equipment is available for foot control of a tape or audio file, allowing the transcriber to start or stop at will without taking his or her hands off of the keyboard.

Organizing qualitative information is also important. Labeling the tapes and transcripts with information about when the interview or focus group took place and any other identifying information is important—and page numbers can help relocate key passages. (Focus group transcripts, by the way, should include remarks made by the group leader or researcher in case there's later an issue of how the questions were asked, how the problems were presented, or the nature of the "probes" used to stimulate discussion.) Just remember that your transcript is unlikely to be perfect. Natural conversation contains far more gaps, omissions, misstatements, and errors than you may have ever realized.

The main function of software designed for qualitative analysis is organizational. It will not do the transcribing or the theme identification automatically. However, some researchers find this software useful for reorganizing the material by theme or at least for relocating examples of themes that have been identified. Ordinary word-processing software can be used this way as well, by making use of the search function, if codes for themes are embedded in the transcript text.

Observation and participant observation data and interview notes should also be labeled and dated. It is always good practice to make some notes about the setting of your project, as well as what happens there. You may wish to return to the same data years later, and you might be surprised at how many details can be forgotten in the meantime. Describing the setting is also good practice for writing the research report, as your audience will be complete strangers to the context of your project until you explain it, and physical description is important to help someone else visualize the setting. Because field notes are not as systematically collected as (say) interview transcripts— they are more impressions than exact records—they may not be subject to the same types of analysis as transcripts, but the same care should be taken to organize them for future use.

Personal preference will dictate the details of how you use your notes. Some people use a system of keeping direct observations on one side of a two-column page and their own comments, reactions, questions, and later analysis on the other. You might use another color of ink or a highlighter or "sticky" notes for insights that occur to you later in the course of your analysis, as you work toward drafting a descriptive text, or to identify examples that you think might be especially useful.

Identifying General Patterns

Whether you are working with participant observation notes, transcriptions of interview or focus group data, or actual mass media stories or programs, identifying recurrent general patterns (or broad themes) is generally the next goal after getting the material transcribed (if needed) and organized for your analysis. What do people consistently talk about in a given social setting? What aspects of issues are consistently presented in the media? What concerns are common across several different interviewees? At this stage you probably cannot list *all* of these; nor should you try. Let your research question be your guide.

For example, if you are trying to understand how advertising agencies are structured as social institutions and the influences of the external pressures that are on them to be successful, be especially alert to discussions of professional roles, appropriate business strategies, interactions with clients, work task assignments, and other aspects that seem particularly relevant. If you are trying to identify important aspects of media portrayals of doctors, be alert to what characteristics of personality or work style, what shortcomings, and even what physical appearance (including clothing and equipment) seem to appear most consistently and what kind of backdrops are common. If you are trying to find out what role docudramas play in conveying information about real-world issues, listen for statements by audience members that relate fiction to fact or to personal experience. If your study concerns the role that a certain type of media plays in everyday social life, concentrate on the type of interaction observed among study participants and other activities taking place simultaneously, not limiting your observations to direct statements about the media.

A study of the appeals of mystery movies, even if done by someone who is not a movie buff, might be approached in terms of narrative structure. How does the typical mystery movie seem to "invite" or encourage reader involvement and particular interpretations? Mysteries often end by revealing that the apparent solution is not the real one. We intuitively understand why this makes good entertainment; nevertheless, this could be an important observation in another way if it helps you understand the *cultural* appeal of the mystery movie. How consistent is this pattern, and how does it seem to structure the audience's involvement with the film?

It is characteristic of qualitative studies that different observations of the same social setting can use slightly different methods and can ask and answer different types of questions. One study about the role of daytime dramas in the lives of office workers might look for recurrent themes or patterns in the office workers' personal reactions to these programs and the structure of their interactions and discussion with one another. Another could be more concerned with the content themes in the programs themselves than in interviewees' comments about them. Remember, while qualitative work owes much to the efforts of the early ethnographers, today's media studies—even qualitative ones—are usually more focused.

Identifying More Specific Themes

In a purely qualitative study, this identification of important general patterns relative to your research question may be the last major stage of the analysis itself. However, if you decide to pursue the development of a more systematic description that can be tested across coders and yields numerical data, use of grounded theory analysis (that is, the constant comparative method) is the logical next step.

Let's say you are conducting a study of the themes commonly addressed by popular music of the 1960s. You want to be able to relate these themes to the historical unrest associated with that decade; perhaps you will be able to document a change in these themes between 1960 and 1970 that will demonstrate the relationship between social change and popular culture. You have chosen the 10 most popular songs of each decade on the basis of sales charts. Preliminary analysis suggests that your unit of analysis should be the theme rather than the song, because some songs seem to have more than one theme, and it is difficult to judge whether one is always dominant.

This analysis has also given you some very general ideas about the general types of themes likely to appear, such as romantic love or antiwar politics.

In a grounded theory analysis, you begin by assigning the initial data (whether themes from an interview, a discussion, or, in this case, song lyrics) to a few tentative categories and then continually add new data, asking at each stage whether the new data reasonably seem to fit the old categories or whether a new category—or sometimes a revision of an earlier one—needs to be constructed. For example, your first example of antiwar politics turns out to have a strong secondary concern with rebellion more generally. Is that a new category or the same one? This is a judgment call. As you move through the data, if you find additional examples that seem to reinforce the existence of two separate themes (antiwar politics and general rebellion), then you might maintain two categories. If not, you might decide to collapse them. Meanwhile, other themes will continue to emerge as you work through your data set.

Grounded theory analysis, if implemented with care, is both very taxing and extremely systematic. At each stage of looking at new data, you must ask if the categories being used "fit" or if the new information is really different enough to call for the creation of a new category. Then when a new category is created, a review of the material that has already been classified can be called for to see if instances that occurred earlier might possibly have been overlooked so that the categories are consistent throughout.

The goal is to use consistent categories in a systematic way but at the same time allow them to emerge from the data, rather than imposing your preconceived ideas that may misrepresent what's really going on. This allows you to be true to the worldview of those being studied and at the same time to be systematic throughout the analysis of an entire body of data. The results of grounded theory analysis can be summarized numerically. Even though the frequency tabulations that result shouldn't be considered "measurements" in the sense that scales and indexes are, they are still very useful for communicating the regularity with which certain themes reemerge in a data set in comparison to others. In addition, if the category definitions are sufficiently explicit, these can form the basis of an intercoder reliability check.

OTHER FORMS OF ANALYSIS

This chapter has hardly exhausted the possibilities for qualitative analysis of media-related material, whether from media products themselves, from social settings that involve the production or consumption of media products, or from other sources. Two alternatives that will not be dealt with here in much depth include visual analysis and the idea of a "close reading" (sometimes called an "ethnographic reading") of media material.

Analyzing Visual Material

Analyzing visual data is potentially many times more complex than analyzing written words. No single, well-accepted, widely tested, systematic social scientific approach to the study of visual content predominates, although there are many rich traditions in the humanities that can be drawn upon. Visual presentations contain rich symbolism, suggest subtle reactions and interactions, and present other complicated patterns in ways that we do not always know how to summarize or articulate in words in an adequate way. We certainly don't know how to assign numerical values to most of the interesting things about visual content. It is therefore doubly important that the analysis of visual information be guided by a theoretical perspective and a specific research question; otherwise, the number of potential observations that could be made is practically infinite. Doing justice to the study of visual symbolism within the scope of this book is not practical; however, a few key practical considerations are discussed here.

Where video recordings are used as resources for this type of analysis, several viewings are advisable. Check your notes from the first time around against your observations the second time. Are they accurate? Are important verbal and visual data recorded as carefully as possible so you can make use of them in your analysis? Do you have any new or different impressions the second time? Use the advantages of modern video technology (VCRs, DVDs, and so on); play, replay, and replay again segments that seem especially important. Watching visual material for research purposes can, quite frankly, be exhausting; it is very different from watching as an audience member for the purpose of being entertained or informed.

Another dimension involves consideration of the technical aspects of the visual presentation itself and how these elements help convey certain moods or suggest certain audience interpretations. What does a "slow fade" or a certain kind of camera angle suggest to the viewer? How are visuals used on the evening news? Do these draw attention to certain aspects of a story? What are the characteristics of the standard shot of a national newscaster on location at a catastrophic event? Are there unique technical elements to the way, say, sports events or news about war are presented? Are these the same, or are they different? To the extent they might be the same, you might be justified in asking why. Does this tell you something about your culture, or is it an accident of technology and media tradition?

"Close Readings"

One way to approach the qualitative analysis of media data—whether visual, like a film, or textual, like a novel or news story—is by adopting a participant observer stance *to the act of reading or viewing*. Above, you encountered *close reading* as a descriptive term for an ethnographic approach to studying media content. "Reading" does not have to refer only to interaction with a written text, however. The idea is simply to experience a piece of media material (such as a text, a program, a film, or an advertisement) in the same way that a participant observer might experience a particular social setting. Be alert to your own reactions. How did the material make you feel? What did it remind you of? Why does the material appear to be compelling—or unsettling?

While opinion might differ as to whether this should actually be considered a form of ethnography, data from a "close reading" should be analyzed like any other attempt to adopt an "insider stance" with respect to an experience. In this sense it is closely parallel to participant observation of a social setting.

WRITING DESCRIPTIVE SUMMARIES

For qualitative researchers, the analysis of data and the effective construction of verbal summaries of those data are closely connected. Qualitative data must be presented in a way that appropriately represents what has been discovered. In addition, the representation must convince those who read your work that your analysis has validity. Here, your skill as a writer is very important, for whereas quantitative studies can rely on numbers, tables, and statistical tests to give as accurate as possible an account of what was discovered, qualitative studies use description (with cogent examples) to communicate results. Only your verbal descriptions are available to the reader as an explanation of the conclusions drawn. In effect, putting together a descriptive account is almost inseparable, in qualitative work, from the actual analysis of data.

In a sense, the descriptive account of a qualitative research project is a persuasive project. You have identified important themes and patterns in a complex series of observations. You have invested much work and great care to be sure your conclusions are justified. Now you must persuade your potential readers that these themes and patterns are actually present in the data and not figments of your own imagination. At the same time, you must write in a way that is true to the point of view of those you are studying as well as to your own observations of the data. You must organize the material so that the reader will "see" the same answer to your original research question that you saw. You want to give as much detail as possible, but at the same time you cannot literally report everything you observed, or your reader will be overwhelmed.

The "Insider" Viewpoint

All qualitative research involves looking at social phenomena from a new point of view. In order to get this far in your qualitative project, you will have had to get "inside" your own data and learn to look at the world from someone else's cultural perspective—whether that meant adopting the viewpoint of members of a social group you studied, understanding things as they look from the perspective of an institution that played a key role in your case study, or perhaps adopting the vantage point of the creators—or consumers—of a particular kind of media product. Now your job is to communicate this "insider" view to your readers.

You are really speaking for those you studied, in a sense—giving their point of view a voice. What does the world look like from this other vantage point, whether that of a media producer or a consumer? What's important, and what's less so? Are there important distinctions made between, say, groups of people, positions on issues, media genres, or types of events or activities that are different from the ones you yourself make?

This chapter has concentrated on the development of themes in qualitative research, whether extracted from interviews, focus groups, observational data, or media material. Your summary should present these themes in a way that makes them vivid and convincing for someone else yet remains true to the reality of what you found. While this task is more art than science, here are a few pointers.

Making Use of Background Information

Perhaps you've completed a qualitative case study of a key media event. Here you need to give your reader the background and history necessary to make sense of it. Whether you are studying a national issue or a local one, you can't assume that your readers have followed the general developments with as much attentiveness as you have. Don't assume that your readers have enough background knowledge of the case. Describe important events that preceded the actual period that you studied, and give a chronology leading up to your study period. Background information provides the context for your later discussion of the results of your analysis, whatever data you use to reconstruct the sequence of events.

If you are focusing on a particular social setting, such as a media institution, the same idea applies. Tell your reader what the social setting is all about—when the organization or institution was created, how many members or employees it has, how it sees its own mission or role in society. What if your study involves qualitative analysis of media data rather than a social setting or case? The same principle applies. Assume that your readers are reasonably smart people, but don't assume they are familiar with the media material you're about to describe. Research is increasingly a global venture. Tell them that *The New York Times* is an elite daily newspaper in the United States or that *Sesame Street* is a children's educational show on U.S. public television, even if these things seem obvious. Who are the publishers or producers? Who is the intended audience?

For something very well known, a short paragraph or so of background material may do. But don't skimp in describing the general outlines of the media material itself. Is there a stock format for the programming with which you're concerned? Who are the key characters or personalities?

If you're working with print or television material, describe it. Your reader will need to understand if the magazine you're studying is written for conservative housewives or "career girls," and the best way to convey this is descriptively. What's a typical cover like, or a typical table of contents? Does television programming in your study follow a well-recognized genre, such as a sitcom or a reality show? What kinds of advertising are carried, even if your main focus is on other content? If you have studied a neighborhood and the role media products play in giving it a sense of identity, tell us about the neighborhood—its history, demographics, and current challenges. If yours is a case study of a particular media event or controversy, where did this take place? What are the politics behind it? What are the characteristics of the city, town, or village involved?

Include a clear statement of the research question. Consider using statements in the form of hypotheses to clarify your thinking (including its link to theory) and communicate this more clearly, even though you're not using a formal hypothesis-testing research model. You will also include a review or discussion of the academic literature (others' work that has helped shape your own, particularly with respect to theory), just as is done when reporting a quantitative study (more details of the conventions for reporting the results of research—those that apply to both qualitative and quantitative work—are presented in the final chapter).

Explaining and Exemplifying Patterns

Remember that thematic analysis (whether or not you are using a grounded theory approach) is generally at the core of qualitative research. Unlike quantitative researchers, you can't rely on numbers, tables, or statistical tests. You must use your own best judgment about what is going on and which parts of it might be important. Having introduced your research site to your readers, your next task is to convey to them the themes or patterns that you've determined best characterize your observations. Here the important thing is to provide detailed examples that will demonstrate to your readers that the patterns you've extracted are good interpretive abstractions from what you've actually observed.

Let's say you're describing a series of focus groups conducted to help you understand how different groups of people are reacting to news of the war in Iraq. You've noticed a repetitive pattern of relating this news to what they know of earlier wars and other national crises. This could be an important key to understanding how public opinion is formed in these cases; historical analogy is probably an important strategy that news audiences use to make sense of current events. What parts of the analogy seem to be most important? As much as possible, let your reader share with you the sense of discovery of this theme. Give enough descriptive examples from specific group discussions that your reader will be convinced of the appropriateness of your conclusions.

You don't need *dozens* of examples of a particular theme or other finding, but you do need two or three strong ones. It is customary when reporting transcribed conversations or discussion to reproduce the original speech as closely as possible, including mistakes and hesitations. You can assume your reader understands that conversational speech is not grammatically perfect, so the use of *sic* should be minimized. Ellipses (. . .) can be used to indicate pauses; unclear portions of the tape should be shown with bracketed question marks, something like this:

Uh, it reminded me of . . . like hearing about Kennedy's assassination, er [?] something like that, I guess.

In this example, the speaker is actually talking about his or her own experience of an event and comparing it to another, similar experience ("like hearing about") rather than commenting on the event itself. If part of a pattern, this might be something you would want to draw out in your written discussion as a conclusion about how people make sense of new events.

Quoted pieces of conversation can help demonstrate how media experiences are responded to as though they were part of everyday life. For example, here is a transcript of a conversation between two office workers regarding their daily "soap":

A: What happened to Joe? I thought he'd come back.
B: Ah . . . he turned back up; he was in Chicago with his old girlfriend, but it didn't last.
A: Well, I'm glad of that!

Here, Speaker A is speaking just as though Joe is someone she knew and cared about as a real person. The connection between "real life" and the soap-opera fantasy appears seamless. Other examples of this kind would help the researcher *show* the reader how this works.

Often, in presenting qualitative data from interviews, focus groups, or observations, the best approach is to walk through each theme, one by one, and explain what it consists of. Then give a few key examples of each. This is a good approach to the presentation of media content, as well.

Media Content Descriptions

Descriptions of media content in qualitative research should be approached similarly. If you are arguing that your analysis has revealed a certain series of themes in the content you have analyzed, illustrate your assertion with key examples, and do not be afraid to make them vivid ones. Make your readers aware of how details of the presentation might affect audience responses:

The film opens with the camera panning across the empty desert until a shimmering lake, surrounded by a strip of green and dominated by two metal towers, comes into view. The contrast between the desert "waste-land" and the artificial oasis leaves an unmistakable imprint.

or:

The typical homicide story in this paper is in some way bizarre or grotesque; run-of-the-mill murders don't generally get covered. Characteristic stories found in this content analysis described a homeless man burned to death, the apparent hate-crime beating death of a gay man, and a 7-year-old victim of child abuse.

If you have used a grounded theory approach, you will also have numbers with which to work. Be careful not to treat these too much like measurements. They are only descriptive categorizations that you've assigned to qualitative data and then counted for your own convenience (and that of your readers). Most statistical tests will not be appropriate, although nonparametric comparisons using statistics such as chi-square comparisons might be very useful in some cases. While it may do damage to insights about some subtle dimensions, summarizing qualitative data in quantitative form is a shorthand technique for reducing complex information to something you can communicate easily. The danger is, of course, that you will lose the advantages of qualitative research (richness of detail, depth of insight). Combine charts or tables giving frequency data with descriptive summaries that present more purely qualitative results.

RELATING DATA TO CONCLUSIONS

At this point, it will help to return to your original research question and the theoretical understanding you have of your research problem. Are the themes and patterns that you expected to find actually there? Or did your results surprise you? What have you learned that you did not anticipate? It is through asking and answering these questions that qualitative research contributes to theory building.

Many research problems appropriate for qualitative study call first and foremost for a descriptive answer from a particular point of view. For example, what is the worldview of today's corporate executive like? How do talk shows portray social issues, and how might this influence their audiences? How did the safety of nuclear power plants in the state of Washington creep into the news following Chernobyl? What is the general tone of blog discussions about today's political candidates? Usually, though, there should also be a theoretical purpose to such studies.

Do your data suggest a confirmation, a revision, or a rejection of theory? Here the thinking is much like the hypothesis testing typical of quantitative research. If you began an agenda-building case study with a theory that states that agendas are built through complex interactions among many social institutions, including the media, are your findings consistent with this? Or did you find that some one institution (perhaps a media institution, perhaps not) seemed to take the lead to a greater extent than you anticipated? If you began a study of an international news-gathering organization with theory that suggested why this organization might produce particularly ethnocentric news, was this actually the case, or not? If you began researching children's use of video games, thinking that they are more likely to reinforce aggressiveness than cooperative play, is this actually what you found?

Your job here is to represent your honest interpretation of what you found. Especially in interpretive, qualitative research, you may need to struggle to separate editorial opinions about what *should* have happened in a particular case, how we *should* represent particular groups or ideas, or how a certain kind of organization *should* function from your presentation of the data you found and conclusions you drew. Statements like these are not inappropriate *as part of the discussion;* however, all "should" questions should be recognized as ethical positions, not dispassionate observations.

Many researchers recognize an ethical obligation to do research that bears on real-world problems, but this does not reduce the ethical obligation to offer analysis that sets aside judgments about "correct" solutions. Many qualitative researchers reject the idea that their work should be "objective" in the sense embraced by quantitative researchers; this is a key distinction between them. However, this does not mean that qualitative research is free of the obligation to ground conclusions in empirical findings.

The "ethnographic stance" involves setting aside one's own personal preconceptions, as well as the preconceptions characteristic of one's own culture. Even when working entirely within your own culture, you can learn much about yourself as well as much about others by having some practice in adopting someone else's point of view.

Qualitative research contributes to building a body of accumulated knowledge not by formal hypothesis testing but by more free-ranging exploration of actual social practices. The structures of social organizations, the deeper meanings of media products, and the patterns of political events are all extremely important social phenomena to understand—and extremely difficult to reduce to measurable variables. Qualitative research—primarily inductive rather than deductive—also helps generate new theory that can be tested either quantitatively or through additional qualitative studies.

Important Terms and Concepts

Sensitizing concept

Social setting

Transcription

Exercise

Qualitative analysis techniques can be used for many forms of data, including interviews, focus groups, observations, or media content data. Media content data, however, is the most readily available of these. For this exercise, please choose a specific form of media content that interests you and that has qualities you believe lend themselves to qualitative (rather than purely quantitative) analysis. This might involve a particular television series, a type of magazine or book or film, talk radio programs, newspaper articles or broadcast news programs, popular music, Internet content, or any other media product that interests you. Base your choice of material on an underlying research question or expectation about the particular type of content you have chosen.

1. Choose at least three to six closely related examples of media material that especially interests you with respect to your research question. Be sure to choose multiple examples of a comparable type of content (such as six ads for a similar product). In some cases (books, Web sites, magazines, newspaper articles or news broadcasts, films, music) finding six examples should not be difficult. In the case of broadcast material such as radio or TV programming, it may be more difficult over a short period of time unless you choose content that appears often (such as a local evening news broadcast) or is available by commercial rental (some popular TV series). For these longer-form items, three examples would be enough.

2. By means of a "close reading" of this content, identify some broad general categories for content. Then, using a "grounded theory" approach, identify more specific themes and categorize your material accordingly. For broadcast material, it is best to work with a video recording, although you can also try working with careful notes made while watching.

3. Can you identify any theoretical significance for the results of your analysis? Your instructor may want to have you turn in your analysis and this discussion as a short paper for course credit or may allocate time in class to discuss making this inductive link between theory and qualitative data.

PART IV

Research in Broader Context

Contemporary Trends
and the Dissemination
of Research Results

CHAPTER 10

Research Horizons

Opportunities and Challenges

This chapter introduces some of the opportunities and challenges on the horizon for media researchers. New technologies seem to be transforming everything, especially the field of media communication, and media research is shifting to keep pace. In an increasingly globalized, so-called "**postmodern**" world, positivism faces new challenges, including those from intercultural, developing-world, and feminist perspectives. Not only are scholars questioning the authority of some of our traditional research approaches, but we are also increasingly conscious that social science cannot resolve most issues of policy and ethics that confront us today—it can only inform our decisions. Communication researchers are asking whether new forms of deliberation are needed that can help democracy function better, and whether these might include media-based solutions. These are the issues that will confront the field in the 21st century.

NEW MEDIA TECHNOLOGY

Research, like society, does not stand still. The explosion of new technology and consumer electronics has affected almost all areas of modern life but especially the areas of communication and information. The computer, until recent decades, a tool primarily designed for accountants and scientists, has become a node on the information superhighway, keeping increasingly mobile families and dispersed commercial enterprises in contact and making a crucial contribution to managing our increasingly global economy. Today's children grow up in an intensively electronic environment in which television is only the beginning; video games, music players, cell phones, and computers are all growing smaller and yet more complex at the same time they are becoming increasingly pervasive. Internet-based social networking sites like MySpace and Facebook have revolutionized the way all of us—but especially younger generations—meet new people, look for jobs, and organize our daily activities. Our entire perspective on media influence and effects is shifting as well.

News has also changed. Mobile equipment facilitates professional video production by small and even single-person teams in some of the most far-flung corners of the world; mobile telephones, satellite networks, and fiber-optic cables support broadband communication networks with capacities unimaginable a few short years ago, including the capacity to transmit live broadcasts from almost anywhere. Citizen journalists can use ordinary cell phones to post snapshots and stories on blogs in an instant or even act as a sort of mini-newswire service by sending these directly to the phones of their friends and acquaintances. Few nations are isolated from today's news network. The lines between news and entertainment (sometimes producing the kind of material referred to derogatorily as "infotainment") are blurred, and the lines between interpersonal and mass media are also increasingly blurred. The future of journalism in traditional media is uncertain, which raises profound new questions of social responsibility and ethics, but it is also a fascinating world to watch—and an amazing research opportunity. Where is today's news media agenda to be found?

Media research methods and mass communication theory have been challenged to keep up with these changes. New media technology is no longer just a footnote to "status quo" thinking and procedures. Nevertheless, our repertoire of methods for studying communication issues and effects has not changed a great deal. Contemporary researchers still use survey methods, observational and interview methods, experimental methods, and content analysis methods to study the role of media in ordinary daily life, the behavior of media organizations, the nature of what they produce, and the long- and short-term influences these products (whatever technology delivers them) may have on people's thinking and behaviors. We do have to be careful not to let our "old media" thinking interfere with our ability to grasp the "new media" environment. Researchers must also cope with new problems, especially issues of sampling. Surveys can no longer hope to reach 50% or 60% of those they contact; many people cannot be reached at all on a conventional land-line telephone, while others still cannot be reached by Internet. Content is no longer accessible through static archives of news messages but has become an ephemeral montage of ever-shifting text and images. The media agenda is no longer apparent to anyone who opens the pages of a major national newspaper but must be seen from the vantage point of a consumer presented with a near-infinite array of choices.

Characterizing Today's Trends

Traditionally, a great deal of media research—especially research on the influence of mass communication media, whether news or entertainment—was based on the so-called "**channel model**" of mass communication. In this model, a single, clearly defined source sends a signal (or message) in a clearly defined channel (such as a mass medium like broadcast television) to a receiver. The receiver could be a single person or many people; the "many" in one-to-many communication was generally conceptualized as a large and homogenous (or "mass") audience. Today this model has been replaced by an entirely different communication environment in which anyone can communicate almost anything to anyone else (or to many other people at once) using any number of electronic technologies. YouTube has made it possible for anyone to aspire to be a broadcast journalist, and Internet blogs make everyone a potential journalist.

While some individuals are **early adopters** who embrace every new technology with enthusiasm and others are slower to adopt or even actively resistant to change, clearly the media environment has changed for everyone. Even traditional media such as magazines, entertainment television, and the advertising they carry are more often targeted at specialized audiences, not a generic "mass." The distinction between "one-to-one" and "one-to-many" communication processes is now a continuum.

Nevertheless, some have benefited more than others by this revolution. The economic and technological changes that have come with today's **Information Age** may have exacerbated the differences between the "information haves" and the "information have-nots" of a generation ago. Some segments of the economy have grown while others have shrunk. Some parts of the world have media environments that are changed to a lesser extent than others, whether due to government policy (e.g., in controlled-media environments, such as that of North Korea), degree of general economic development and communication infrastructure (e.g., in much of Africa and parts of Asia and Latin America), or both (e.g., in mainland China, although this "sleeping giant" is changing very quickly).

Even within a single country, including those with highly developed economies like the United States and some countries in Western Europe, divides persist and may even be growing between the "richest" segments of the population and the "poorest," in terms of access to information and technology as well as income. A significant gender divide existed in the use of computer-based information technology in the early years of Internet use, when computers were still for geeks and nerds, and although this is much less noticeable today, concerns remain about disparities of access associated with gender, race, ethnicity, and nationality, as well as those associated with economic status and educational achievement.

The phrase **media convergence** refers to a variety of trends that are linking different kinds of media and technologies. One aspect is the migration of traditional media like newspapers and radio or television stations onto the Internet. At first this tended to take the form of Web sites that reproduced the day's content, sometimes with little originality, making possible **asynchronous** reception and the ability for news workers to make instantaneous updates around the clock. Increasingly, however, both traditional news organizations and new ones have invested in producing journalists capable of generating "cross-platform" content created by reporters with the skills to create stories that can be presented in text, video, and multimedia simultaneously.

The best of today's Internet-based news sites make real use of the Web's capacity, whether enhancing or competing with traditional media, rather than simply duplicating the day's news from a print, wire, or broadcast source in another medium. Using new communication technology, citizen journalism is being integrated into daily news organizations in many communities—whether through providing opportunities to comment on published stories or through citizen production of original content on local events. At the same time, while co-ownership of papers and stations has always been controversial because of its implications for controlling the diversity of views available to news consumers, technological convergence may exacerbate the formation of ever-larger media conglomerates.

It is not just traditional news and Web-based news products that are converging. Now the cell phone and the computer are also converging, as are the computer and the television set. Imaginary "virtual worlds" like Second Life®, once frequented only by multiplayer game enthusiasts, are readily accessible to anyone with a relatively ordinary computer and a cheaply available broadband Internet connection. If "RL" (or "real life") doesn't appeal, the alternative—complete with an active economy, a well-developed system of property ownership, and a complex level of social organization—is waiting to provide the escape. What will this development do to our ideas about "media effects"?

Electronically available versions of much conventional library content, including that in historical archives, exist alongside public-access informational databases like Wikipedia that are written anonymously by anyone. Together these mean answers to most factual questions are almost immediately available—but are the answers correct? This new environment demands new information-processing skills of consumers who must sort the real from the wished-for, the imagined, and even the malicious in this "brave new world" of near-infinite information.

The popular music industry is being transformed by the ready availability of file sharing, Internet marketing, and other downloading alternatives to shopping, both legal and illegal, taking place within and across national borders. Book and periodical publishing have been transformed as well by the concept of technology-based "on demand" and "open access" alternatives. News aggregation sites like Yahoo!® and Google™ that do not produce much (if any) of their own news may have independent influences on the national and international news agendas that may be driven by quite different values from those of the traditional news organization. And all of this is probably only the beginning.

New Ideas for Media Research

Media research has struggled to adapt its theories and methods to this still-emerging, ever-converging world in which not only are the lines between various traditional mass media being erased but so are the lines between journalism and entertainment, news and opinion, reality and fantasy, and interpersonal and "mass" communication. What does it mean to take a "sample" of the content of the Internet—or even of an individual Web site? There is simply no clear fixed "population" of information items from which to choose. How do we assess what "the media" are transmitting, when today's technology means that any individual has such a vast sea of material from which to choose—or that individuals can so readily produce their own news if they don't find what interests them? More important, what are the crucial research questions we should be asking about this remarkable new information and communication environment?

Some of these trends (particularly the sampling issues) present profound challenges for the application of social science research methods to the world of new media. But at the same time, the transformations we are experiencing also produce vitally important new research questions, a number of which are suggested by the trends described here. For example, how is online news content different from, or the same as, the news content of traditional organizations?

What are the consequences (good and bad) for the diversity of voices we hear? Are our traditional "news values" and journalistic ethics being eroded by the ready availability of news produced by anyone? Or are these trends adding valuable new perspectives, in effect destroying the **hegemony** (or domination) of older news monopolies?

The list goes on. What is happening to information and knowledge gaps between "haves" and "have-nots" in this new world? Do the new media actually produce more diversity and a stronger checks-and-balances system on government—or only an avalanche of unproven gossip and trivia? What are the effects on other institutions, ranging from libraries to music labels? And what does all this mean for the individual media consumer or the individual author or artist or musician? In the end, is democracy being destroyed or reborn?

Of course, not all of these questions are directly researchable by the methods of social science. Nevertheless, in many significant ways the same theories and methods used to understand traditional media can be used to understand these new forms. If violence on television is a social problem, violence in video games may be a problem in the very same way—some are concerned it may be a worse problem because of the increased engagement and realism these games (and their online analogs) provide. Asking questions about the differences between old and new media tests our theoretical understanding of how media work against new situations and so contributes to the accumulation of social scientific knowledge.

New Methods for New Media?

Do the new media need to be studied by new methods? Chances are, we will continue to use our existing methods, but we must think creatively about how to adapt them to the changes in our field. "New media" can mean everything from broadband cable, satellite TV systems, and high-definition digital television to computer-based video and multimedia systems to broadband phone lines and cellular telephones that take pictures and send text to new means of marketing and distributing music and film. It is a pretty good bet that by the time this book is printed, there will be other, even newer examples that do not even receive mention in this chapter. Yet from the view of the social scientist, all of these changes provide new opportunities to observe, experiment with, sample, and evaluate people's use of technology to communicate.

What do these developments have in common? One of the ways we might think about new media for research purposes is to consider exactly what it is that makes them "new." Most of these technologies and systems have the shared feature of being more personalized and less "mass" than traditional media. This is sometimes referred to as demassification (Rogers, 1986). In print- and Web-based journalism in particular, **hyperlocal** news targeted at a smaller geographic area is an emerging trend. Smaller suburban newspapers may be experiencing a renaissance, even while some major urban dailies may be dying. Advertisers have learned that it is more efficient for them to reach those specific audiences most likely to be interested in their products. Public relations professionals seem increasingly to understand that there are many "publics," not one monolithic "public," and that they need to target their messages appropriately. These are trends that can be observed and documented through our existing methods, such as ethnography and content analysis.

The fact that new media tend to blur the distinction between mass and interpersonal communication is also a crucial shared characteristic. The existence of millions of personal e-mail accounts means that advertising, public relations, and political messages—not to mention news itself—can be spread without relying on traditional media in any direct way. The proliferation of special-interest blog sites means that political messages of interest only to a small minority of the population spread especially rapidly, and even though this may involve a small group, it may be a highly influential group for particular issues. The ways that "demassified" messages spread through social networks, the credibility of information received through alternative channels, and the influence these messages carry represent a rich arena for new media research that should be able to make good use of our existing methods, including surveys and experimental approaches.

Research designs will need to reflect the contemporary media landscape. Instead of trying to study "the public" or "the news agenda" as though there were only one public and a single agenda, researchers of the future will want to concentrate on particular audiences—their uses of media, their responses to messages, and their perceptions of what matters. This will be especially true of smaller-scale studies likely to be undertaken by beginning researchers. Case study research on how particular organizations and groups make use of new technology is one promising frontier. With so much variation in individuals' own media environments, studies of selectivity and its impact will become increasingly important, as will studies of the "uses and gratifications" new media provide for their users. The study of specific interpretive communities that share a cultural or political identity will become more important, occupying a "middle ground" between studies that focus on the individual media producer or consumer and studies that assume a monolithic "mass" audience.

Survey research presents a special challenge and quite possibly an exception to the idea that our methods do not need to change. In addition to the proliferation of cell phones, sometimes in preference to conventional land-line phones, survey researchers must contend with other new technology such as caller ID and call blocking systems that allow electronic screening of incoming calls. But survey response rates have been dropping for some time, due not only to these new technologies but most likely also to respondent "burnout" in reaction to repeated contacts—including those from market researchers or political campaigns, as well as academic researchers. Going back to door-to-door, face-to-face surveys seems impractical in today's mobile, urban societies where those willing to open their doors to unknown individuals for any purpose may be increasingly rare—and not everyone is at home during the day to begin with. Eventually, Internet-based surveys may take up the slack, but at present not everyone has access to, or uses, the Internet, and it is still not clear how the integrity of sampling methodology can be maintained using this alternative, whether for surveys of people or of content.

Research on Technology and Its Adoption

Research that is specifically concerned with how new technologies are adopted and their likely impacts on society is called **technology assessment**, sometimes abbreviated "TA." We can probably expect this form of research to become more important in media studies as our media continue to become more complex and ever-evolving. TA has a long history outside of media studies, with connections to fields such as policy studies, engineering, and the sociology of technology. TA uses primarily the same social science methods with which you are already familiar from this book. A form of policy research, TA tries to project the impact and evaluate the wisdom of particular choices about technology, ranging from nuclear power to word processing.

The design and evaluation of new electronic information systems—the kinds of alternatives traditional news organizations have been struggling to create—can also benefit from social and behavioral science research on human-computer interaction. Largely experimental, research in this area is sometimes done within departments of computer science but would benefit from media studies expertise. Those next-generation media developers who are most successful will go beyond being impressed by novel technology in and of itself and will start asking how technology can deliver needed information to their audiences more effectively—whether at the hyperlocal or at the global level. Case studies of organizational innovation should also give us new insights into these dynamics.

News organizations have traditionally given their audiences some of the information they *ought to have* as well as some of what they want, however. First Amendment protections in the United States derive from the recognition that journalism serves crucial democratic purposes. Research is needed on the ways that the traditional functions and core values of journalism are evolving. What are the news values that are shaping the 21st-century news agenda? As these methods did for the media of the 20th century, content analysis and ethnography will help us answer this question. In pursuing such questions, we need to address not only what works but also what is seen as socially responsible.

Many of the big issues associated with new technology are policy, regulatory, business, or ethical issues that cannot be directly resolved by the gathering of any empirical data, whether qualitative or quantitative. Nevertheless, social science methods have a big role to play in allowing us to make informed judgments about how best to manage our technological future—as entrepreneurs, as journalists, and as citizens.

RESEARCH IN A GLOBAL VILLAGE

Today's media research is headed in a number of new and important directions. As Chapter 2 explained, research methods (like all other cultural practices) have social and cultural origins. In turn, social trends influence methods. While science itself was originally an invention of White males, feminist and international-intercultural perspectives on communication research look in new ways at the challenges and opportunities posed by new media technologies. Media scholar Marshall McLuhan (1989) called contemporary society a "global village" in which mass media serve the traditional function of the storyteller—and in which the entire globe seems to have shrunk to the scale of a village as a result of accelerating changes in media technology.

The Feminist Contribution

In recent decades, a handful of **feminist** scholars have argued that much of modern science has been done from a subtly **masculinist** (or male-biased) point of view (see Keller, 1985). This perspective does not entail a blanket rejection of the fruits of scientific knowledge, especially where these make clear contributions to our quality of life, but it does entail a recognition that social values and political forces have shaped (at a minimum) the *kind* of science that we have today, an assertion that many sociologists of science would support. The feminist critique represents a relatively early recognition that science (including, of course, social science) incorporates a point of view. Today's world is said to be "postmodern." One dimension of postmodernism is the rejection of the "modernist" assumption made by a rapidly industrializing world that science and technology are necessarily the superhighway to truth and progress. A blind commitment to the assumptions of positivism (see Chapter 1) is no longer universal; truth in the postmodern world is recognized as having many faces.

Feminist researchers in social science are often (although by no means always) conflict theorists, as their work is directed in large part toward understanding how the power of men has been maintained, over time, within society (for an excellent discussion of the variations of perspective within feminist analysis, see Steeves, 1988). Both the privilege accorded to science and the definitions of reality offered by the media have historically contributed to the power differential that separates the genders. Feminist scholarship and research is to some extent distinct from feminism as a political movement, but there is a clear connection between the two. Feminism as a political movement argues for the rights of women. Feminist scholarship and research looks at the means through which these rights have historically been denied and tries to understand the social dynamics involved.

In mass media studies, the very limited types of images of women and definitions of their appropriate roles that have been presented in many media portrayals, in both entertainment media and news, and the historical limitations on women achieving their full potential in mass communication careers are both seen as parts of this problem. Although there is still a long way to go, increasing attention in mass media research to gender issues—gay and lesbian as well as feminist perspectives—is a present-day reality.

For many feminists, the purpose of understanding how women have historically been denied power and the ways that they have successfully resisted this denial is to help work toward women's further **empowerment** in the future. For researchers, this perspective offers another lesson. Research proceeds from a point of view. Just as news may never be "objective," research is not free from the cultural assumptions of the researcher—or the broader society of which he or she is a member. For example, the problems chosen for research reflect a particular set of priorities, even if the methods do not (itself arguable). In science generally, much research effort is directed toward controlling or dominating nature in some way. Some feminist critics of science believe this is an inherently masculinist goal—that women are more likely to find working *with* nature rather than *against* it preferable. One root of our present environmental challenges could be this persistent attempt to conquer the natural environment in preference to learning to live within—and with—it.

Research that divides the world into researchers and those who are the objects of the research is similarly seen by some feminists as yet another attempt to dominate and to maintain an artificial separation between some (more powerful) people and other (less powerful) ones. Some feminist scholars reject the **subject-object distinction** inherent in quantitative work. Does feminist mass communication research actually require different methods? Not necessarily, but some feminist researchers are more interested in how the world looks *from a point of view* than *from an objective stance*, which they may dismiss as illusion. Understanding how the world works from a particular point of view may be more consistent with qualitative than with quantitative methods. Qualitative methods, after all, were developed specifically to understand cultural differences.

International and Intercultural Media Research

The reminder from feminist scholarship that the researcher's own cultural biases influence the way that he or she thinks about research problems is also extremely important in international and intercultural communication studies. **International communication** generally refers both to the study of communication that crosses the borders of separate nations and to the study of the ways that mass media systems differ from one country to the next (sometimes called comparative media systems). **Intercultural communication** refers to communication between different cultural groups, including that between members of different national cultures but also communication by, among, and about different ethnic groups within multiethnic societies.

Both areas of study require special attention to how ethnocentric assumptions can interfere with effective communication and, just as feminist scholars have argued with specific respect to women's roles, perpetuate limiting stereotypes and the traditional power of some groups at the expense of others. The study of international and intercultural communication systems also reminds us that U.S. and other Western media systems, the legal and political systems in which they operate, and our expectations about their roles in society are unique to our own culture, not shared around the world (see Hachten, 1987, for more information on how these systems vary).

If you are a mass communication student in a country with a strong "free press" tradition, you may be surprised at what you might learn from looking at press systems around the world and their legal justifications. No one system is considered the ideal system everywhere in the world, and some do not consider press systems like that in the United States particularly "free" because of their heavy dependence on information from government sources and on revenue from advertising. On the other hand, there are many situations around the world in which the press is still heavily controlled by government coercion or direct censorship. Journalists' lives are often at stake.

The bottom line is that assumptions about how media systems "should" work are culture-bound and may vary as much as the realities of how they actually do work. Research in the international/intercultural area is concerned in part with these issues.

Research Challenges for International and Intercultural Projects

Doing international or intercultural studies sometimes poses special methodological challenges. Even for those with the requisite language skills, it is not always easy getting access to broadcasts and publications from outside one's own country in order to do content analysis, for example. In the so-called "developing" world, the meaningfulness of survey data is open to question; samples may not be as representative, and respondents may be less familiar with survey procedures. Also, the practical problems posed by the cost and difficulty of international travel, language and cultural barriers, and obtaining permissions for research in a foreign country are all too easy to underestimate, even in today's world. Compromises are sometimes essential. Researchers whose home countries are in the less developed world—and who may therefore be in the best position to do local, culturally sensitive work—sometimes lack the financial and other resources for research afforded those in the developed world.

Although international and intercultural communication studies use the same methods as other mass communication studies, they must be especially sensitive to cultural variation in the interpretation of survey or interview questions and in expectations about how the media function. To take just one simple example, the role of the print press in a developing country with a low literacy rate—where only elites can read—is not the same as its role in an industrialized Western democracy. This will complicate any attempt at comparing the two societies in terms of media content or structure. Radio may dominate television broadcasting in some areas, and Internet—while increasingly available—may function only intermittently or at lower speeds.

An important issue in international/intercultural communication is the effect on a culture of imported media products. When village farmers in India watch *I Love Lucy* or *Little House on the Prairie,* how does this influence their worldviews and their perceptions of themselves? On the one hand, it is so difficult to evaluate the effects of media even within a single culture that the problems of studying this type of "effect" across cultures seem overwhelming; on the other hand, the appeal of this "natural laboratory" for understanding media effects is enormous. The quantitative, often positivist, hypothesis-testing model used in much media effects research in the United States may fail to transfer to such situations. Rather, case studies based on techniques like participant observation are much more likely to yield meaningful insights.

Ethnic Diversity Within Pluralistic Societies

Today's modern pluralistic societies are increasingly ethnically diverse, in part a consequence of globalization and its impact on international migration, and communication systems must allow for this. Practical business objectives like being able to advertise new products effectively to diverse audiences, as well as social ideals such as the promotion of democratic dialogue that is inclusive rather than exclusive, depend on communication that can reach multiethnic audiences. Fortunately, pluralistic societies such as the United States and the United Kingdom are beginning to respond to this challenge, although these responses are still incomplete.

How do the mass media in the predominately Anglo culture of the United States represent African Americans, Spanish speakers, Asians, or Native Americans in entertainment programming? Are these minority perspectives appropriately represented on the news? Are advertising messages reaching these groups, or are they sometimes offensive to them, even unwittingly? Are there minority as well as majority journalists, writers, editors, producers, and announcers? And just what images of minority groups *should* the media be expected to provide?

One African American in the United States might think entertainment television's *Sanford and Son*'s portrayal of a ghetto junk dealer is an honest and positive portrait of a minority businessman who has succeeded within the boundaries of his own circumstances; another might think the same image is insulting and embarrassing. One might think *The Cosby Show*'s portrayal of a middle-class African-American family is exemplary; another might think it suggests an unrealistic ideal in which race has somehow become irrelevant. Studying these images without making implicit judgments about what they "ought to" look like is difficult. Yet, clearly, mass media images of ethnic minorities may be a powerful influence on stereotypes and expectations that apply to those groups.

Participatory and Community-Based Research

Researchers publish results and build careers on the basis of data they have taken from a particular group of people, often without giving anything in return. They assume that their own research objectives are the important ones, generally without consulting the people they ask to participate in their studies. Is such behavior ethically justified? Such questions have given rise to alternative approaches to setting a meaningful research agenda.

The idea of **participatory research**—research in which those being studied have a voice in the direction the research takes—is one response. This approach to research tries to give research participants more control over their own lives—to empower them rather than to extract information for research purposes without giving anything in return. Those who might otherwise have been seen merely as the "objects" of the research may be invited to define research problems and priorities and to participate as members of the research team. By involving research participants as collaborators, researchers will also gain cooperation and perhaps a more culturally appropriate perspective.

A participatory, community-based approach might involve asking a community what its members believe key problems are and how they might best be understood and then inviting the community's participation in developing solutions. What is the best way to get out HIV/AIDS information to those in the community who most need it? How is the community represented in existing local media, and what would it take to get a community newspaper off the ground? How could local women most effectively publicize a support group? The community may or may not be a geographic one; it might consist of homeless people in the United States, for example, or slum dwellers in South Africa.

ETHICS IN RESEARCH: A FURTHER NOTE

Journalists, public relations practitioners, and advertisers all have professional **codes of ethics** that govern their professional behavior. All three of the fields this book has referred to as "foundational" in terms of their contributions to our field's most commonly utilized methods also have extensive codes of ethics that apply specifically to the conduct of research. The American Psychological Association, the American Sociological Association, and the American Anthropological Association each publishes its own discipline-specific code of ethics on its Web site, as does the American Association for Public Opinion Research and many other social science research organizations. These codes are consistent with the regulations that govern formal human subjects board (IRB) reviews but go beyond them in many areas. Students and instructors using this book are urged to consult these codes for general guidance about the types of ethical issues that can arise as a result of research activities.

While its code is not as extensive as the codes that have been developed over a longer time within these organizations, the Association for Education in Journalism and Mass Communication, which is the major professional organization for university professors and other scholars engaged in research about mass communication, is currently in the process of developing a similar code that will cover research activities among others. The International Communication Association and the National Communication Association also address issues of research ethics on their Web sites.

Research participants (human subjects) contribute time and attention to help projects reach their goals; these contributions, which are often unpaid, should not be wasted. While compelling current events sometimes send researchers into the field quickly, subjects should not generally be asked to participate in projects that are so hastily conceived that the results are unlikely to be useful for publication, whether in a thesis or in a formal article in an academic journal. Not all research is publishable, of course; sometimes mistakes are made despite the most careful plans—a computer crash might destroy a data set, for example. (See also discussion of negative results below.) In general, though, the willingness of research participants to volunteer for our studies should not be taken lightly. Once we have collected human subjects data, most social scientists agree that we have an obligation to disseminate them, and journal publication is the most common means of doing this.

Even where human subjects are not involved, as with content analysis projects, researchers are still bound by a broad range of ethical principles. Generally speaking, publishing scientific results is an ethical obligation of scientists and social scientists, not just a "publish or perish" requirement of universities. Part of the job of a researcher is to move knowledge forward and to give other scholars, and where possible society at large, the opportunity to benefit from their results.

A few of the major areas where ethical difficulties routinely arise for aspiring scholars, whether students or professors, are addressed below. These discussions are intended only as general introductions to some of the most common problems, not as a substitute for good judgment or for consulting one or more of the ethics codes published by research organizations such as those mentioned above. Many situations are not so clear-cut as those discussed below.

Fraudulent and Misleading Data

As science has become more competitive, news reports of scientists who alter their data to fit their theories have become more common. Obviously, this is both unfortunate and blatantly unethical. Nevertheless, it is worth underscoring the reality that in social science, as in other fields, accusations of research fraud occur with some regularity. Sometimes fraud can occur without the researcher even being aware of it; interviewers or survey workers assigned a quota of questionnaires to complete may cave in to the temptation to fill out the forms themselves, for example. Good research management includes the kind of training, supervision, and oversight that makes such events reasonably unlikely.

More commonly, researchers may be tempted to slant data to support a cherished hypothesis or ignore results that contradict their favorite theory. This is very easy to do without trying to defraud. Research reports have, in a sense, a persuasive intent; having achieved a certain result, the researcher presents the data in a way that will help others also recognize the achievement, and the tendency to put that accomplishment in the best possible light is common—almost expected. However, authors of research articles should still strive to do justice to possible alternative interpretations of the data. Only a fine line separates honest advocacy for the value and perceived meaning of research results from active misrepresentation.

A related but more subtle problem is that a study consisting entirely of negative results—one that failed to provide sufficient evidence to reject any null hypothesis—would often be considered unpublishable, even if the researcher would like to publish it. This means (in effect) that if 99 reasonably well-designed studies produce no evidence in support of a given hypothesis, but a single study does provide such evidence, only the study that provides supportive evidence is likely to see print. It could well be that this study is the one out of a hundred studies that produced the result in question strictly by chance (an example of Type I error), but it is the only one likely to appear in the published literature. This is certainly not an example of fraud or misrepresentation, but it constitutes an important general bias in academic publishing.

Most media research studies that follow the hypothesis-testing model result in some hypotheses being supported while others are not. Commonly, both are included in the resulting article. A large proportion of media research is exploratory, descriptive, or interpretive; these approaches do not generally test hypotheses, so the problem of negative results does not arise in quite this form. Even so, academic publishing remains biased toward those studies that produce positive new results. Since no design is ever perfect, the rule of thumb is for researchers to always be as aware as possible of the limitations of the design and data and to be candid about reporting these.

The Peer-Review Process

Blind peer review (Chapter 4) is a highly respected system for judging the quality of research papers submitted for publication. However, it is not perfect. Editors know who has submitted each paper and how prestigious an institution they represent, and they have a lot of discretion as to which reviewers to choose for a particular manuscript. Some reviewers are tougher judges than others. Many submissions fall into a gray area, such as those that receive both positive and negative reviews. And both editors and reviewers may have strong, even unconscious preferences regarding the types of problems or methods chosen—in addition to making conscious judgments about the "fit" of an article to the mission of the journal.

Journal reviewers are expected to decline to review papers where there is a conflict of interest (for example, they recognize the likely author and have had a previous collaborative or professor-student relationship with him or her). They are also expected to keep the contents of the paper and the result of the review confidential. However, it is not unusual for scholars submitting papers to be concerned that their work might not get a fair evaluation or even that someone might use their idea without giving them credit. Nevertheless, peer review is the best system we have available for fair and impartial manuscript review.

Science journalists often compete with one another to get out stories about the most compelling new scientific "breakthroughs," yet a number of leading journals in science and medicine routinely refuse to publish research papers reporting results that have been released to the mass media before undergoing peer review. Although this seems to go against the scientific ethos calling for open dissemination and sharing of information, releasing results of scientific research that have not been peer reviewed may be considered misleading. This is especially true in the case of information (like the results of medical studies) that might affect people's important personal decisions. (For an extended discussion of the ethics of scientific publishing in general, see LaFollette, 1992.)

Authorship Credit

Issues of authorship, and the order of authorship, receive a lot of attention in the academic world. It is through authorship that researchers get professional credit, the recognition of their peers, and the opportunity to build a scholarly reputation; very often publication authorship is the main foundation for salary raises and promotions as well. The order of authorship (if there are multiple authors) should reflect the degree of each author's contribution, from greatest to least in most mass communication journals (although some fields treat this element differently). A thesis or dissertation is a student's own intellectual work; in most cases, papers resulting from a thesis or dissertation will list the student as the first author. Occasionally, coauthors who believe they have made roughly equal contributions will choose to list themselves alphabetically, most likely with a brief footnote of explanation. A team of two or three researchers working closely together may make an agreement to rotate authorship.

Different subdisciplines and even different institutions may have slightly different traditions regarding authorship. However, simply doing some of the work for a research project reported does not automatically qualify someone for authorship. Someone whose help is confined to the routine aspects of a project (say, a laboratory technician in biology, a computer programmer for an experiment in psychology, or a survey interviewer in a media studies project) but who did not make a *substantial intellectual contribution* to the project generally should not expect to be listed as an author.

Because someone in this category is often someone who has been paid for his or her labor on the project, the "work for hire" test is sometimes suggested as a way to resolve authorship disputes. However, this does not always work. Perhaps the lab technician, the programmer, or the survey worker actually participated more fully in developing the research design, above and beyond what he or she was paid to do. Scholarly collaborators at much higher ranks may also get paid for their participation, and this certainly does not disqualify them from authorship. In the end, this is another judgment call, and one that sometimes becomes contentious.

It is generally inappropriate for a researcher (at whatever stage of his or her career) to expect to be made an author of a research paper without having made a substantial intellectual contribution. Usually this means the researcher helped in a major way with the conceptualization or design, the data analysis, or the writing of the paper. A casual conversation about the project over coffee is not usually enough. If asked, scholars should decline to be listed on papers where they were not significantly involved with the research. There are other ways to acknowledge more limited collegial contributions, such as contributing an idea for the literature review or the analysis or helping to edit a draft.

Rarely, someone in a position of authority will put pressure on a more junior scholar to include his or her name on a paper; also rarely, junior scholars may seek senior scholars as coauthors not for their help but in the belief the names alone will help them pass the peer-review process more smoothly. Both of these are highly inappropriate. All researchers should also decline to be listed on papers if they do not have the time or opportunity to read what has been written, even if they helped with the project in earlier stages, as all authors are responsible for the integrity of the research and the contents of any publication on which they are listed.

Should students help with a professor's own research project for a grade or for extra credit, when the research will be published under the professor's name alone? This is another gray area because it depends on the nature of a student's contribution and the extent to which the purpose of the involvement is to educate the student as opposed to getting the professor's work done. In most cases, at least a footnote acknowledging such a student by name would be included. The important thing is to communicate clearly about what the expectations are. Student researchers in particular are urged to seek a clear understanding of authorship plans whenever they collaborate on their professors' projects.

Data Ownership

Another area where disputes can arise is the question of **intellectual property rights** to data or results. Researchers are obligated to make data from federally funded research available to other researchers once they have taken a reasonable amount of time to analyze it for themselves. This most typically applies to large-scale surveys, the unnecessary repetition of which is especially costly, but the policy is not limited to surveys. Many researchers will voluntarily share data from other studies (not just those that were federally funded) with their peers, so long as subject confidentiality is not violated. Sometimes this requires separate human subjects or IRB approval by the institution of the person who plans to do the reanalysis. Of course, the original researcher would receive some kind of acknowledgement in any new publications.

Another set of issues surrounds ownership of data paid for by private industry. If a newspaper corporation funded a university study of what today's newspaper readers most want in a paper, the data would most likely belong to the corporation unless there was a prior agreement to something else. Genuine potential for conflict exists in such situations. The newspaper may not want other papers—especially competing ones—to benefit from the research that it funded. This seems fair, but the researcher may want to publish the results, whether because of a perceived obligation to disseminate research to his or her peers or for the benefit of his or her career. All of these motivations are legitimate. As with authorship, the best thing is to work out the arrangements in advance.

It is also important to acknowledge funding sources in all research publications. This is not only to give credit where credit is due; it is also to let the readers of the research know of any potential biases. Historically, some of the research that has suggested that the media's negative effects are quite limited was funded by the entertainment industry. This certainly doesn't make the results incorrect, but research consumers (such as policy makers, parents, and others concerned with possible negative effects) certainly need to understand where the money came from. Survey questions in particular often contain subtle slants that influence the answers they generate, which is why American Association for Public Opinion Research guidelines require the identification of funding sources in any reports or releases about survey research.

Occasionally, funding sources might have an interest in suppressing research results. A researcher who takes funding from anyone for a project that has any chance of generating controversial results—or results that may not be consistent with the interests of the funding source—is especially urged to have ownership rights to the data and publication rights spelled out in advance. While very rare, industrial interests have also been known to attempt to redirect or suppress research that does not put them in a favorable light, even if they have not paid for the research. We might think this happens only to scientists, but social scientists have also been put in this position.

Important Terms and Concepts

Asynchronous	Intellectual property rights
Channel model	Intercultural communication
Code of ethics	International communication
Early adopter	Masculinist
Empowerment	Media convergence
Feminist	Participatory research
Hegemony	Postmodern
Hyperlocal	Subject-object distinction
Information Age	Technology assessment

CHAPTER 11

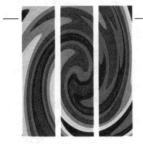

Writing and Presenting the Research Report

Journal articles, conference papers, technical reports, and other research publications are at the core of the research community in mass communication, just as they are for other scientific and social scientific disciplines. It is in these forums that new ideas are heard, good work is rewarded, research priorities are set, and problems and trends are discussed. Often, a paper presentation at a research conference represents the first public hearing that a researcher's new work gets. This can be a traditional oral presentation on a panel with others, usually about 10 or 15 min, or it can be in the form of a presentation at a **poster session** in which a visual representation (emphasizing tables, charts, bullet points, and other visual elements) does most of the work. Slots in the pages of journals and on conference programs are awarded competitively, based on the quality of the papers submitted for consideration.

A common sequence of events for student-written research is for an article to begin its life as a final paper in a course, then be revised and expanded for submission to a conference, and then be revised again for submission to a journal. Between initial presentation and publication, the improved paper may move from presentation at a local conference to presentation at a regional or national one. At each stage, the written report provides the opportunity to receive feedback from an instructor or a set of reviewers, which helps the researcher to continually improve the final product until, ultimately, it is ready for publication. This sequence of events leading to eventual publication is more common for graduate students than for undergraduates; however, an increasing number of opportunities are available for undergraduate researchers to present their research work as well. Of course, you may be more interested in simply finishing an empirical paper to meet the requirements for a research course. But the basic format and approach are the same.

Research articles had their historical origin in letters written by researchers (including naturalists, astronomers, and explorers) to the earliest scientific societies, starting in the 17th century. At that early point, there were relatively few professional scientists; almost everyone was an "amateur" who either was good at raising money or had quite a bit of his own. From the beginning, these communications were designed for an audience of the researcher's peers, those familiar with the research process and highly concerned with all of the methodological details and theoretical implications the work entailed. Readers often wanted enough detail to try to replicate the experiments or observations themselves, so research reports could not be just abbreviated accounts but had to describe the methods used as well. These early letters were circulated within the societies and eventually evolved into the "scientific journal" format that we know today.

CONSTRUCTING THE RESEARCH PAPER

Beginning research students writing research reports often have difficulty with the conventions, especially if they have been well trained in the art of journalistic writing. A research report is more like an ordinary term paper than a piece of journalism, but it has a distinct style of its own. Since the purpose is for other researchers to be able to scrutinize the study being discussed, every decision and its justifications and implications should be documented, and every source consulted must be cited and referenced with extreme care. Sentences may need to be longer to accommodate all this detail, and paragraphs may as well.

Often, scientists (including social scientists) are disappointed with mass media coverage of science because journalistic stories simply cannot include all of the qualifications and other discussion that scientists consider completely essential—and are used to seeing in published research articles. Yet research articles *cannot* be wordy—space is often at a premium, and there are tons of detail to be crammed in. These articles need to be both comprehensive and very carefully put together.

Because of the necessity to use no more space than necessary (many journals and conferences have strict length limits), the writing has to be very succinct. This also serves the needs of busy researchers who need to absorb the key information quickly. Unfortunately, the result is often so dense that beginners find the material tough going even to read, let alone to write.

Organization

Research papers have a prescribed format that varies only slightly from discipline to discipline and usually includes an **abstract** or a summary, an introduction, the literature review, a detailed description of the methods, the results, conclusions, and usually a concluding discussion where there is a little more freedom to move beyond the data to an interpretation of their meaning. Some ethnographic and other qualitative work, like history, can have a much more flowing narrative structure, but most of these elements are still present. If a paper is destined to be submitted for publication, consult an issue or two of the most likely journal to find out what its editors expect. Conference organizers often keep archives of previous years' papers; while these tend to vary more in form and style, they are still worth scanning through to get an idea.

Abstract. The purpose of the abstract is to provide a concise, one-paragraph summary of the problem, the method, and the results. Abstracts are republished in sources like *Communication Abstracts* (for the interdisciplinary communication literature) and *Dissertation Abstracts* (for doctoral dissertations in any discipline), in other library databases, in conference archives, and on journal and publisher Web sites. They become excellent tools when doing library research because they give far more information than titles and authors alone yet allow researchers to identify the most relevant papers quickly. If you want people to read your research, write an informative abstract.

Keywords. Some journals also ask authors to suggest keywords that can be used for indexing the article in an index to that particular publication (if one exists—for example, on the publisher's Web site) or in library indexes.

Introduction. Begin by explaining your general research problem in broad terms. Why is it important? Is there a social, historical, cultural, legal, or policy context that readers should know about? Was there a special opportunity available that inspired the study or an overarching theoretical question or practical need? Give your reader as good an idea as possible of what inspired the kind of a study you did. You can cover the technical details later, but first, readers want to know why you initiated this particular project—as opposed to pursuing some other opportunity. Explain in general terms the goals of the research, as well as its context. For participant observation or other ethnographic work, you will need to include some background on the culture, group, organization, or setting you studied.

Literature review. After the introduction, discuss succinctly but in detail the research literature that you looked at in preparing to investigate your problem. Devote a few sentences or more to each study that you used to gain insight into yours, and emphasize the specific findings that helped shape your own research design. Literature reviews are generally organized chronologically (from earliest to most recent), but they can also be organized along the lines of theory versus methodology or in any other way that will help your reader make a logical connection between your study and those that have gone before. Sometimes literature reviews that are especially comprehensive and identify gaps in the research literature can be published as independent papers. These are sometimes called "bibliographic essays," especially in humanities fields.

Methodology. This section describes exactly what you did in sufficiently specific terms so that the reader can judge the reasons for and adequacy of your choices. First, you may find it effective to summarize your general goals and the ways that the literature review suggested you could best develop them. Then, list your research questions and (if your project included them) your hypotheses. Many studies include both research questions for exploration and hypotheses encapsulating specific expectations to be tested against the data.

If your project was based on testing specific hypotheses, restate the theoretical justification for each one, and then state each one of them clearly in exactly the form in which you will be testing it. Research questions can be presented the same way. Then describe and justify your methods—both your choice of a general methodological approach and your specific decisions—about variables, measurements, population, sampling, statistical analysis, social setting, the case, or the choice of media material. Of course, every study will not include all of these, but you need to include all relevant ones for your own study. Make it clear exactly what data you collected and exactly what was done with them, including (here if not elsewhere) any important gaps, uncertainties, or limitations.

Results. Next, describe your results in detail. For quantitative work, include tables and charts as needed to summarize and communicate the numbers; include the results of statistical tests, but do not stop there. Tables should stand on their own and be intelligible to someone who has not yet read the text, so label everything carefully. But each table should also be called out and described in the text and its contribution made clear. Analyses resulting in only two or three numbers do not need their own table but can be incorporated directly into the text. For qualitative work, you may also need tables if you have used a "grounded theory" approach. Either way, provide adequate descriptions for qualitative work, with definitions and typical examples in the form of direct quotations from media or transcript material for each theme identified.

You should give your readers enough information to reach the same conclusions as you did, based on giving them the opportunity to briefly review the same data. If you have hypotheses, walk through each one in terms of the findings of your study; research questions are sometimes treated the same way. The results section may take more space than any other section of the paper.

Conclusion. Finally, write a meaningful conclusion that summarizes your results. What are the most important things you learned? What are their significance? Which ideas were turned upside down, and which were upheld? All methods have advantages and limitations; this is a good place to discuss significant flaws and data limitations, if you have not already done so. Keep your conclusion focused on what the data can actually support, as well as what they failed to support.

Discussion. The conclusion and discussion are sometimes combined (or the conclusion might be the last section of the "results"). However, the discussion is best kept as a separate section because here is where you have the freedom to go beyond the literal interpretation of your data, so it helps if the borders between speculation and empirical evidence are firmly drawn. If your sampling was not quite representative, if your method didn't work as you expected, or if your understanding of the problem turned out to be less than perfect, what would you do better next time? If some of your hypotheses did not receive support, is there an explanation that originally escaped your attention or a flaw in your original design you overlooked?

Perhaps even more important, do your data and conclusions suggest the need for changes in government policy, public education, or media organization operations? Do they tell us something significant about ourselves as a culture or about human society in general? You can take something of an editorial approach as long as your general direction is justified by the data you've collected and presented—and as long as you can keep the discussion short enough to meet the journal or conference requirements for overall paper length. This is often the place where the implications for either social policy or professional practice are set forth.

Last but definitely not least, it is customary in this section to suggest what research should come after this one to fill in some of the gaps the study you are describing could not—whether you complete this next study yourself or someone else picks up the thread. This is an important opportunity for thoughtful reflection and articulation of next steps with respect to the original goals you included in your introduction.

Writing Style

Some research articles can be tedious and boring to read, but please remember that this is *absolutely not necessary*. This material must be complete and thorough; it is written for a very specialized audience consisting of other researchers—your fellow students, your instructor and his or her colleagues, and other people around the world who study, teach, or do research about mass communication. You can assume that the audience for your results is reasonably well acquainted with what social science research is and why research on the mass media is so important. These audience members are also likely to be critical judges of the decisions you have made in developing a research problem, choosing a method, and using it to reach conclusions. Your job is to explain how these decisions were reached—including your first one, the choice of a research problem—and anticipate their objections. But you can aspire to do so in an engaging way. Research of any kind is a detective story. Use the element of suspense to your advantage.

Your task is to "tell the story" of your research project—how it evolved, what previous projects influenced it, and what you found out. In a sense, a research report is a persuasive project; you must persuade your readers that your problem is important and your results are sound (even where they may be imperfect). Although there is some variation in scholarly journals with respect to details of the format that should be used (and your instructor's preferences may also vary), the basic goal is the same.

Be clear and direct, and defend your choices. Some research choices are made on practical grounds. Perhaps a certain publication collection was available to you, or you had an unexpected opportunity to observe a particular media organization. This kind of reason is fine, so long as the opportunity was used to answer an interesting or important question. Remember to be honest about imperfections in the design or execution of your project—*all* research has them.

Citations

Citing references appropriately is a critical component of scholarly writing because the building of new research results on top of old, resulting in the development of cumulative knowledge, is such an important characteristic of the scientific enterprise. Citation style varies from journal to journal. Some use a footnote style that is probably similar to one you used in high school or college English classes. More typical, however, is some variation on American Psychological Association style, the style in which the author and year of publication are contained in parentheses as they have been throughout this book. This is an efficient and effective approach for most research work; year of publication provides important context for your readers.

The exact format of research articles and some details of citation style vary depending on the journal publishing them. The number of journals in our field is expanding to the point it is increasingly difficult to point to only a few key examples, but studying a few issues of those journal publications that are locally available to you will help you begin to develop a sense of each one's preferences.

Technical Reports

Many forms of research are first reported in technical reports rather than published journal articles. This can include market research reports or other "in-house" research designed primarily for a commercial purpose and a less technical audience. Media managers and marketing specialists are not always as interested in details of research methods or advanced analysis, but they are concerned with the results and their practical implications, so discussions of methodology should be limited and emphasis placed on applications to business decision making. These reports should acknowledge major limitations just like more theoretically driven research, however.

Technical reports have one major advantage over journal articles. Since they are generally published for limited distribution, space constraints are less severe. While technical details are not the main point, more space can be devoted to presenting raw results.

ABOUT CONFERENCE PRESENTATIONS

Conference programs, like the contents of scholarly journals, are generally decided by blind review; conference organizers, like journal editors, almost always provide authors with copies of the anonymous written comments from reviewers. Good, detailed, constructively critical reviews are invaluable, even when rejection is recommended. Some conferences specifically provide for undergraduate or graduate student contributions; a few even provide special prizes for winning papers from students, and a handful might concentrate exclusively on undergraduate research work.

Paper competitions for conferences create a great deal of work at one time for reviewers; as a result, it is not unusual for conference reviews to be a bit more abbreviated than the reviews that would be received from a journal.

Rejection is always disappointing, but even so this experience provides the opportunity to learn from the comments reviewers offer. Unfortunately, some good papers are never presented or published because there is no appropriate forum. Others have conceptual or methodological problems that cannot be overcome. But in many cases, persistent, aspiring scholarly authors will eventually be rewarded with success. Conferences are the logical places to start.

Both regional and national research conferences are available, and sometimes local ones are sponsored within a specific state or on a single campus. Regional and local meetings represent a smaller geographic area, of course, and are therefore a good bet for the beginning researcher seeking a first forum to present his or her work. Regional conferences are sometimes associated with regional journals. Bigger annual meetings have more presentation slots to give away, however, with most of the larger ones typically attracting hundreds of scholars. Unfortunately they can be expensive to attend, but your college or university should be able to help in many cases.

If one of these organizations is meeting near you and you are especially interested in research, talk to your instructor about attending, even if you're an undergraduate beginner and even if you're not ready to present your own research. If you are a graduate student in particular, you should plan to go. You will learn more about research in a couple of days than you would ever have thought possible.

Alternative Conference Presentation Formats

Poster sessions, as mentioned early in this chapter, are becoming more common as an alternative to the traditional 10- or 15-min oral presentation. Poster sessions are a tradition borrowed from the natural sciences. Most readers of this book will have seen student science fair posters and other research posters from science students and faculty, often decorating the halls of science and engineering departments.

At some conferences, posters used to be considered "second-tier" presentations, with oral presentations reserved for papers seen as more important or better developed, but this is not always the case anymore. Poster sessions have some distinctive advantages. Some kinds of research in social as well as natural science lend themselves well to a visual presentation. One other important reason why this option is becoming more popular is because of the increased opportunities for interpersonal interaction it provides. Interested scholars can seek out posters about research that interests them, and both presenter and audience have more opportunities for discussion than they might in a formal oral session.

Some conference organizers continue to experiment with other alternatives. Roundtable discussions are a less formal alternative designed to stimulate thinking among the participants. Whereas a typical panel usually includes three to five paper presentations, a round table may include many more participants. Yet other formats allow a larger number of speakers to make very short oral presentations, followed by opportunities for face-to-face interaction between presenters and audience members.

Whatever the format available to you, these opportunities to hear about others' research in person and share your own with a wider audience are crucial to the way our field—like so many others—moves forward.

A CONCLUDING NOTE

The report of a study that began life as an unpublished course paper and was then photocopied for discussion might be accepted for presentation at a research conference and then be revised for submission to a research publication. The result may not be instant success; some good journals may have acceptance rates of 10% or less of manuscripts submitted. But at each of these stages, feedback and criticism (both formal and informal) can help the author revise the paper appropriately for eventual publication. Publication is important, not just to fulfill the administrative and bureaucratic demands of university managers but because this is the way scholars leave a legacy for the future. Good journal articles shape the work and thinking of those the authors have never met, sometimes for many years.

Above all, study the *best*—not the worst—scholarly writing! Research discussions do not need to be obtuse, although many of them are written for those interested in, and familiar with, highly technical debates. They do not need to be dry or boring. You considered your research problem interesting enough to spend time, energy, and thought exploring it. Now your job is to convince others that this was a wise choice and to tell the world what you found out.

Important Terms and Concepts

Abstract

Poster session

Appendix

Table A1   Random Numbers

0430	2613	7878	5595	8076	3068	4113	7962	4989	3987
6095	8618	7024	5831	8995	0902	3972	4894	2153	5764
6720	4690	2123	7101	1166	0087	3042	4745	4690	3173
8948	4609	9126	2814	8383	2951	1958	8212	4131	5313
3268	0189	9175	0473	4295	2993	7027	4153	3864	7542
5473	1540	5681	3933	7826	3823	9933	3101	6742	2364
2951	2169	3096	8663	8147	5255	1756	0650	8493	7024
1031	4981	9118	7969	2688	8229	2863	5320	6124	9920
6010	3219	2640	2737	6055	7298	7628	8430	8159	8506
7534	1369	9935	4358	1490	3193	2906	8893	6850	0891
1529	4760	9897	8352	9742	3222	4402	5286	7490	8293
8640	4369	2154	0167	8358	4086	2082	4454	8300	6078
4802	5490	5571	5666	2838	6789	4990	4780	8211	9244
5575	7527	5181	5048	6590	2984	3675	3713	9279	2444
8567	8238	4885	2201	9949	6557	9036	0762	5741	0075
3274	7170	8828	3802	8740	0349	3301	0854	6672	7755

(Continued)

Table A1 Random Numbers (Continued)

7241	5444	3332	9411	0974	9305	1968	6590	2879	8846
9775	0637	0620	3371	1320	2326	5367	2505	7106	8327
5967	8343	1255	6275	8485	2979	4725	8253	1482	7908
7751	6866	9343	2573	9731	6516	8446	2564	4320	5098
5351	8360	4701	0334	6325	6623	5137	9967	3771	2139
9489	7125	7285	6006	9644	8078	4301	8991	7505	7908
4123	5242	6491	7400	5045	7933	0171	4898	3955	2712
6300	7627	8988	6159	9272	7495	1516	3011	4975	1997
8692	3259	4187	0708	1821	5341	9440	0223	3858	0821
3971	0814	5119	6038	1296	2652	0170	3593	1459	0425
1458	9604	6418	7922	3438	3212	8105	6187	9651	2711
1532	5944	6461	2186	6531	9642	7027	4512	1871	1547
4358	4732	2836	7479	7775	9372	5429	3719	3704	0959
4771	3705	1207	6469	3964	3735	6951	6726	1822	6737
8320	3056	6632	6155	3391	6854	2468	7444	0255	3133
0780	1789	7331	2176	2761	8899	6595	9499	3543	5813
4070	5232	3454	6773	8100	2066	1208	3083	6906	8123
5346	1848	1476	0788	5314	8818	2993	6710	8478	8989
9998	3687	9759	6679	2548	1029	3827	7357	1508	7640
3645	8649	3296	0892	7380	0197	4126	0455	6421	0426
2557	6761	7808	5045	9141	5541	4223	6136	9505	4995
1087	9755	4751	5061	2832	4231	1508	7534	0844	5725
6355	5538	2461	5869	0447	6704	1861	2725	8901	8212

8426	6186	9022	1265	8066	7173	8981	0181	0794	0397
3513	0498	9207	7115	3367	8342	0415	4787	7058	6874
8415	9346	4334	2976	3382	5732	4626	8733	5606	0797
5604	4248	5282	1402	4514	2419	9922	0440	3763	4844
3293	0554	1972	9984	1488	1936	0002	4826	8885	4399
0482	6386	7228	6668	5710	7267	1942	7027	4138	9070
4496	8432	0507	5735	8649	3503	4284	4731	2598	8563
9909	4716	7697	8245	5921	3583	7679	4077	1490	4665
8029	7193	5378	7464	5161	8795	4537	2816	8367	6919
8435	7008	0739	8069	8406	0862	1831	1584	5723	8733
4520	9775	0803	8260	7956	4495	6670	6761	6847	4544
1306	1189	5731	3968	5606	5084	8947	3897	1636	7810
0422	2431	0649	8085	5053	4722	6598	5044	9040	5121
6597	2022	6168	5060	8656	6733	6364	7649	1871	4328
7965	6541	5645	6243	7658	6903	9911	5740	7824	8520
7695	6937	0406	8894	0441	8135	9797	7285	5905	9539
5160	7851	8464	6789	3898	4197	6511	0407	9329	2265
2961	0551	0539	8288	7478	7565	5581	5771	5442	8761
1428	4183	4312	5445	4854	9157	9158	5218	1464	3634
3666	5642	4539	1561	7849	7520	2547	0756	1206	2033
6543	6799	7454	9052	6689	1946	2574	9386	0304	7945
9975	6080	7423	3175	9377	6951	6519	8287	8994	5532
4866	0956	7545	7723	8085	4348	2228	9583	4415	7065

(Continued)

Table A1   Random Numbers (Continued)

8239	7068	6694	5168	3117	1586	0237	6160	9585	1133
8722	9191	3386	3443	0434	4586	4150	1224	6204	0937
1330	9120	8785	8382	2929	7089	3109	6742	2468	7025
2296	2952	4764	9070	6356	9192	4012	0618	2219	1109
3582	7052	3132	4519	9250	2486	0830	8472	2160	7046
5872	9207	7222	6494	8973	9545	6967	8490	5264	9821
1134	6324	6201	3792	5651	0538	4676	2064	0584	7996
1403	4497	7390	8503	8239	4236	8022	2914	4368	4529
3393	7025	3381	3553	2128	1021	8353	6413	5161	8583
1137	7896	3602	0060	7850	7626	0854	6565	4260	6220

Table A2   Critical Values of Chi-Square

Degrees of Freedom	Level of Significance		
	0.10	0.05	0.01
1	2.706	3.841	6.635
2	4.605	5.991	9.210
3	6.251	7.815	11.345
4	7.779	9.488	13.277
5	9.236	11.071	15.086
6	10.645	12.592	16.812
7	12.017	14.067	18.475
8	13.362	15.507	20.090
9	14.684	16.919	21.666
10	15.987	18.307	23.209

Degrees of Freedom	Level of Significance		
	0.10	0.05	0.01
11	17.275	19.675	24.725
12	18.549	21.026	26.217
13	19.812	22.362	27.688
14	21.064	23.685	29.141
15	22.307	24.996	30.578
16	23.542	26.296	32.000
17	24.769	27.587	33.409
18	25.989	28.869	34.805
19	27.204	30.144	36.191
20	28.412	31.410	37.566
21	29.615	32.671	38.932
22	30.813	33.924	40.289
23	32.007	35.172	41.638
24	33.196	36.415	42.980
25	34.382	37.652	44.314
30	40.256	43.773	50.892
35	46.059	49.802	57.342
40	51.805	55.758	63.691
45	57.505	61.656	69.957
50	63.167	67.505	76.154
55	68.796	73.311	82.292

(Continued)

Table A2   Critical Values of Chi-Square (Continued)

Degrees of Freedom	Level of Significance		
	0.10	0.05	0.01
60	74.397	79.082	88.379
65	79.973	84.821	94.422
70	85.527	90.531	100.425
75	91.061	96.217	106.393
80	96.578	101.879	112.329
85	102.079	107.522	118.236
90	107.565	113.145	124.116
95	113.038	118.752	129.973
100	118.498	124.342	135.807
110	129.385	135.480	147.414
120	140.233	146.567	158.950
130	151.045	157.610	170.423
140	161.827	168.613	181.840
150	172.581	179.581	193.208
200	226.021	233.994	249.445
300	331.789	341.395	359.906
400	436.649	447.632	468.724
500	540.930	553.127	576.493

Note. The statistical tables in this appendix are adapted from material in *Handbook of Statistical Tables,* by D. B. Owen, 1962, Reading, MA: Addison-Wesley. Copyright © 1962 by Addison-Wesley Publishing Company, Inc. Reprinted courtesy of the publisher.

Glossary

Abstract   Concise written summary of a research article. Often appearing at the beginning of full-length articles published in academic journals, abstracts are also used in conference programs and indexes to the research literature to facilitate searches.

Academic journal   Publication that contains primarily or exclusively research articles. Almost all well-respected academic journals are blind reviewed; that is, research articles are accepted or rejected based on the opinions of researcher-reviewers who don't know who wrote them.

ANOVA   Abbreviation used as shorthand for analysis of variance. ANOVA distinguishes among categorical independent variables in terms of the strength of their contributions to the variance in a continuous dependent variable and identifies interaction effects.

Applied research   Research done primarily to answer a question of immediate practical significance (for example, to make a business decision). Good applied research uses theory; its main purpose, however, is solving immediate problems rather than advancing understanding of theoretical issues. (See **basic research**.)

Asynchronous   Communication that takes place at the convenience of the communicator or the receiver (outside of "real time") rather than instantaneously or according to a fixed schedule. E-mail is asynchronous, for example, because messages can be read and responded to at any time of the receiver's choosing.

Attitude   Persistent, consistent, evaluative response to an object, a person, or an idea. Attitudes are considered difficult to change; they can be positive or negative.

Basic research   Research done primarily to answer a theoretical question. Good basic research addresses important questions; its main purpose, however, is advancing our understanding of theoretical issues rather than solving immediate problems. (See **applied research**.)

Behaviorist   Researcher (or research project) characterized by an emphasis on readily observable behaviors rather than internal thoughts and feelings, an outgrowth of behaviorism in the field of psychology.

Bell curve   So-called normal distribution. Many naturally occurring variables, such as height and weight, follow this curve; some artificially created variables, such as intelligence, are constructed to approximate the same shape. The mathematical properties of normal distributions are well known, which is important for statistical inference. (See **normal distribution.**)

Blind review   Process through which articles describing research projects are evaluated by reviewers who do not know who wrote the paper. The goal is a review unaffected by personal friendships or the reputations of either authors or their institutions. (See **peer review.**)

Case study   Research design that focuses on one or more specific institutions or events (cases). Case studies are carried out with the intention of shedding light on general processes, but the results are not necessarily generalizable in the statistical sense.

Categorical   Data from variables whose values are categories, like color, shape, or name. Some categorical data are also ordinal, meaning they can be arranged in a logical order; otherwise, the data are nominal. (See **nominal, ordinal.**)

Cell   For a frequency distribution involving two or more variables, a category defined by particular values of each of those variables. The total number of cells is the product of the possible values of each variable. (See **contingency table, cross-tabs.**)

Census   Complete count of a population. Where a survey is based on a partial count, or sample, a census tries to include all members of the population.

Channel model   Early model of media processes that first conceptualized mass communication as involving a source, a channel, and a receiver.

Chi-square test   Test for whether two frequency distributions are alike or different. The data for a chi-square test can be nominal or ordinal rather than a higher level of measurement.

Cluster analysis   Statistical technique for separating cases into clusters based on shared characteristics; useful for subdividing audiences.

Codebook   A reference document summarizing definitions used to assign items from open-ended survey content or media content analysis and other related text (e.g., focus group transcripts) to specific categories (generally, assigning numeric identification) for purposes of further analysis.

Code of ethics   Set of rules specifying appropriate professional behavior. Many professions (including journalists, medical doctors, attorneys, and researchers in a variety of fields) have their own codes of ethics.

Coding   Assigning numerical codes to raw data for purposes of analysis. Values for nominal variables can be assigned numbers so that computers can more easily be used to process the data, even though the particular values assigned are completely arbitrary.

Coefficient of determination   Amount of variability (or variance) in one variable that can be predicted based on knowledge of the values of another variable. The coefficient of determination is the square of the correlation coefficient.

Collective behavior   Behavior that is characteristic of groups, such as crowd behavior, rumor transmission, or public opinion formation. Collective behavior cannot be reduced to the actions of individuals considered in isolation.

Confidence interval   Range of possible values that we believe a variable might reasonably be expected to have in the population, based on results from measuring that value in a sample.

Confidence level   Probability to be achieved that the results observed did not occur by chance. The researcher chooses an acceptable level in advance; it is usually 95% or 99%; 90% is sometimes considered acceptable for exploratory research on new problems.

Conflict theorist   Social scientist who emphasizes the existence of conflict and competition in society, as opposed to one who emphasizes stability and harmony.

Confounding variable   Variable that has not been included among those measured in an experiment and is not otherwise controlled but that has an influence on the dependent variables. Confounding variables make the interpretation of results difficult or misleading.

Constant comparative method   Method for developing categories from the data in a qualitative study rather than defining them in advance based on the researcher's preconceptions. As new data are analyzed, the categories are continuously reviewed and refined, with news added as needed. (See **grounded theory**.)

Content analysis   Collection and analysis of data about media content. No single method or technique for content analysis exists; it can be quantitative or qualitative, theoretical or applied.

Contingency table   Table (or series of tables) giving frequency distributions for two (or more) variables simultaneously (such as age and gender) showing the value of each variable contingent on the value of the others. Each category defined by particular values of the variables (such as women in their 40s) is called a *cell*. (See **cell, cross-tabs**.)

Continuous   Data that result from measurements on a continuous scale, as opposed to categorical data. Interval and ratio-level measurements yield continuous data. (See **level of measurement**.)

Control group   In an experimental design, a group of subjects to whom no treatment is applied. Control group measurements tell the researcher what the values of dependent variables might have been if no experimental manipulation of an independent variable had taken place.

Control variable   Element in an experiment that needs to be controlled (held constant, randomized, or statistically factored out) in order to accurately observe the separate effects of specified independent variables on dependent variables.

Controlled experiment   Experimental design that uses a control group and/or other means, such as statistical controls or the physical control of laboratory conditions, to isolate the effects of the independent variables so they can be measured accurately.

Convenience sample   A sampling technique that relies on conveniently available participants, such as students in a class or shoppers who volunteer. While a convenience sample is not random, convenience sampling is often a practical necessity. It is not always a bad choice, depending on its relevance to the research question.

Correlation coefficient   Measure of the amount of change or variation in one variable that is associated with change in another. If two variables are highly correlated, extreme values of one will commonly be associated with extreme values of the other. Most correlation coefficients (such as Pearson's r) assess linear relationships only. (See **linear relationship, Pearson's r.**)

Cross-tabs   Common short version of "cross-tabulations," the analysis of frequency data for two or more variables considered in relation to one another. Data from cross-tabs analyses are generally presented in contingency tables that show the values of each variable contingent on the value of the others. (See **cell, contingency table.**)

Cultural relativism   Recognition that moral and ethical standards vary across cultures. A cultural relativist recognizes that behavior considered deviant or wrong in one culture may be acceptable or even demanded in another.

Cultural studies   Branch of communication scholarship that looks at the mass media as products of a particular cultural tradition with a certain set of ideological beliefs. The cultural studies approach originated primarily in Great Britain.

Culture   Shared knowledge held by members of a social group; the knowledge that is necessary to function appropriately and effectively as a group member, including shared beliefs, values, behavioral norms, and communication conventions.

Deductive   Making a specific conclusion based on general premises. Hypothesis-testing research tests propositions based on general theories and is therefore considered deductive.

Degrees of freedom (*df*)   Number of values of a variable that can be said to be free to vary—that is, that could take any possible value without changing important characteristics of the data set. The value of *df* is important to the interpretation of statistical tests.

Demassification   Term that describes the way media technology sends messages that are increasingly tailored to the individual, often actively chosen by the receiver. The Internet does not send the same message to a large "mass" of people but allows users to select messages that interest them, for example.

Demographics   Basic, largely standard, descriptive variables used to describe key characteristics of human populations, such as gender, age, ethnicity, income, education, and religion. Can be used as a check that a sample is roughly representative of a population.

Dependent variable   Variable whose value we expect will change when experimental treatments are applied (or when the values of independent variables otherwise change); outcome variable that is affected by the factors we are trying to assess.

Depth interview   Interview designed to explore someone's point of view in detail. Unlike survey interviews that ask as many people as possible a short series of identical questions, depth interviews are flexible and lengthy; they usually involve fewer respondents.

Descriptive   Study designed to describe a particular sequence of events or social setting rather than to test theories of causation. Many descriptive studies are qualitative, but survey research is also primarily descriptive in most cases.

Descriptive statistics   Statistics intended to describe a set of numbers accurately and succinctly, such as the mean value of a variable as a measure of central tendency. Inferences about causation are not normally possible purely on the basis of descriptive data.

Dichotomous categories   Categories used in a situation where a variable takes only two values, such as gender or the answers to yes-or-no questions.

Directional hypothesis   Hypothesis that includes a statement about the direction of a relationship as well as its existence. For example, a hypothesis that says that older children understand advertising better than younger children is directional.

Discourse analysis   Method for looking at argumentation and dialogue in a systematic way. This idea is similar to that of *rhetorical analysis*, and some scholars use the terms interchangeably.

Discriminant analysis   Statistical technique for identifying the characteristics that most reliably separate one group from another. For example, discriminant analysis might be used to determine what attitudes and opinions best predict political party preference.

Early adopter   Person who tends to adopt a new technology soon after its appearance, unlike a "laggard" who does not adopt until the technology is already in wide use. Early adopters may have different personality characteristics than late adopters.

Empirical   Based on data obtained from direct, systematic observation rather than reasoning or speculation. Both qualitative and quantitative research that relies on systematic data collection and analysis is empirical.

Empowerment   Giving more power to, or enhancing the power of, a group of people. Participatory research is one form of research that is designed to empower those being studied. (See **participatory research**.)

Ethnocentrism   Tendency to look at things only from one's own cultural perspective. Some social science research and some news accounts are ethnocentric in that they do not take into account cultural variation in values or beliefs; ethnocentric accounts judge others by the standards of one's own culture.

Ethnography   Rich, holistic description of all aspects of a culture; originally, this almost always meant an anthropologist's description of a non-Western culture.

Ethnomethodology   Study of the ways in which the members of a particular culture make sense of their social environment. Ethnomethodology is a field rather than a method of study; ethnomethodologists commonly use qualitative techniques.

Explanatory   Study designed to identify or to test theories about causation. Explanatory studies can be either qualitative or quantitative; however, experimental approaches involving precise measurements are most commonly said to be explanatory.

Exploratory   Research designed to understand a new problem rather than to rigorously test hypotheses or produce a definitive description of a social setting. Exploratory research is inductive. (See **inductive**.)

Factor analysis   Statistical technique for identifying a limited number of factors that might lie beneath a complex set of interrelated variables.

Feminist   From a woman's point of view. Research and scholarship, as well as political activity, can be feminist in this sense; when used in this way, the term implies a theoretical rather than a political position, although the two are often linked.

Field experiment   Carrying out an experiment under natural (or "field") conditions. For example, observing the introduction of a new type of technology in a media organization is a kind of field experiment.

Focus group   Discussion group created for the purpose of research. Focus groups can be used to assess people's reactions to products, messages, or ideas.

Forced-choice question   Question with a limited number of answers from which respondents must choose. A yes-or-no question is a forced-choice question, as is a question that requires someone to choose his or her ethnicity from a list of alternatives provided or indicate agreement on a scale with a certain number of points.

Frequency distribution   Simple count of the number of times that each item in a set of categories appears—for example, the numbers of men and women in a particular experiment or the numbers of people receiving each of the possible letter grades on a test.

Functionalist   Social scientist who focuses on the way in which various social institutions contribute to the stability and harmony of the social system, as opposed to one who primarily analyzes sources of conflict.

Grounded theory   A method for deriving categories from a qualitative data set rather than relying on preexisting assumptions. This method allows for the systematic, inductive development of theory from qualitative data. (See **constant comparative method.**)

Hegemony   Political domination; in media studies, this term usually refers to the pervasive dominance of a particular ideology or belief system across a range of mass communication messages and media within a particular society or culture.

Holism   Study of cultures or societies as integrated wholes; the belief that studying particular characteristics of social groups as isolated fragments can be misleading.

Hyperlocal   Term referring to news coverage that focuses on a small, local, geographic area and target population, such as a school district, neighborhood, or very small town.

Hypothesis   Statement logically derived or deducted from a theory. Experiments are designed to test carefully constructed hypotheses; if done correctly, their findings help support, refine, or reject the theory. (See **deductive.**)

Independent variable   Variable whose value is altered, or manipulated, systematically in an experiment to observe whether changes in a dependent variable result. In survey research, independent variables cannot be manipulated but are identified based on expected theoretical links to dependent or outcome variables.

Index   Numerical scale used, for convenience, to represent a variable that has not been measured directly. For example, grade point average might be used as an index of academic ability, but it is not a direct measure.

Inductive   Reasoning from the specific to the general; the development of theory based on observations rather than through testing hypotheses. Many descriptive studies are inductive.

Inferential statistics   Statistical techniques designed to allow the researcher to draw conclusions (that is, to test hypotheses or to estimate population values) based on limited information (generally, information from a sample).

Informant   Someone who participates in an ethnographic study by providing data in response to the researcher's questions; a source of cultural information from an "insider's" perspective.

Information Age   The present era in the most economically developed nations; believed to be different from the previous Industrial (or "Modern") Age in being characterized by an economy and lifestyle in which information and information technology are the driving forces. (See **postmodern**.)

Instrument   Tool used for measurement. In social science, this term most commonly refers to a paper-and-pencil- or Web-based tool, such as a questionnaire on which the respondent provides answers.

Intellectual property rights   Ownership of information. In research, questions about who has the right to examine or analyze data or publish the results are intellectual-property-right issues. In applied research, a client who has paid for the data collection may retain these rights.

Interaction effect   Effect on a dependent variable resulting from the interaction of two or more independent variables; effect of one variable may only occur when the value of the other is within a certain range, for example.

Intercoder reliability   Measure of the extent to which two or more coders agree on the classification of material into categories for research purposes. In media research, these measures are most commonly used in content analysis but can also be used in the analysis of qualitative data from interviews and focus groups.

Intercultural communication   Communication among members of cultures or subcultures; the study of the issues that arise in communication among people of different cultural or ethnic backgrounds, whether or not media technology is involved.

International communication   Communication across national boundaries; the study of the issues that arise in communication of this type, including consideration of the variations in media systems and philosophies that exist among contemporary human societies.

Interpretive   Research, usually qualitative, in which the reactions and interpretations of the researcher are seen as an integral part of the methodological approach rather than as a source of subjectivity or distortion.

Interpretive community   A group defined by values and beliefs or other common influences that predispose its members to understanding media messages in a particular way, such as members of a particular religion or those having a particular political ideology or lifestyle.

Interval   A type or level of measurement in which every unit represents the same distance, size, or other measure but which does not include a true zero point, inhibiting the researcher's ability to calculate statistics, such as ratios or arithmetic means.

Intervening variable   Variable believed to mediate, change, or control the influence of an independent variable on a dependent one. For example, perhaps the income of parents does not directly influence the income of their children, but it influences educational achievement, which in turn influences their children's income (the dependent variable).

Interview schedule   List of questions for use in a semistructured or depth interview. Unlike survey questions that are designed to be asked in the same order in the same way of each respondent, an interview schedule (also called an interview guide) is flexible.

Labeling theory   Theory that says that how people and their behavior are labeled or categorized creates social expectations that influence future actions. For example, those labeled deviant will begin to act according to others' expectations.

Level of measurement   Usually divided into nominal, ordinal, interval, and ratio, this term refers to the degree to which a particular measurement has certain properties that some types of statistical tests require. Nominal and ordinal data are categories; interval and ratio data represent scale measurements. (See **categorical, continuous.**)

Likert scale   Series of questions answered on a numerical, usually 5- or 7-point, agree-or-disagree scale. Likert scale items must be chosen according to a specified procedure; however, the term is often used more broadly to refer to all questions asked in this general form.

Linear regression   Technique for developing an equation that best represents a linear relationship between continuous variables; it predicts the value of a dependent variable on the basis of one or more independent variables.

Linear relationship   Relationship between two variables that can be described by a straight line on a graph where the vertical axis of the graph represents one of the variables and the horizontal axis represents the other.

Margin of error   Range of likely population values for percentage data. If 60% of people sampled agree with a statement and the margin of error is calculated as 2%, the population value is believed to be between 58% and 62% agreement.

Masculinist   Done or said from a male point of view; promoting male values; sexist. This term is usually used to indicate the opposite of feminist or the absence of feminism.

Mean   Average value in a set of numbers derived by summing all scores and dividing by the number of scores. The mean is the most common measure of central tendency.

Measure of central tendency   Standard approximation of the most typical, common, central values in a frequency distribution from which most scores do not vary by extreme amounts. The mean, median, midpoint, and mode are all measures of central tendency.

Measure of dispersion   Standard approximation of the extent to which scores in a distribution deviate or vary from the typical, common, central values. Variance and standard deviation are well-known measures of dispersion used with continuous data.

Media convergence   The tendency for previously distinct media channels to merge as a result of technological change, management philosophy, and ownership patterns. For example, computers and the Internet now deliver material from both print and broadcast organizations; if a television station and a newspaper are owned by the same corporation, they are likely to share a Web site.

Median   Score in a frequency distribution above which half the scores fall and below which the other half fall. If there is an even number of scores, the median may be chosen as halfway between the two scores in the middle.

Meta-analysis   Combining data from multiple previous studies to yield new results. Often done with survey data, sometimes this term refers to combining results from multiple similar experiments. Because more data are available, results from meta-analysis may be statistically significant in areas where the original studies were not.

Method   A general data collection strategy underlying the choice of particular research techniques. Often used interchangeably with the term *methodology*.

Mode   Most common score in a frequency distribution. For example, the modal age among college freshmen is probably 18, although the mean age is probably a good deal higher.

Multifactorial   Involving numerous independent variables or treatments ("factors"). Multifactorial experimental designs can be extremely complex.

Multistage sampling   Sampling at several different levels, points, or stages. For example, sampling from a list of all counties in the United States and then sampling the populations of the counties selected is two-stage sampling.

Multivariate analysis   Any statistical technique, such as multiple regression (linear regression using multiple independent variables) or multivariate analysis of variance, designed to study relationships among numerous variables simultaneously.

Negative correlation   Relationship between two variables in which an increase in one is associated with a decrease in the other. For example, number of hours spent watching television might be associated with a decrease in children's school performance; number of hours spent exercising might be associated with a decrease in weight.

Nominal   Data based on classifying cases into meaningful categories that cannot be ranked or ordered in a logical way from lowest to highest. Eye color is an example of nominal data, as is ethnicity.

Nonparametric   Refers to a large group of statistical techniques that make minimal assumptions about the data to which they are applied and that can be used with nominal data, data for which the shape of the frequency distribution is unknown, and other special cases.

Nonverbal communication   Communication that takes place without words; "body language." This can include facial expressions, gestures, and even posture; some nonverbal communication is unconscious.

Normal distribution   Distribution that many naturally occurring variables follow. Many statistical tests rest on the assumption that the data to which they are applied are normally distributed. (See **bell curve.**)

Norms   Rules or guidelines for behavior accepted in a given culture. Anthropologists and sociologists have pointed out that norms are a key characteristic of every society; the mass media help establish these behavioral expectations.

Null hypothesis   Exact complement (or opposite) of the hypothesis. Statistical tests test null hypotheses rather than hypotheses themselves; only if the data clearly force rejection of the null hypothesis are they said to support the hypothesis.

One-tailed test   Statistical test based on the assumption that the hypothesis is directional. Where there is good justification for this assumption, it is easier to meet the criteria for rejection of the null hypothesis. (See **two-tailed test.**)

One-way ANOVA   Analysis of the relationship between the values of a single categorical independent variable and variance in a dependent variable. (See **ANOVA.**)

Open-ended question   Interview or survey question where a list of possible answers is not provided and the respondent makes a free and spontaneous choice as to what answer to give; the opposite of a forced-choice question.

Operationalization   Finding a way to measure or assess a variable; turning an abstract concept into a variable defined so that empirical data can be collected to measure it.

Ordinal   Data in categories that can be assigned to a logical rank order from lowest to highest with no assumption about the exact distance between each category and the next being equal.

Parameter   True population value; the theoretical value that a census would produce and that inferences from sample data are intended to approximate.

Parametric   Type of statistical test that makes specific assumptions about the variables and parameters being approximated. Use of parametric tests is normally restricted to interval and ratio data.

Participant observation   Qualitative research technique associated with ethnography. In participant observation, the researcher tries to become a member of the culture being studied, and his or her own reactions become part of the analysis.

Participatory research   Research that takes into account the goals and wishes of the people being studied; a reaction against the tradition of researchers pursuing their own goals without considering the effects on people who are the objects of their study.

Path analysis   Technique based on correlational data that tries to establish which among a set of interrelated variables are most reasonably thought of as causes and which as effects; requires a theoretical as well as a statistical foundation.

Pearson's _r_   Common correlation coefficient used with interval or ratio data. Like those for most other correlation coefficients, values for this statistic range from +1 to –1, with 0 indicating no relationship between two variables.

Peer review   System through which articles intended for publication in academic journals, papers intended for presentation at academic conferences, and grant applications are reviewed by specialists with appropriate expertise. (See **blind review**.)

Pilot study   Small-scale study designed to generate ideas, refine techniques, and test methods prior to initiating a larger-scale project.

Population   The larger group of interest that is sampled for study. A population may consist of people (adults, voters, residents of a particular area, and so on) or other items, such as messages (news articles, magazine issues, e-mails, advertisements, Web pages, and so on).

Positive correlation   Relationship between two variables in which an increase in one is associated with an increase in the other. For example, number of hours spent studying might be associated with children's better school performance; number of calories consumed might be associated with higher weight.

Positivist   Proponent of stance asserting that the goal of social science is precise, objective, empirical measurement of the phenomena of interest and that this goal is attainable.

Poster session   Special session at an academic meeting in which researchers display poster presentations describing their research. The use of poster sessions allows more researchers to describe their work in a short period of time and to interact with others.

Postmodern   The current era, characterized by shifts in cultural identity, eclecticism in art and literature, and challenges to both traditional and "modern" beliefs, all associated with globalization and cultural self-awareness. The term attempts to capture a variety of seemingly unrelated phenomena and is used in very different ways by different scholars. (See **Information Age.**)

Posttest   Test or other measurement administered after the treatment in an experiment. Posttesting reflects the effects of the treatment and the conditions that were already present, plus any changes that might have occurred incidentally during the experiment.

Pretest   Test or other measurement administered before the treatment in an experiment. Pretesting reflects the effects of conditions that existed prior to the experiment. (Pretesting can also mean prior testing of survey questions or questions to be used in an experiment to ensure they are unambiguous and clearly written.)

Pretest-posttest design   Experimental design in which the measurement of the dependent variable takes place both before and after the administration of the treatment (manipulation of the independent variable).

Probability sampling   Form of random sampling used to select participants in an experiment or a survey. In probability sampling, every member of the population has an equal chance of being included in the sample.

Psychoanalytic   Concerned with analyzing unconscious processes. Now primarily a branch of psychotherapy and subject to various critiques, historically the psychoanalytic approach contributed much to our general knowledge of human psychology.

Qualitative   Any method for doing social science research that uses general observations, depth or semistructured interviews, and verbal descriptions in place of numerical measures. Qualitative research does not generally rely on probability sampling, although participants can be chosen randomly.

Quantitative   Any method for doing social science research that uses numerical counts or measures and statistical analysis in place of verbal, textual, or visual material. Quantitative research generally relies on probability sampling, although convenience samples (nonprobability samples) can also be used.

Quasi-experiment   Social science research that follows the general principles of experimental research but does not meet all of the conditions for maximum experimental control. For example, subject assignment to conditions may not be random.

Quota sampling   Sampling technique based on filling quotas for age, ethnicity, gender, and so on. While not as satisfactory as probability sampling, this technique is often more practical, especially for market research.

Range   Difference between the lowest and the highest scores or values obtained for a particular variable. In a distribution with a lowest score of 10 and a highest score of 80, the range is 70. Range is a measure of dispersion that can be used with ordinal data.

Ratio   A type or level of measurement in which each unit represents the same distance, size, or other measure and which includes a true zero point, which makes it possible for the researcher to calculate such statistics as ratios or arithmetic means.

Reductionism   Approach to research that emphasizes the study of component parts instead of the whole; usually used critically: Quantitative techniques are seen as reductionist in comparison to qualitative ones.

Reflexivity   In research, this term refers to our attempts to turn our methods of study and analysis back on our own societies or, more specifically, on our own theories and ideas. More generally, reflexivity is used in a number of different ways, sometimes referring to the self-awareness characteristic of contemporary society.

Reification   Treating imaginary things as though they are real; usually used critically: Some opinion research reifies the existence of attitudes, treating them as concrete objects rather than as researchers' abstractions.

Reliability   Whether or not repeating the same measurement or experiment can be expected to yield the same or similar results. For quantitative research to be meaningful, reliability must be reasonably high.

Representative sample   Sample that is as similar as possible to the population. This can be achieved through probability sampling, quota sampling, or some other means. If the sample contains close to the same proportions of various demographic groups as the population, the sample is usually assumed to be representative.

Research method   Basic strategy for obtaining empirical data, whether quantitative or qualitative. Surveys, experiments, participant observation, and focus group work are all examples of research methods. (See **method, technique**.)

Research question   Formal statement of the question a particular study is designed to answer. Unlike a hypothesis, which posits a specific assertion to be proved or disproved, a research question is more open-ended.

Respondent   Someone who participates in a survey or in other similar research by answering questions (responding); the term for a study participant that is most commonly used in sociology.

Response   Behavior that occurs as a result of a particular stimulus. In behaviorist psychology, the researcher is concerned with observable behavioral responses, not internal emotional or cognitive states.

Response bias   Tendency to give the researcher what he or she wants; a bias toward the answers believed to be seen as "correct," socially appropriate, and so on.

Response rate   Proportion of people in a sample who are ultimately included in a study (such as a survey). Historically, low response rates have been interpreted to mean a study is likely to be unreliable; however, with response rates dropping, this principle is being reconsidered.

Sampling distribution of means   Distribution of all possible means that might have been obtained if successive samples of the same size had been drawn. Even where data are not normally distributed, this distribution is usually normal.

Sampling frame   Source of the sample; the list of population members from which the sample is chosen. For example, all people listed in a telephone book, all registered voters, or all families with children enrolled in a particular school might be chosen as the sampling frame.

Scale   A numerical measurement made with units of consistent size, such as a measurement of length made in inches or meters, of time in seconds, or of weight in pounds or grams.

Semantic differential   A type of question used in a survey or an experiment in which research participants are asked to indicate how they feel about a particular object or person by choosing a point on a line separating two adjectives. The adjectives are pairs of opposites, such as *cold* and *warm* or *honest* and *dishonest*.

Sensitizing concept   A concept that helps direct social science research, especially qualitative research, toward particular elements. Not a fully developed theory in itself, a sensitizing concept (such as power, gender, or media representation) nevertheless points to areas that deserve special attention on the basis of our theoretical understanding of society. (See **theoretical concept.**)

Snowball technique   A means of recruiting research participants for studies of specific groups in situations where random sampling is not practical. Each participant is asked to suggest several additional people falling into the same group who could be invited.

Social construction   Generation of a shared reality through communication and other social interaction. Sometimes called *constructivism*, this term refers to a theoretical position that emphasizes how social life influences our perceptions.

Social psychology   Branch of either sociology or psychology that is concerned with the psychology of human social groups, including the ways in which group membership affects individual thought and action.

Social role   Prescribed way for someone in a given social relationship to act. Father, secretary, teacher, and friend are all examples of social roles; norms for individuals acting in these roles are more specific than the general norms of the society.

Social setting   Particular social situation used as the object of a research study; these can be social institutions, whether a large organization, such as a media institution, or a smaller one, such as an individual family, or places where people congregate and interact, such as a supermarket, a hospital waiting room, or a movie theater.

Standard deviation   Square root of the variance of a distribution; a common measure of dispersion. For known distribution shapes, such as the normal distribution, the number of scores falling within a certain number of standard deviations from the mean is also known.

Standard error   The estimated standard deviation of the sampling distribution of a particular population measurement that has been based on a sample. Most commonly, this refers to the standard deviation of the sampling distribution of the mean, that is, the standard error of the mean.

Statistical significance   Confidence level achieved by a particular statistical test. An acceptable confidence level should be chosen in advance; test results are then evaluated as to whether they do or do not achieve statistical significance at the chosen level.

Statistical test   Technique for determining whether a set of data do or do not support a particular hypothesis. Based on a particular confidence level, a statistical test asks whether observed results might have occurred by chance.

Stimulus   Event occurring in the environment that causes a response. In behaviorist psychology, study is limited to observable stimuli and the visible behavioral responses they produce. However, stimuli can also be internal.

Subculture   Specialized culture that exists within a larger, more complex one. The existence of ethnic subcultures, professional subcultures, and so on is characteristic of modern pluralistic societies; this feature can complicate communication.

Subject   Participant in an experiment; the term commonly used in psychology for a research participant.

Subject-object distinction   Division between the social scientist as researcher and the people he or she is studying. The status of this distinction is a matter of some debate among philosophers of social science and critical scholars.

Survey   Series of questions asked of a sample of people believed to be representative of a larger population. Surveys may be in person, by telephone, or by mail; a variety of sampling techniques are used to choose the respondents.

Symbolic interactionism   Branch of sociology that is concerned with the roots of self-identity and social meaning in the symbolic communication and other interaction that occurs between two or more individuals.

Systematic random sampling   Sampling in which the first element is chosen randomly, a specific number of elements are then skipped over before the second element is chosen, and so on; used where the sampling frame is a list, such as a telephone book.

t **test**   Statistical test for comparing two means. Although special tests are available for other situations, such as ANOVA, a simple *t* test should only be used in the two-mean situation.

Technique   Procedure that is part of or that contributes to a method. The term is more specific than *method* or *methodology*. For example, most statistical procedures are more accurately described as techniques rather than methods.

Technology assessment   The application of social science methods to the understanding of the likely social effects of introducing a new technology. This term can also encompass the projection of likely environmental and/or economic effects.

Theoretical concept   An abstract idea or principle that may be the beginning of a theory but that does not yet specify a cause-and-effect relationship or another fully developed explanation for social phenomena. (See **sensitizing concept**.)

Theory   Explanatory idea that helps account for empirical data. Although the types of theories used in qualitative versus quantitative work and the ways these theories are tested differ, explanation is always the goal.

Time-series analysis   Set of techniques for attempting to determine the relative order of items in a complex sequence. For example, content analysis might ask whether a particular theme was more common before or after certain historical events.

Transcription   Word-for-word typescript recording conversational data from interviews, focus groups, or other verbal communications. Transcription is one way to put a qualitative data set into a format that is conveniently available for systematic analysis.

Treatment group   In an experiment, the group exposed to one or more manipulated independent variables in order for the researcher to observe whether predicted changes occur in one or more dependent variables. For example, exposure to different types or sources of information might change the opinions of those exposed. The term may derive from medical experiments in which the "treatment" is a drug or procedure designed to cure a disease.

Triangulation   Using substantially different methods to study the same problem, such as a combination of qualitative and quantitative approaches.

Achieving parallel results with different methods vastly increases the researcher's confidence in those results.

Two-tailed test   Statistical test that evaluates a nondirectional hypothesis, such as a hypothesis of difference. In a two-tailed test, extreme values in either direction will result in rejection of the null hypothesis. (See **one-tailed test**.)

Type I error   Rejection of a null hypothesis that is actually true; the acceptance of a hypothesis that should not have been accepted. The probability of Type I error is set by the researcher; it is the complement of the confidence level.

Type II error   Acceptance of a null hypothesis that is actually false; the rejection of a hypothesis that should have been accepted. The probability of Type II error is related to the statistical power of the test used and the confidence level.

Unidimensional   A characteristic, such as an attitude variable or a personality variable, that is best represented as a single factor, as opposed to one that is actually a composite of two or more interrelated factors.

Unit of analysis   The type of individual case or unit around which a study is organized. In survey research, this generally refers to the individual survey respondent—although it can also refer to a household, an organization, and so on. In content analysis, the unit of analysis can be an entire publication or program, or it can be an individual article or broadcast.

Unobtrusive observation   Observation in which those being observed are not aware of the researcher's presence. Unobtrusive observation in public places is generally considered legal but always poses ethical questions.

Validity   Whether the researcher is measuring or observing what he or she thinks is being measured or observed. Misleading survey questions, initial observations of a poorly understood culture, or experiments based on erroneous reasoning all lack validity.

Value system   What is thought to be important or valuable in a particular culture; what is considered worth pursuing and preserving; what gives life its meaning.

Variable   Characteristic that can be measured or assessed empirically; an abstract quality that can take on any one of two or more values in a given instance.

Variance   Amount of variation in a set of data; a standard measure of dispersion that is the square of the standard deviation. Variance is related to the distribution of the area under a frequency curve. (See **standard deviation**.)

Yates's correction   Adjustment necessary for a chi-square calculation when there is only one degree of freedom—that is, when a two-row–by–two-column table is being analyzed.

References

Azjen, I. (1991). The theory of planned behavior. *Organizational Behavior and Human Decision Processes, 50,* 179–211.

Bandura, A. (1977). *Social learning theory.* Englewood Cliffs, NJ: Prentice Hall.

Berger, P. L., & Luckmann, T. (1966). *The social construction of reality: A treatise in the sociology of knowledge.* Garden City, NY: Doubleday.

DeFleur, M., & Ball-Rokeach, S. (1989). *Theories of mass communication* (5th ed.). New York: Longman.

Gans, H. (1979). *Deciding what's news: A study of* CBS Evening News, NBC Nightly News, Newsweek *and* Time. New York: Pantheon.

Geertz, C. (1973). *The interpretation of cultures: Selected essays.* New York: Basic Books.

Gerbner, G., Gross, L., Morgan, M., & Signorielli, N. (1986). Living with television: The dynamics of the cultivation process. In J. Bryant & D. Zillman (Eds.), *Perspectives on media effects* (pp. 17–40). Hillsdale, NJ: Lawrence Erlbaum.

Glaser, B. G., & Strauss, A. L. (1967). *The discovery of grounded theory: Strategies for qualitative research.* Chicago: Aldine.

Hachten, W. A. (1987). *The world news prism: Changing media, clashing ideologies.* Ames: Iowa State University Press.

Jowett, G., Jarvie, I. C., & Fuller, K. H. (1996). *Children and the movies: Media influence and the Payne Fund controversy.* New York: Cambridge University Press.

Keller, E. F. (1985). *Reflections on gender and science.* New Haven, CT: Yale University Press.

Kuhn, T. S. (1970). *The structure of scientific revolutions* (2nd ed.). Chicago: University of Chicago Press.

LaFollette, M. C. (1992). *Stealing into print: Fraud, plagiarism, and misconduct in scientific publishing.* Berkeley: University of California Press.

Lang, G. E., & Lang, K. (1983). *The battle for public opinion: The president, the press, and the polls during Watergate.* New York: Columbia University Press.

McLuhan, M. (1989). *The global village: Transformations in world life and media in the 21st century.* New York: Oxford University Press.

Merton, R. (1968). *Social theory and social structure.* New York: Free Press.

Minium, E. W. (1970). *Statistical reasoning in psychology and education.* New York: John Wiley.

Noelle-Neumann, E. (1984). *The spiral of silence: Public opinion, our social skin.* Chicago: University of Chicago Press.

Owen, D. B. (1962). *Handbook of statistical tables.* Reading, MA: Addison-Wesley.

Potter, W. J. (1994). Cultivation theory and research: A methodological critique. *Journalism Monographs, 147.*

Radway, J. (1984). *Reading the romance: Women, patriarchy, and popular literature.* Chapel Hill: University of North Carolina Press.

Rogers, E. M. (1986). *Communication technology: The new media in society.* New York: Free Press.

Shoemaker, P., and Reese, S. (1996). *Mediating the message: Theories of influence on mass media content.* New York: Longman.

Shoemaker, P. J., Tankard, J. W., and Lasorsa, D. L. (2003). *How to build social science theories.* Thousand Oaks, CA: Sage.

Siegal, S. (1956). *Nonparametric methods for the behavioral sciences.* New York: McGraw-Hill.

Steeves, H. L. (1988). What distinguishes feminist scholarship in communication studies? *Women's Studies in Communication, 11,* 12–17.

Tremayne, M. (Ed.) (2006). *Blogging, citizenship, and the future of media.* New York: Routledge.

Tuchman, G. (1978). *Making news: A study in the construction of reality.* New York: Free Press.

Webb, E. J. (1966). *Unobtrusive measures: Nonreactive research in the social sciences.* Chicago: Rand McNally.

White, D. M. (1950). The "gate keeper": A case study in the selection of news. *Journalism Quarterly, 27,* 383–390.

Yin, R. K. (2008). *Case study research: Design and methods* (4th ed.). Thousand Oaks, CA: Sage.

Index

Numbers in bold indicate glossary terms.